Breathe Underwater

Becoming Saturated with the Gospel of Grace

Janalee B. Smith

Breathe Underwater

Becoming Saturated with the Gospel of Grace

Copyright © 2020 Janalee B. Smith

All rights reserved

ISBN 13: 979-8-7057532-1-5 (Paperback Edition)

Cover design by: Sarah Kennedy Irwin

Contents

Dedication

David C. Smith, you loved me when I was not lovely and have ever since forgiven me freely and served me fervently. With much wisdom and sacrifice, you have promoted and protected an environment of encouragement, unconditional acceptance, and open communication within our home. I love you most dearly my faithful friend!

Crossroads, in the years we've walked together, I've been challenged by, deferred to, believed in, prayed with, built up, and fought for more times than I can count. Thank you for your investment in me and the kingdom.

Rich Williams, you believed in me, saw the very best in me, and called it out long before it became a reality. To see the light of God in others, no matter how dim, requires supernatural vision. It is a life-giving gift, one which you have employed with great power and grace.

Rebekah Olson, what would the world do without people like you? Thank you for your keen insights, attention to detail, and patient service to me!

Jeff Nuovo, thank you for offering your careful inquiry and humble curiosity in the creation of reflection questions. May the Holy Spirit utilize your good and thoughtful questions to inspire, encourage, convict, and grow.

Disclaimer

I esteem the authors and teachers quoted within these pages, but the reader ought not interpret the presence of a quote as a complete endorsement of their lifestyle, ministry, or theology. It was not my goal to write an original work as much as a good and honest one, therefore, I have unashamedly utilized the words of others where they have spoken more succinctly or accurately than I. Please do not read more into these quotes than what was intended.

Introduction

*"Come and hear, all who fear God, and I will tell of what He has done for my soul." (Ps. 66:16)*I met Jesus in the same manner as the woman at the well. He went out of His way, went before me, into the forbidden and stigmatized country of the damaged and dysfunctional, and waited for me to arrive. His timing was impeccable. I was busy trying to meet my needs and quench my thirst in my own messed up way when He scandalously and personally intercepted me with an offer of something more and something better. Just one encounter with Him, one sip of His living water, and I was hooked; completely lovestruck and forever changed.

What followed was a complicated journey of discovery and healing. It was a divine romance set amidst profound disruption. My world was shattering, but my heart was mending. I was losing ground circumstantially but making headway spiritually, trudging through the valley of the shadow of death while learning to hear Him, believe Him, and follow Him.

As the circumstances of my life became more and more compounded and the circle of onlookers grew, I anxiously waited for God to take the ashes of my broken life and fashion them into something beautiful. Because I knew that God keeps His promises and delights to deliver His people, I eagerly waited for the day when I could tell my triumphant story of divine rescue. But in the waiting, God's loyalty and intimate affections for me outweighed the black clouds of loss and uncertainty. And I could wait no longer. I penned the first pages of this book and stuck them like stakes in the ground to declare my gratitude and adoration for the God who risked His reputation and regard for a woman like me. Putting pen to paper was a drink offering and a sacrifice of praise to the Lover of my Soul.

So, without a before-and-after picture to boast of or an outline to follow, I began to tell the story of God's great and gracious rescue of my heart. As an act of worship, I sat myself down to testify of the grace that is available in the suspense-filled in-between times of our lives; of the love that upholds us in the meantime. Breathlessly, like that Samaritan woman, I've run back to my people announcing that there is a God who loves sinners, who reveals Himself to outcasts, who provides abundance in times of famine, and who welcomes all who are thirsty to drink from His eternal well of paradigm-shifting, soul-changing love.

It is my prayer that God would use me as an object lesson, a source of encouragement, and even a bit of provocation for you. May you become more and more convinced of His peace that defies comprehension, His goodness that sweetens the darkest of hours, His power that exceeds our limitations, and His love that transforms our hearts.

With Love,

Janalee

Chapter 1

The Third Option

Virtually Saved

I think we should start a support group for those of us with complicated testimonies. After hearing countless stories of radical conversions, I've always felt a bit sheepish about mine. I had no sudden transformation, no spectacular light bulb moment, no before-and-after makeover to point to. As I've told it, *"I grew up in a perfect Christian family and accepted Christ at the tender age of five."* I had just learned to tie my shoes, for Pete's sake; what's there to tell? I understood that Jesus was God, perfect in every way, and willing to take upon Himself my death sentence. That sounded like a good deal to me, so I signed up – pretty simple and a bit uneventful. Mine was a childlike faith, right?

While it's true that I had very little time to make much of a mess of my life before Christ entered the scene, I sure did find ways to create mayhem after that point. Like many who have accepted Christ as a young child and grown up in the Church, I understood grace for salvation, but had no idea how to apply that grace for living. So, I did all I knew to do. I embraced the truth of the cross and then went on to sanctify myself. I felt it was my duty to perform as an "obedient" Christian according to the code I extrapolated from my culture and from Scripture. I studied, I prayed, I evangelized, and I served, but I did so out of my own strength. I attempted to reach God by building my own tower of Babel, and I failed miserably. I went through my teen years, college years, and early years of marriage and motherhood desperately hungry for spiritual transcendence, purpose, intimacy, and an authentic relationship with God, but could not find a way to reach Him that didn't involve formulas to follow. I checked all the boxes in my attempts to develop an impressive Christian resume but had no joy or peace. What I did have was a bucket full of spiritual bondage. I was living a duality. I was somewhat like a Pharisee: addicted to my own merit. So, there you have it. Don't you think a support group might be a good idea? We could call it 'Virtually Saved Anonymous'. Hello, my name is Janalee and I was virtually saved. Here's my story.

Game Over

It was a crossroads, the end of a strangled struggle and the beginning of a new way of life – one that many of us promote, but few have actually experienced and none of us can completely apprehend. It awakened me to a paradigm that changed my view of reality: required more than I possessed, none of what I knew, and absolutely all that I am.

It all began one beautiful, very dark summer night when God called my bluff and pulled me out of my slumber. As my husband and children lay sleeping soundly in their beds, I sat at the kitchen table with a cup of tea, in hopes that it would ease the bitter ache in the pit of my stomach. I rested my weary head in my hands and pondered. Silence was rare in our busy little house, but in that moment, it wasn't appreciated. Like any other mom of young children, I would have found a break from the chaos and constant demands fantastic on any other occasion, but it was wasted on me. It only seemed to amplify the pounding of my anxious heart. It wasn't the first night I had spent alone in the silence. My calendar was filled with them and they were increasing in intensity and frequency.

What was my problem? Good grief, everything was fine! I was fortunate enough to have all that I needed and most of what I wanted. I was a stay-at-home wife and mother with a husband and two children who loved me. I had a little time and a little money, loyal friends, a good church family, a solid upbringing with lots of moral and Biblical teaching, ministry opportunities, and even some hobbies. Nothing seemed to be out of order, so what could explain my panic? As I scanned through my mental files searching for red flags, I came up with nothing but a series of carefully covered tracks. There was no logical explanation for the music of impending doom that was playing in my head and had increased to deafening levels. There was no talking myself back into my happy place. I couldn't console myself with Band-Aid promises to be a better mom, be a better housekeeper, or drop that last 5 pounds. My meticulously crafted task list wasn't providing me with the confidence and satisfaction I thought it should. And as I added more and more to my job description – my makeshift identity – it just got harder and harder to keep up. All I could sense was, GAME OVER!

The Third Option

Despairing and tearful, I turned my attention to the Father and confessed the fear that was gripping my heart. I described it as if I was stranded in the middle of the ocean. Hopeless and weary from years of trying to stay afloat, fighting against the colossal waves, I was sure I would drown. I just couldn't swim any longer. What was I to do?

Fortunately, He didn't tell me to snap out of it or pull myself up by my bootstraps. That might just have pushed me over the edge. Having already lost heart, I think I would have given up and checked myself in somewhere or hid in my closet until the second coming. Instead of trite and pseudo-inspiring rubbish, I received these life-giving words: *"Stop striving and learn to breathe underwater!"* I couldn't help but laugh. What does one do with a statement like that? *"Learn to breathe underwater"*? No one can *breathe* underwater and why would anyone set out to learn the impossible? It sounded like foolishness to me, a riddle, or perhaps even spiritual nonsense intended to pacify me.

No, I didn't understand that night, but one thing resonated within me. I'd been holding my breath for years, and I couldn't do it anymore. There was a glimmer of hope in the possibility of a third option.

Option One: Sink.
Option Two: Swim.
Option Three: Breathe underwater?

In that moment, the idea was intriguing enough to stall my demise. Expectant and pondering, I slept that night.

What I didn't understand in my hazy panic, but came to understand in time, was that I had long before bought into a self-focused, graceless gospel of works. I never doubted my need for salvation, nor did I doubt Christ's sufficiency to redeem my soul from hell. But I did not understand the grace available to me that was essential if I was to *"work out"* my salvation (Phil. 2:12). I was holding my breath while waiting for eternity, living in survival mode because I, like you, was incapable of earning God's approval. God invited me that night to die to my self-righteousness and embrace the full gospel of grace. *"Stop striving and learn to breathe underwater."* The suggestion was absurd, but it did dismantle my armor, and that was enough —for then. My hopeless worldview was exposed for what it was: empty and completely void of life. Naturally I was left feeling unfulfilled, insignificant, insecure, and exhausted. No wonder I had sleepless nights!

Sadly, the gospel of works is our default setting. Ever since man lost his communion with God at the fall, he has tried to reach Him, or perhaps just secure His blessing and favor, through performance. It's as ancient as Cain, who offered a faithless sacrifice, and as close as our prayer life. A works orientation is hardwired into our sin nature. It is the norm, the lie that undergirds every world religion, and it walks a thin line of co-dependence with the programs and institutions of the Church.

In his book *Waking the Dead*, author John Eldredge says that religiosity is alive and well in many churches today: *"Christians have spent their whole lives mastering all sorts of principles, done their duty, carried on the programs of their church…and never known God intimately, heart to heart."*[1]

My dear friend Tana says she experienced it this way:

> *I was spiritually dying under the weight of methods of men, formulas by Pharisees (of which I was one), doctrines of do-gooders, lies of legalism, committees of the committed, stream-lined by strategies, regulated by rituals, and dominated by self-determination.*

Pastor and teacher Henry Blackaby likens such an approach to idolatry. In his book *Hearing God's Voice,* he shares his view:

> *Many Christians conclude that the only relationship they can have with God will be found in obeying biblical commandments and teachings. So, they invest their lives earnestly trying to follow the rules and admonitions they find in Scripture. This can lead to ritualistic, legalistic religion. This stagnant approach to worship has no more life to it than worshiping idols. Those who worship a lifeless, silent God, embrace a lifeless religion that offers nothing but silence. The Christian life is meant to include so much more.*[2]

The good news is that God sent His Son to overturn that world system and put an end to our hypocrisy. Singer/songwriter Bono says it well:

> *You see, at the center of all religions is the idea of Karma. You know, what you put out comes back to you: an eye for an eye, a*

tooth for a tooth, or in physics; in physical laws every action is met by an equal or an opposite one. It's clear to me that Karma is at the very heart of the universe. I'm absolutely sure of it. And yet, along comes this idea called Grace to upend all that 'as you reap, so you will sow' stuff. Grace defies reason and logic. Love interrupts, if you like, the consequences of your actions.[3]

In His mercy, God defied logic and interrupted my religious life! That night was the catalyst that finally brought me to a point of surrender: acknowledging my inadequacy, my emptiness, and my need for utter reliance upon a God who desires all of me. Praise God for His kindness that leads us to repentance. His kindness to me was insomnia. It stripped me of my coping skills until I was willing to admit my need for an absolute rescue. He saw my useless battle to survive a performance-driven life and He heard my cries for help, but He didn't pull me out of the water. Although I pleaded, He didn't give me the strength to swim harder. He did not send me a lifeboat or even so much as a floatation device. What He did was bring me to the end of my own resources so that I would release the death grip I had on my life. Then He introduced me to grace and set me on the road to healing. It happened to me as it did the psalmist who declares in Psalm 118:5, *"In my anguish, I cried to the Lord and He answered by setting me free"* (NET).

But get this: the insomnia continued. It actually got worse for a time. Looking back on it now, I see that it was one of the greatest spiritual blessings of my life. First, being in a constant state of sleep deprivation taught me to rely upon God's grace in my role as a wife and mom. Being a "good" mom, as I had previously defined it, went out the window. I had to look that failure straight in the face and say "goodbye". Anything good I managed to accomplish for my family would have to come from the strength, love, and wisdom He provided. Secondly, because I wasn't about to vacuum at 3 a.m., I started using that time to pray and read. And I began to listen. In the stillness of a sleeping house, I developed a sensitive spirit, a longing for His grace-filled presence, and an ear for His voice. He was teaching me to trust, to endure, and to abide! The Father became a person to me, and in the light of His presence I saw the indisputable reality of my loneliness without Him. I saw the poisoned well of neediness I had filled with self-sufficiency instead of His personhood. Praise God, He saw it all along and was disciplining me so that I would receive Him. And He did so with tenderness, not condemnation. As I responded to Him, I discovered Him to be the God of the Psalms who delights in us, who desires our brokenness and promises things like restoration, joy, and security in Him.

<u>Questions for Reflection</u>

1. *How would you describe Janalee's dilemma at the beginning of the chapter?*

2. *What solution did God offer her?*

3. *What was the significance of having a third option?*

4. *How was insomnia a gift?*

Tethered to Discipline

A few million Israelites would relate.

> *Remember all the way which the Lord your God has led you in the wilderness these forty years, that He might humble you, testing you, to know what was in your heart...And He humbled you and let you be hungry, and fed you with manna which you did not know, nor did your fathers know, that He might make you understand that man does not live by bread alone, but man lives by everything that proceeds out of the mouth of the Lord.* (Deut. 8:2-3)

Just like He did with the Israelites, our Gentle Shepherd grew in me an understanding of my need for Him. And I welcomed His "manna" because of the solitude and violent hunger I had found in the wilderness. The literal meaning of manna is *what is it?* How appropriate to a discussion of grace – the great mysterious provision of God. Grace doesn't feel like a rescue to those of us who are clinging to illusions of self-sufficiency. Unmerited favor is as foreign to us as manna was to the Israelites. But when our faces are planted in the stench-filled reality that we are perishing, grace becomes the wildest rescue, daily sustenance, and the very gift of life. Given the right provocation, we will take a bite! Psalm 34:8 says, *"O taste and see that the Lord is good; how blessed is the man who takes refuge in Him!"*

This is where we tend to get confused. Take a closer look and you'll see that this passage in Deuteronomy 8 sits just a few verses away from the Judaic law. In the same chapter that God told the Israelites He wanted them to gain their sustenance from Him alone, He introduced a conditional system that regulated their behavior! The law demanded nothing less than perfection, being filled with "if…then" statements that promised blessing if commands were obeyed and cursing if not. The weight of the Law was crushing and there was no grading on a curve. As Paul says in Romans, the Israelites were weighed down *"under the Law"* and it was a burden they could not carry.

Let us not read these sections of the Law and assume that God is only pleased by our strict performances. Even if they were able to perfectly abide by the Law, the Israelites stood guilty before Him. Good behavior cannot compensate for an evil heart. Thus Jesus called the Pharisees *"whitewashed tombs"* (Matt. 23:27). In His Sermon on the Mount, He told the people that their righteousness must *surpass* that of the Pharisees if they were to have a part in the eternal kingdom. Why? Because the Pharisees obeyed the letter of the Law, but their hearts were far from Him. Jesus fought fiercely against the Pharisees, who heaped burdens upon those who wanted to please God. They misrepresented Him and cheapened things like forgiveness, the sacraments, and spiritual disciplines. Jesus pointed out their deceitful efforts in John 5:39-40: *"You search the Scriptures, because you think that in them you have eternal life; and it is these that bear witness of Me; and you are unwilling to come to Me, that you may have life."*

Within the harshness of the Law, God revealed a layer of His unfathomable wisdom. Paul tells us in the book of Galatians that the Law was a *"tutor"* that led the Israelites to repentance. In Romans 3:20 he says, *"...because by the works of the Law no flesh will be justified in His sight; for through the Law comes the knowledge of sin."* The Law was not intended to condemn man, because he already stood condemned. Neither was it intended to provide man with a merit system by which he could climb a staircase to heaven. Make no mistake about the fact that salvation has always been based upon grace by faith in Jesus' perfect work. The Law was intended to bring failure and an awareness of our brokenness- a total lack of confidence in the flesh.

Because the law of works is our default setting, it takes an act of God – the failure of the flesh – to awaken us to grace. Men and women in every age recount the same story. Paul speaks of it in Romans 6-8.

> *Wretched man that I am! Who will set me free from this body of death? Thanks be to God through Jesus Christ our Lord! So then, on the one hand I myself with my mind am serving the law of God, but on the other, with my flesh the law of sin. There is therefore now no condemnation for those who are in Christ Jesus.* (Rom. 7:24-8:1)

Hudson Taylor spoke of his experience like this:

> *When my agony of soul was at its height, a sentence in a letter from dear McCarthy was used to remove the scales from my eyes, and the Spirit of God revealed to me the truth of our oneness with Jesus as I had never known it before. McCarthy, who had been much exercised by the same sense of failure, but saw the light before I did, wrote: "But how to get faith strengthened? Not by striving after faith, but by resting on the Faithful One." As I read, I saw it all! If we believe not, He abideth faithful. I looked to Jesus and saw (and when I saw, oh, how joy flowed!) that He had said, "I will never leave thee." Ah, there is rest! I thought. I have striven in vain to rest in Him. I'll strive no more. For has not He promised to abide with me – never to leave me, never to fail me? And, dearie, He never will.* [4]

Without a doubt, grace is embraced by those who have transferred confidence in their flesh to a full confidence in God. Consider what Jesus says in Matthew 11:28-30: *"Come to Me, all who are weary and heavy-laden, and I will give you rest. Take My yoke upon you and learn from Me, for I am gentle and humble in heart, and you will find rest for your souls. For My yoke is easy and My burden is light."* The offer is rest for our souls, and we obtain it as we tether ourselves to the sufficient sacrifice of Christ rather than the burdensome weight of the law.

In the time of Jesus, a young ox was tied to an older, stronger, faithful one in order to be broken in. The yoke was placed upon both, but the weight of it settled upon the older ox. The yoke served to keep the younger one on course. If he struggled for independence and tried to go his own way, the heavy yoke would become a burden to him and he would exhaust himself. The much easier course for him was to follow the lead of his faithful mentor who carried the burden for him. And so it is with us. Jesus carried the weight of our punishment for sin. He paid our debt so that we could have favor with God. We no longer need to carry that burden and try to earn righteousness or God's love. We only need to walk with Him in surrendered obedience, something which is no longer a burden, something we are now empowered to do. *"And for this purpose also I labor, striving according to His power, which mightily works within me"* (Col. 1:29). *"For this is the love of God, that we keep His commandments; and His commandments are not burdensome"* (I John 5:3).

True Obedience

Luke 10:38-42 recounts a familiar story:

> *Now as they were traveling along, He entered a village; and a woman named Martha welcomed Him into her home. She had a sister called Mary, who was seated at the Lord's feet, listening to His word. But Martha was distracted with all her preparations; and she came up to Him and said, "Lord, do You not care that my sister has left me to do all the serving alone? Then tell her to help me." But the Lord answered and said to her, "Martha, Martha, you are worried and bothered about so many things; but only one thing is necessary, for Mary has chosen the good part, which shall not be taken away from her.*

Admittedly, I have succumbed to sudden and temporary states of irrationality prior to the arrival of house guests. I have gone to great lengths in my zealous pursuit of the perfect visit. Someday remind me and I'll tell you about the nights I've stayed up cooking casseroles, cleaning porches, sewing curtains, building bookshelves, painting walls, and bleaching carpets. I've been so worn out by the preparations that I didn't enjoy the visit!

Even so, if I was Martha, I might have felt diminished by Jesus' correction. She was striving to take care of Him and His companions. Her efforts were sincere, and we all know dinner doesn't appear out of nowhere. Someone must prepare it. The mundane tasks that consume our days do matter! But Martha's service was driving her to distraction. She had become so consumed with caring for others that she forgot her greater need and priority. She didn't understand what was expected of her. Jesus corrected her by redefining her terms. He pointed out that her service was born of worry and a troubled spirit. She was *"worried and bothered about so many things; but only one thing is necessary"*.

Men and women both fall prey to distractions. We do well to remember that God empowers us with His grace to do all that He commands us to do. Self-directed action, no matter how good and sacrificial, is a draining way of living because it is completely devoid of grace. Moreover, it is autonomous action and therefore independent of God. Such efforts may make us feel safer at times, and certainly may impress some around us, but they display a lack of faith and a spirit of pride. In fact, that is the very definition of disobedience. As Paul says in Galatians, it is a *"perverted gospel"* (Gal. 1:6-7 NIV).

Mary chose what was better. Living by the true Gospel of grace is not living as a slave to a set of rules and regulations in an attempt to either appease the wrath of God or obtain perfection and favor with Him. It is a receptive and responsive leaning of our heart toward Him. Such a posture is not a burden. It is a relationship of trust and submissive dependency. It is not living in utter abandonment of clear commands in Scripture, nor is it gaining a sense of identity from a perfect adherence to them. Both are idolatrous ways to live independently of God. Living according to the true Gospel, true obedience, and grace-filled living means one thing: knowing the indwelling, transforming, all-sufficient Spirit of God and living each day utterly constrained by Him.

Philippians 4:13 says that we can do all things through Christ who gives us strength. We are not limited to doing those things which we are gifted to do or which our natural talents allow. By His power, we are to do all that He determines according to His will and purposes. For we have died, and our life is buried, swallowed up with Christ. Our resources – time, effort, gifting – all belong to God. The question then becomes: what is He asking us to do? Not: what do we have the *ability* to do, or what is it that *needs* to be done? We are always perfectly equipped for whatever tasks He has for us. We may not succeed in the eyes of man, but we can be sure that He will accomplish what He sets out to do.

If I were one of the onlookers at Jesus' crucifixion, I would have been quite befuddled by the announcement, *"It is finished"* (John 19:30). I may have taken a good look around me and questioned Him a bit. I may have been disappointed. From my vantage point, Jesus sure did leave a lot of work undone. He did not heal all the sick. He did not provide for all the poor. He did not vindicate all the victims of injustice and He didn't right every wrong. Yet, according to Scripture, He completed the tasks assigned to Him. His heart may have longed to do more and we know He felt compassion and sadness for what He saw and experienced around Him, but had it been His responsibility He would have surely addressed it, would He not? Instead, with the crowds pressing in on Him, demanding that He meet their needs, He would steal away for a respite with the Father. Unlike us, Jesus was certainly able to meet their needs, but He chose to spend time with the Father to listen and to lay His heart before Him. Christ lived life completely dependent upon the Father through the power of the Holy Spirit. He did nothing of His own initiative. He saw what the Father was doing and joined Him in it. He, who knows our frailty, instructs us to do the same. The Father wisely tells us to enter into His presence for a time of rest and acknowledgment of who He is. We need daily to be reminded of our place before Him. It is from this place that we gain the clarity and the confidence to know and do what He has for us.

We are not greater than Christ! We will leave much undone, but with the time we are given, we can do the tasks which God's grace allows. To access that grace, we must die to ourselves and live in submission to Him: sit at His feet as Mary did, and listen intently. We must sink beneath the waves, embrace the death of our natural ways, and breathe in the living water of His presence. We can trust God for the manna which will sustain us on the journey of each day.

Questions for Reflection

1. ***Jesus tells us to take His yoke, which is easy. What kind of yoke have you been carrying?***

2. According to this chapter, what is grace? What is obedience? Do you agree with these definitions?

3. If salvation has always been based on faith in Christ's perfect work, what was the purpose of the Law?

4. What does it mean to transfer our confidence in our flesh to a full confidence in Christ?

The Gospel of Grace

When the truth of God's grace finally began to settle into my spirit, I felt freer than I ever had before. I felt free from the need to perform for others, free from the failures of my past, and free from fears for the future. I felt like one of those crazy-on-fire, shout-it-from-the-rooftops babes in Christ. Most importantly, I felt free to ask and to receive from the Father the relationship I very much needed.

Ah yes, relationship. How easily we forget what we have been created for and what we have been welcomed into. The relational nature of the Godhead is an illustration and a reminder of both. Every fiber of His being pulsates with the energy of synergistic connection. Afterall, He is Trinity. He is a fellowship of three. The Father, Son and Spirit dwell together in a bond of loving intimacy. He is the triune *"All Y'all"* as my daughter used to say. And this fellowship is what He offers to us. It is part of our original glory. It is eternity set within our hearts: our need for loving, passionate, deep union which He alone can fulfill.

If His loving grace seems more like a measuring stick than a daily ration of manna, you might be missing out. Let us not pick up again the heavy burden of the Law as the Galatians did. They foolishly began by the Spirit and then sought perfection by the flesh (Gal. 3:3). We cannot improve upon our salvation; neither can we improve upon our sanctification. If you know more about Jesus through intermediaries such as pastors, teachers, theology, and books than you know of Him personally, you might be missing out. For the believer, Satan manages to perpetuate distance from God through distractions, falsehoods, and even religion. Our study of Scripture can become an academic exercise where we aim to learn *about* God and His will. So, while our list of good and bad behaviors gets longer with each Bible study, and our heads are puffed up with knowledge, we lose our ability to learn from Him and walk in true freedom.

In his sermon entitled "Problems Arise", pastor and teacher Mike Plunket says this:

> *What I found is that when the trials and conflicts come, you need more than someone else's faith. You need something more than someone else's teaching. You need something more than someone else's story. It's got to be your story. If you think about it, we're not studying a dead teacher. We're not listening to a dead prophet. We're not following a dead religious leader. He's alive. He's risen. He wants to be known! He said that it was better for you that He be at the right hand of the Father because the way He would send His Spirit would be better for you than if He were standing right here with you. So, knowing Him only through a book, or only through someone else's faith, is not His desire. Jesus wants to be known. He wants to reveal Himself to you. He wants to reveal His heart for you.* [5]

Was this blessed union not also the joy set before Christ? The mending of our broken relationship, the reconciliation of God to man: is this not the joy that motivated Christ to endure the cross and its shame? Loving intimacy was both His motivation and His joyous accomplishment. We miss this too easily, because it is the very crux of what was destroyed by sin. The awareness of our need to be filled by the love of God was the casualty of the Fall. Satan's best tactic, the one that defeated mankind, was to separate man from God, his life source. Legalism can result from a lack of intimacy, a lack of fresh encounters with the living God. When Jesus came on the scene, there had been 400 years of silence and the religious Jews were at the height of their prominence. They found a way to insert themselves and their formulas into the silence, and the result was bondage. But this is what Christ came to remedy!

Through the cross, the Father's wrath was satisfied, the Son was glorified, and man was justified; but why? Christ endured the cross with joy because His completed work allows us to rejoin the Triune

God in their cherished fellowship. He sent His very Spirit to us so that we would know Him and be known in our innermost parts. Not only on a good day, not only when we're on time with good hair and attitude in check. Not only when we're successful, popular, and rising above our circumstances. The Godhead, through the Holy Spirit, has set up residence within us as believers, accessible 24/7. He's never hiding, never bored, never remiss, never unavailable, and never silent. This is the grace, the sweet aroma that is manifested through us to those who are being saved and to those who are perishing (2 Cor. 2:15).

What's Your Story?

How shall we divide bone from marrow and rightly discern what is of grace and what is flesh? I spent time with God, read His Word and prayed to Him, and somehow still fell prey to this deceptive gospel of works. I was deceived – and deceived people don't know that they are deceived, do they? Only the Spirit of God can unveil our true motivations, making a clear distinction between what is faithful and what is faithless. But I never bothered to consult Him!

There is a hair's-width difference between the external portrait that is seen in a life of relational grace and in a life of moral self-sufficiency. The motivations are polar opposite, although the behaviors might be identical. This is the point that is so counter-intuitive: *it's not about our behavior.* Failure is sure to follow when we expect grace by faith in what *we* can do, because the true Gospel is grace by faith in *what Christ has done.* It is focused upon life, not behavior. It is born of dependence and rejects all forms of independence. It produces fruit, not performance. It is God-centered and not self-centered. The fruit of a life lived in partnership with the Spirit is unique and life-giving to others; whereas the fruit of a life that is set upon the achievement of significance, security, and personal identity will be marked by stiff performances and a lack of peace and joy, and it will always smell of exhaustion.

Perhaps it could be most succinctly described as walking on the road paved by the blood of Christ, in submission to His Spirit, in brokenness of heart, and in a humble receptive posture. Are you on it?

What is your grace story? Do you have a testimony of what you have done since receiving salvation? Do you have a story of God's compelling work in your spirit? Perhaps you missed the Gospel of grace as I did. Perhaps you also bought into a false gospel and have felt the insatiable hunger it brings. Have you experienced life as the young ox, fighting for autonomy against the yoke of our faithful Mentor? Have you been frenzied like Martha, carrying out works in the flesh with a host of bad theology supported by faulty definitions? If so, take heart; for hope lies ahead. When I reached the end of myself, God spoke to me of my need for Him. I believe He speaks the same to you. The same God who rescued me now whispers your name and tugs at your heart with an invitation to freedom. There is no formula for freedom. It cannot be taught, but it can be experienced by anyone who wishes to live life through the Spirit. Let's discover it together.

> *Thus says the LORD, who makes a way through the sea and a path through the mighty waters, "Do not call to mind the former things, or ponder things of the past. Behold, I will do something new, now it will spring forth; will you not be aware of it? I will even make a roadway in the wilderness, rivers in the desert.* (Isaiah 43:16, 18-19)

Questions for Reflection

1. *What is your grace story?*

2. *How do we access the grace God has for us?*

3. *If we should not ask what we have the ability to do or what needs to be done, what question should we ask? Why should we not live according to our own initiative?*

4. *A greater truth about God's character is that He is relational. How is it significant to you?*

5. *God speaks to us about our need for Him and the freedom He offers, but we don't usually listen until what happens?*

Chapter 2

Counterfeit Grace

A Case of Mistaken Identity

Blame it on Adam and Eve. If they hadn't eaten that apple, then our labor wouldn't be cursed and I wouldn't have been stuck at the office on a rainy winter day wishing for a warm cup of comfort and a flannel cocoon. It took an inordinate amount of strong coffee and some obnoxious music to help me survive the day. But as with all working parents, shutting off my computer and walking out of the office was just the end of my paid job. My yoga pants and animal slippers were still hours away, delayed by the demands of three small children.

My husband's work was close enough to mine that we drove together, and that gave us some time to map out our plans for each evening on the ride home. That night, there were errands to run, so we decided to pick up the kids in one car and take them to their favorite restaurant. Then, after picking up our second car from the repair shop, we would drive home separately. My very kind husband offered to brave the ride home with the children so that I could have a few moments of silence. We all like me better when I've had some time alone.

Despite the soggy conditions, everything went smoothly. But when things go according to plan, that's when it always happens, doesn't it? I followed my husband in that blue car ahead of me, with my wipers on and the radio off. Then he pulled into the parking lot of a Mexican restaurant and parked the car. I assumed he was having trouble with the kids, so I stopped and prepared to take on passengers. I had just put my hand on the door, ready to get out and assist him, when much to my surprise, he got out of the car, walked around to the passenger side, and opened the door for a lovely young woman! I froze in astonishment. That brazen young thing took his arm and they headed into the restaurant!

My jaw was still sitting on the floorboard when my cell phone rang. *"Where are you?"* asked a familiar voice. *"Well,"* I retorted, *"I was following you until you decided to take your girlfriend out for dinner. All I got was McDonald's?"* I held the phone away to protect my ear from his uproarious laughter. Somehow, I had veered from the course, managing to get behind an identical blue car, while my dear, faithful husband was waiting for me at the gas station with three rowdy children in the backseat. By the time we reached home that night, news of my blunder had traveled to our friends. It is now enshrined as one of my husband's favorite "Janalee Bloopers." A little weariness, a little rain, a little traffic, and we had a humorous little mix-up.

After several years of marriage, I realize I should have recognized my husband. I've had a good long time to study that man of mine. I know his disdain for dishonesty, his love for long showers, his weakness for sappy movies, and his struggle to find the right words. He's got a sheepish smile, an absent-minded walk, and a quirky sense of humor. I *know* the man and I love him dearly, but a specific set of circumstances accompanied by my limited understanding of them led me to question him, if only just for a second.

I am a woman of sound mind and I do my best to make good decisions with the information I have. If I'd had another few seconds, I'm sure I would have blinked the fog away and seen that I had detoured from my path and jumped into the wrong story. I think it's fair to assume that another few seconds would have given me enough context to see that my perceptions weren't lining up with reality. But more often than not, a split second is all it takes for us to turn everything upside down and inside out.

In the millions of split seconds of our lives, we perceive, assume, calculate, and respond to all we encounter. In the time it takes to glance across the room or read a bumper sticker, we take in and classify everything around us. And although we do our best with the information we have, we are predisposed to misunderstandings, misuses, false assumptions, prejudicial leanings, and omissions. It's not intentional; it's just human. Our lives often seem like a rainy night filled with heavy traffic and endless errands. We're just trying to get through the day, straining to see clearly through our rain-stained windshield.

I Corinthians 13:12 says that we *"see in a mirror dimly"* and *"know in part."* We cannot see with much clarity. Of course, we do hold within us some insight and understanding, but our individual experiences, our personalities, and our ways of thinking are specific, unique, and therefore somewhat limited. For this reason, things that we don't understand, don't prioritize, or don't have references for simply slip under our radar. While these particular limitations can be burdensome, they are not morally good or bad. They are simply part of our human reality. So here's the rub. Our attempts to answer life's questions from our finite perspective and resolve life's pain with our human resources will fail us miserably.

The Parody of Pain

Pain plays a larger role in shaping our worldview than we would like to admit. It alerts our survival instincts, triggering an automatic response system whereby we become driven to neutralize and/or remedy threats. Whether these threats are real or perceived, our analysis mechanisms shut off and our survival mechanisms turn on. Neither our perceptions nor our resources can be fully trusted when we shift into autopilot because our predisposed tendencies take over, often outranking our rationality. Was it rational to think that my husband would have managed to pick up another woman in less than three minutes, under my watchful eye, and with our children in the backseat? Of course not! In this case, his phone call alerted me to my false reality. But logic has seldom stopped me from taking action when I have felt threatened in the past. If my husband hadn't called, who knows what would have happened first — regaining my senses or making a fool of myself! Sadly, we don't typically ponder our options and pick the course of action that makes the most sense. Our partial-understanding, control-desiring, pain-avoiding, sin-loving responses often supersede our mental capacities and even our spiritual convictions. When pain enters the scene, all bets are off.

Because we are so emotionally driven to resolve painful situations, we will often do so without consulting or informing our conscious mind. We simply react. John Eldredge speaks of this in his book *The Sacred Romance.*

> *To say we all face a decision when we're pierced by an arrow is misleading. It makes the process sound so rational, as though we have the option of coolly assessing the situation and choosing a logical response. Life isn't like that...It feels more like an*

> *ambush, and our response is at a gut level…We may never put words to it…. If you'll listen carefully to your life, you may begin to see how it has been shaped by the unique arrows you've known and the particular convictions you've embraced as a result. The arrows also taint and partially direct even our spiritual life.*[1]

In his teaching on emotional healing, pastor and teacher Mike Plunket describes it this way:

> *Life tends to make us fall apart…shattered into pieces and we don't know any better, so we pick up the pieces and put them back together. We don't know how to assemble a healthy person, so we assemble a person who can function in the moment. The problem is, that function in the moment is actually a dysfunction for the rest of our lives.*[2]

Soulutions

The unexamined life is fraught with haphazardly established function-in-the-moment coping mechanisms I like to call "soulutions". Hidden underneath our religious veneer is a never-ending endeavor to mitigate, self-medicate, and insulate ourselves from pain and plug the holes in our souls. To be sure, we should diligently steward our minds, bodies, and souls with healthy habits, but too often our intention is to secure substitutions rather than exercise stewardship. Too often we limp along with short-sighted, make-shift antidotes to terminal problems under the false assumption that we have the resources to satisfy our needs and repair life's hurts with our own resources. Scripture paints a very different picture. It says that we are dead apart from God, utterly lost and helpless with no means with which to save, protect, heal, or improve ourselves. Total dependence upon God is our only hope, our only source for life and godliness. In our flesh, we have no power or sustainable resources. So, in reality, our "soulutions" function a bit like counterfeit grace. They compete with God as our source for life and healing, and they can insulate us from the pain that would otherwise lead us to Him.

Ray Stedman says in his book *Body Life*, "*In our shallow concern for externals we treat symptoms and not causes. We apply superficial remedies that work only for the moment, if they work at all, and then the situation is worse than it was before.*"[3] We seldom discipline ourselves to reach for what is good, nourishing, and sustainable. More often than not, we reach for comforts that numb us for a moment, but when they wear off – and they always do – we're twice as miserable as before. Any sane person would connect the dots and run for help, but we usually just go back for more. Even then we won't admit it because we've become addicted to them.

I don't suppose most of us would consider coping mechanisms to be idolatry. Perhaps we believe the flesh has some measure of power. Unfortunately, our fascination with self-sufficiency is a fantasy. There's no such thing as a self-sufficient human. We were not created for autonomy. We were created for God's glory. As C.S. Lewis wrote in *The Problem of Pain*:

> They [Adam and Eve] wanted, as we say, to "call their souls their own." But that means to live a lie, for our souls are not, in fact, our own. They wanted some corner in the universe of which they could say to God, "This is our business, not yours." But there is no such corner. They wanted to be nouns, but they were, and eternally must be, mere adjectives.[4]

We are not self-sustaining, self-defining creatures. On the contrary, as Lewis says, we're adjectives. We offer the world a colorful description of the Creator. Like the rest of creation, we were designed for worship (Luke 19:40). The question is: who will we worship? (See Matt. 6:24 and Rom. 1:20-23.)

This is the choice God placed before Adam and Eve in the garden. They could eat from any tree of the garden, except the Tree of the Knowledge of Good and Evil. Doubting God and desiring the way of autonomy, self-determination, and self-sufficiency, they chose the counterfeit. And throughout the ages, all mankind has been presented with the same choice. God gave Noah a boat for the salvation of all who would come to it for shelter. God gave Jonah a whale, and the Ninevites another chance. He gave the Jews the Passover lamb, and the Law and the prophets. And ultimately, He gave Jesus to the world. But just as Adam and Eve rejected God and ate from the tree that brought death, all their children have done likewise. The earliest generations chose the tower of Babel. The Israelites chose the golden calf, then a king, then religiosity, and ultimately Barabbas. We too reach into the bag of human strength and wisdom, calling it ridiculous things like progress, the human spirit, and the American Dream. In so doing, we reject God and agree with the mantra of the enemy. *God is not worthy, I am!* In other words, we reject an opportunity for life and healing, and embrace spiritual bondage instead.

The Anatomy of Spiritual Bondage

Anytime we choose to reject God's love, grace, and truth, and grab for other ways to protect ourselves from pain or secure for ourselves some measure of pleasure, we have committed an act of idolatry which ushers sickness into our souls. Left unattended, it will grow. Even though we are often unaware of these little decisions of the heart, the consequences are real and cascading. The sinful patterns that often emerge from this sickness cannot be remedied by trying harder, by reminding ourselves of what is good, true, and right, or even by repenting for the sin patterns themselves. The split-second, half-witted choices we make in the deep soul must be exposed and surrendered up to God before we can be released from their grip. These choices, my friends, are what make for spiritual and emotional bondage. This is what happens when we forget to take our pain to God, when we fail to yield to His ways, and when we neglect to receive His sufficiency.

Second Corinthians 10 offers some descriptive vocabulary that might help us as we grapple with these ideas.

> *For though we walk in the flesh, we do not war according to the flesh, for the weapons of our warfare are not of the flesh, but divinely powerful for the destruction of fortresses. We are destroying speculations and every lofty thing raised up against the knowledge of God, and we are taking every thought captive to the obedience of Christ...* (2 Cor. 10:3-5)

First, Paul sets the stage by reminding us that we are at war, a reality we would do well to embrace. Then he describes the nature of our battle: a spiritual battle waged within our mind against a true knowledge of God. This battle is fought according to the power of God, and it is fought for His glory. Paul describes what we are up against: *"fortresses"*, *"speculations"*, and *"lofty things."* Finally, he rebukes the Corinthians for making judgments based on appearances (2 Cor. 10:7), which sums up their short-sightedness and ours.

The words *"fortresses"* in the NASB and *"strongholds"* according to the NET come from the original Greek word *kathairesis*, meaning *to fortify through the idea of holding safely.* In simple terms, a fortress is something we attempt to grab hold of, but it ends up having a greater hold on us. It's a dangerous and deceptive sin which we embrace because we think it will supply us with what we want and need.

The next two words, *"speculations"* (logismos) and *"lofty things"* (hypsoma) are the thoughts, reasoning, or judgments set up to protect our fortress. They are the excuses and justifications, the wall of resistance which we throw up anytime our sin is exposed, anytime we experience the natural consequences of it, and anytime we feel the sting of shame or conviction about it. This is the madness of spiritual bondage. It will destroy us, yet we will defend it.

For this reason, Paul points out that self-determined effort and discipline cannot overcome a stronghold (spiritual bondage). We need the precise revelation of God to expose our strongholds, and His supernatural power to eradicate them as we respond in repentance. David knew this, as evidenced by his words in Psalm 51. He wrote this particular psalm in the wake of his sin with Bathsheba. Pouring out his heart before God, he repented for the sin (behavior) that he was aware of: *"Wash me thoroughly from my iniquity, and cleanse me from my sin. For I know my transgressions, and my sin is ever before me"* (Ps. 51:2-3). But he also asked God to uncover the deeper realities of his iniquity, the hidden thoughts and motives within his heart. *"Behold, You desire truth in the innermost being, and in the hidden part You will make me know wisdom....Create in me a clean heart, O God, and renew a steadfast spirit within me"* (Ps. 51:6-10).

Perhaps we could liken spiritual bondage to the high places of the Old Testament. These idolatrous places of worship are mentioned 117 times in the Biblical record. That is too many times for a nation who had been instructed to tear them down before they entered Canaan (Num. 33:52, 55)! In their sordid drama of idolatry and immorality, Israel periodically repented for their sinful ways and recommitted themselves to God. Yet they repeatedly failed to destroy the idolatry of their hearts, evidenced by the continued existence of the high places. With the exception of Josiah (2 Kings 23:19) and Hezekiah (2 Kings 18:4), even righteous kings failed to rid the nation of these pagan shrines (Jehoshaphat in 1 Kings 22:43, Jehoash in 2 Kings 12:3, Azariah in 2 Kings 15:3–4, and Jotham in 2 Kings 15:34-35). We often do the same, focusing on sin management, behavior modification, and coping skills rather than going for the source of the problem: the spiritual bondage of the heart. Until we invite God into those dark places and repent for what only He can reveal, our secret thoughts and intentions will continue to have a powerful influence over us.

Questions for Reflection

1. *Why are coping mechanisms, or "soulutions" as Janalee likes to call them, likened to counterfeit grace?*

2. *What should we do with our pain?*

3. *What is spiritual bondage?*

4. *Why do sin management, behavior modification, and coping skills not solve our sin problems? What do we need to do instead?*

5. *Is the Holy Spirit revealing any thoughts or intentions that need to be addressed? If so, what are they?*

The Unholy Trinity

Sometimes, our spiritual bondage is more complicated than just a subconscious reaction to pain or a fleshly desire to satisfy our own wants and needs. Sometimes things are not as simple as we would like them to be. Quite naturally, we assume that every thought and temptation is our own, that we get ourselves into these fixes alone. But that's not always the case. While we are perfectly capable of rebellion, manipulation, and deception without any provocation at all, sometimes we have an unseen accomplice. The Bible informs us that man is not alone in his rebellion against God. The battle wages within and without. According to Scripture, we're up against the flesh, the world, and the Devil. Acknowledging all three forces in our spiritual struggle and recognizing their collaboration is vital. Here is what Scripture says.

- **The Flesh:** The book of Romans explains the implications of man's fall from a doctrinal point of view. Chapters 3 and 5 tell us that the *"first Adam"* brought sin into the world, and all people since then have been born dead in sin. Jews and Gentiles alike are under sin. Romans 3:10-12 says, *"There is none righteous, not even one. There is none who seeks for God; all have turned aside, together they have become useless..."* Simply put, sin brought death and destruction to mankind. The *"second Adam,"* Christ, brought healing and restoration to those who would trust in Him, yet we still live with a flesh that is fallen. Our new nature resonates with the truth of God. Our redeemed self loves the Lord, desires what is good and holy, and longs to please Him and live according to His ways. This is our new identity and our truest self. Yet, in our flesh, we are rebellious and resistant to God. As believers, we are no longer identified by this old nature and its sinful desires, but if we do not daily and decisively put it to death, we will become weak and carnal, living in subjection to that which brings death. Galatians 5:17 says, *"For the flesh sets its desire against the Spirit, and the Spirit against the flesh; for these are in opposition to one another, so you may not do the things that you please."*

- **The World:** Just as mankind fell into the slavery of sin, creation has also been subjected to corruption. Romans 8:20 says, *"For the creation was subjected to futility, not of its own will, but because of Him who subjected it..."* The earth is cursed and set against man's dominion, but we are not waging a spiritual battle against the earth. Therefore, "the world" is not usually a literal term referring to creation, but actually means the entire fallen human system. While the flesh is the internal set of evil desires, the world is the external system of wickedness, encompassing those who have not been made right with the Father through Christ. From the world comes the lust of the eyes, the lust of the flesh, and the boastful pride of life (1 John 2:16).

- **The Devil:** Ironically, the cursed serpent who was found guilty of deceit and sinful enticement in the Genesis account has managed to find a place of prominence in our world. Both man and creation are subjected to his temporary reign here on earth. The apostle

John says, *"We know that we are of God, and that the whole world lies in the power of the evil one"* (1 John 5:19). Paul calls the Devil the *"god of this age"* in 2 Corinthians 4:4(NET). We are living in enemy territory, aliens and strangers in a lost land. We're playing a game of double jeopardy. Because Christ was victorious over sin and death, our eternal destiny is tied up with Him and we are no longer captives of Satan. Instead, we are his targeted enemies. And our constant waywardness provides him with ample ammunition for his bloody battle. So, we are hated for our spiritual redemption, and we are exploited for what remains of our flesh!

Here, in part, is the point of contention for many of us. Christ's work on the cross was perfect and complete. When He declared, *"It is finished"*, it was because He had accomplished the mission for which He was sent (John 19:30). But does this mean that the war is over, that we no longer wrestle with these three forces of evil? Yes and no. Yes: because of what Christ did for us, we can have victory. No: victory is not automatic. It will not be granted to us without our participation. Salvation offers us far more than we realize and far more than we actualize. It offers us freedom from the sins that have been modeled to us; freedom from the trappings of sins committed against us; freedom from our own sin; and freedom from the anguishing snares of the enemy. But that freedom comes to us as we move to the rhythms of God in submission to His Spirit. Specifically, we are told to walk by the Spirit and to deny our flesh (Gal. 5:16, 24); to love God and not the world (1 John 2:15); to submit to God and resist the schemes of the enemy (James 4:7). None of these things are accomplished automatically or without our intentional participation.

We might like to believe that our inner world is private property, but all three of these forces can attack us on a conscious and subconscious level, enticing us with opportunities to rebel against God. Therefore, we can succumb to deep and binding agreements with all three, whether they are operating independently or in concert. According to Karl Payne in his book *Spiritual Warfare*, we will need to become discerning and take up arms against these forces if we hope to live victoriously.

> *The world, the flesh, and the Devil are each real, and each represents one third of the spiritual warfare pie that Christians must learn to recognize and confront...Each piece of this pie*

represents opponents equally capable of destroying our testimony for the Lord Jesus Christ. Consequently, to ignore or to glorify one part of the warfare pie at the expense of the other two is a tragic mistake.[5]

Robertson McQuilkin has said, "*It seems easier to go to a consistent extreme than to stay at the center of biblical tension.*"[6] This is certainly true of spiritual warfare! There are churches, and perhaps even denominations, that overemphasize the work of the Devil and downplay the enticements of the world and/or the lusts of the flesh. But more commonly there is a reluctance to acknowledge, study, or teach on the work of the Devil. Pastors and counselors receive little to no instruction or training in the subject of demonic activity, and sound lay materials are similarly sparse. Books, articles, and blogs dealing with the flesh and the world abound but finding non-sensational material on the Devil and his demons is far more difficult.

The paradoxical confusion is not usually over the New Testament writers' awareness of spiritual warfare, but rather over the relative silence of the Evangelical church in North America about it, despite Scripture's testimony to its reality. Why so hesitant to train people to distinguish between the various tactics and warfare strategies of the world, the flesh, and the Devil?[7]

We might be a little skittish about the demonic, but Scripture is not. It paints a vivid picture of who the Devil is and what he actually does. Consider the following:

Tempter

- *Stop depriving one another, except by agreement for a time, so that you may devote yourselves to prayer, and come together again lest Satan tempt you because of your lack of self-control.* (1 Cor. 7:5)
- *Then Jesus was led up by the Spirit into the wilderness to be tempted by the devil.* (Matt. 4:1)

Opportunist

- *Be of sober spirit, be on the alert. Your adversary, the Devil, prowls about like a roaring lion, seeking someone to devour.* (1 Peter 5:8)
- *But whom you forgive anything, I forgive also; for indeed what I have forgiven, if I have forgiven anything, I did it for your sakes in the presence*

of Christ, in order that no advantage be taken of us by Satan; for we are not ignorant of his schemes. (2 Cor. 2:10-11)

- *BE ANGRY, AND yet DO NOT SIN; do not let the sun go down on your anger, and do not give the devil an opportunity. (Eph. 4:26-27)*

Deceiver

- *And the woman said, "The serpent deceived me, and I ate." (Gen. 3:13)*
- *But I am afraid lest, as the serpent deceived Eve by his craftiness, your minds should be led astray from the simplicity and purity of devotion to Christ. (2 Cor. 11:3)*
- *But the Spirit explicitly says that in later times some will fall away from the faith, paying attention to deceitful spirits and doctrines of demons... (1 Tim. 4:1)*

Liar

- *You are of your father the Devil, and you want to do the desires of your father. He was a murderer from the beginning and does not stand in the truth because there is no truth in him. Whenever he speaks a lie, he speaks from his own nature; for he is a liar, and the father of lies. (John 8:44)*

Accuser

- *Then he showed me Joshua the high priest standing before the angel of the LORD, and Satan standing at his right hand to accuse him. (Zech. 3:1)*
- *Now the salvation, and the power, and the kingdom of our God and the authority of His Christ have come, for the accuser of our brethren has been thrown down, who accuses them before our God day and night. (Rev. 12:10)*

Persecutor of the Saints

- *Do not fear what you are about to suffer. Behold, the Devil is about to cast some of you into prison, that you may be tested, and you will have tribulation ten days. Be faithful until death, and I will give you the crown of life. (Rev. 2:10)*

Clearly there is a larger and long-overdue discussion to be had here. But limiting ourselves to the issue of spiritual bondage, we can conclude that our flesh has wicked desires, the world dazzles us with wicked possibilities, and our enemy looks for vulnerable opportunities where he can utilize these forces to lure us into treasonous agreements.

Unknowingly, we can take part in his schemes and agree with his deceptions and distortions. Have you thought about who he is and the role he might be playing in your negative self-talk, your addiction, your bitterness, or your temper? We're going to be pretty confused about this life, and pretty ineffective in our spiritual battles, if we don't take our enemy into account. To put it bluntly, considering the possibility that the Devil may in fact be involved in our spiritual bondage may be uncharted territory in our Western church culture and it may push the envelope of our theology, but it is highly relevant to our current struggles.

The Second Great Awakening

When God interrupted my performance-driven life and introduced me to His life-giving, soul-satisfying Gospel of grace, it was the beginning of a new work in me. This was my "First Great Awakening", but only the first phase of a much longer journey. A few short months after I joyfully discovered and embraced this new way of life, my husband and I entered a season of significant difficulties. It felt as if we were thrown headlong down a long and winding staircase of disaster. We were pounded by one blow after another until we hit bottom. It was four miserable years, and the consequences dragged on for another seven. It certainly felt severe —but it was a severe mercy. In His goodness, God crushed our little house built upon the sand, because it couldn't stand. We didn't have a chance in this world with the relationship we had, with the baggage we were carrying, or with the tools in our toolbelt. Relying upon our own understanding and our own resources was all we knew to do, but it was treasonous, and we serve a jealous God.

Thus, He orchestrated that tumultuous storm to get my attention. Once He had it, He showed me three things:

- **First,** I had not been guarding or attending to my heart. He began to reveal areas where I had been hurt or wounded, areas where I had been vulnerable and failed to go to Him with my pain. Instead I had tried to protect myself.
- **Second,** like most of us, I had not recognized or refuted the work of the enemy. Because I don't possess the resources to heal myself or protect myself from pain, I ended up embracing the enemy's

counsel. I took every thought that raced across my mind and every feeling that bubbled up from my heart as if it were my own. I never thought to ask the questions: *Where did that come from? Is it mine? Is it true, good, and right?* Not only did I not ask questions, but I never put up a fight. I didn't take these thoughts captive, didn't challenge them, even if they were dishonest or destructive. I simply owned them, agreed with them, completely oblivious to the cascading impact they would have.

- **Third**, I was practicing superficial repentance. Although these were inadvertent choices of my heart rather than willful choices of my mind, they established a foothold or place for the enemy's influence. My unrepentant sin gave room for him, giving him opportunity to add fuel to my fleshly desires. The result was a cycle of habitual sins I felt helpless to break. Even worse, they produced a hardness in me toward God, and robbed me of His felt presence. Despite all this, I wanted more in my relationship with God and repeatedly repented for my bad behavior, but it didn't do much good. My repentance was sincere, but sadly insufficient and thus yielded short-lived victories. This is because my behavior was motivated by or symptomatic of the soul sickness in my heart (Matt. 15:1-20). I needed to repent for the thoughts and intentions of my heart, not just for the manifestations of them.

God used the pain of our circumstances to expose my brokenness and then He invited me into wholeness. Bit by bit, He led me to deep and abiding repentance, then ushered in His healing presence, bringing peace and comfort where there had been only fear and pain. As Job 5:18 says, *"For He inflicts pain and gives relief; He wounds and His hands also heal."* I will walk through the gates of glory praising God that He loved me where I was but did not allow me to stay there. Because of His jealous affection, He pursued my heart with gentle persistence. He moved me beyond the grace of relief, the grace that freed me from a performance-driven life and invited me into the grace of healing.

Questions for Reflection

1. *Have any of the pieces in the spiritual warfare pie been neglected in your spiritual life?*

2. *The unholy trinity of the flesh, the world, and the Devil entice us with opportunities to rebel against God. What does Scripture say we must do to get out from under their influence?*

3. *Why is repenting for our bad behavior insufficient?*

4. *What were the three things Janalee was ignoring in her spiritual life?*

The Other Side of Grace

The grace that had come to me by sinking below the waves and dying to my self-sufficiency was no longer enough. There was more to be had in my relationship with God, and a new kind of grace was the path to get it. I needed to learn how to survive and thrive while developing untried muscles and operate in a distinctly different form of grace. I needed to learn how to breathe underwater.

Quite frankly, the grace I initially received was a welcomed relief and felt much like a soft whisper and a loving embrace. My "Second Great Awakening" grace was nothing like that. It was a rude kind of awakening that felt more like having someone rip the blankets from me and splash a cup of cold water in my face. It gave me a good whiff of the mess I had made. It took me firmly by the hand and walked me through the valley of the shadow of death, until I was willing to give up my idols and resist the enemy's influences. It embraced pain with a purpose. It wasn't cheap grace. At times, it felt very weighty as it broke through my decidedly hard heart and presented me with opportunities to choose truth or falsehood, God or idols, life or death (Deut. 29). It required me to participate in the battle for my heart, my soul, and my healing. It was a harder pill to swallow, but a truer rescue for sure.

Let us embrace the high purpose of grace. It does not exist to overlook sin. It exists to welcome us into a relationship with God, and to fiercely protect that relationship! Praise God for the soft grace that mends us when we are brokenhearted, and for the hard grace that injures us when we are hard-hearted.

Hear me on this. My God did not shame me. He did not condemn me. He is compassionate toward us, even in our sin. It is because of His love that He reveals our sin. And in so doing, He always shows us the way out. Every time the Holy Spirit convicts us of sin, He also invites us to receive more grace, more love, and more freedom (Gal. 5:1). According to the book of Luke, Jesus declared this to be part of His ministry. When He introduced Himself to the Jews and launched His public ministry, He stood in the temple and read from the book of Isaiah, *"The Spirit of the Lord GOD is upon me, because the LORD has anointed me to bring good news to the afflicted; He has sent me to bind up the brokenhearted, to proclaim liberty to captives and freedom to prisoners; to proclaim the favorable year of the LORD..."* (Is. 61:1-2). He then went on to declare that He was the fulfillment of this Scripture.

Do You Want to Be Well?

One of our daughters had a fierce love for her pointer finger. She sucked the life out of it for several years and refused to give up the habit. After she'd fallen asleep one night, I went into her bedroom with the hope that I could pry that finger out of her mouth, but the more I pulled, the harder she sucked. After a rousing game of tug-of-war, she ended up sitting upright in her bed, still fast asleep, with that finger affixed to the roof of her mouth! Sometimes, we just don't want to let go of our habits!

Even though He came to heal and to save, Jesus still asked the afflicted if they *wanted* to be made well. He never asked if they had enough faith. He never asked if they thought they deserved it. He never balked at the enemy's claims to the person. He simply asked if they would choose to give up their sickness and submit their will to freedom. It's a good question, because sometimes we like our sickness. Sometimes we like our chains. Perhaps we like the attention, the familiarity, or the excuses. Regardless, our idols give us just enough benefit to keep us from reaching out to God. John Eldredge says:

> *Rescuing the human heart is the hardest mission in the world.*
> *The dilemma of the Story is this: we don't know if we want to be*
> *rescued. We are so enamored with our small stories and our false*

gods, we are so bound up in our addictions and our self-centeredness and take-it-for-granted unbelief that we don't even know how to cry out for help. And the Evil One has no intention of letting his captives walk away scot-free. He seduces us, deceives us, assaults us – whatever it takes to keep us in darkness.[8]

We must admit that we doubt God's ability to sustain us better than our idols do. But then what do we do with Romans 8:31-32? *"If God is for us, who can be against us? He who did not spare His own Son, but delivered Him for us all, how will He not also with Him freely give us all things?"* These are not lofty and unattainable promises available only to the most spiritual among us. We, in our human experience, can know Him and actualize His promises. But we cannot experience the life lived through the Spirit *while* we are living for idols of our own making.

Too often we want deliverance from the pain we're in, but we don't really want deliverance from our idols. Remember the Israelites? They walked around with PTSD, romanticizing over leeks, onions, and garlic. Labor camps in Egypt, now those were the glory days, right? Like abuse victims or prison inmates so often do, they had so identified themselves with their bondage that they did not know how to live free, and they were too afraid to try. If God had not stepped in and confined them to the wilderness, they would have gone back to Egypt!

There is no way to escape the fact that our will must be committed to freedom. After all, it was by an act of our will that we chose the bondage we're in right now, whether we were aware of it or not. Being committed to freedom is not common. Commonly, when we speak of our spiritual bondage, we say things like, *"I'm struggling with anger issues…or lust…or an addiction."* But we aren't usually struggling in the true sense of the word. According to the Oxford Dictionary, to struggle is to *"make forceful or violent efforts to get free of restraint or constriction."*[9] So when we say we're struggling with something, are we exerting great effort to rid it from our life and soul? Because, if we aren't risking life and limb to get free, we're just sitting in it. We're just suffering the consequences of our choices and alternating between moments of self-pity and self-loathing. We may hate the consequences, but we have chosen them over the process of getting out of whatever holds us captive. And we will continue like this until the pain of staying the same outweighs the pain of change. Then, and only then, will we truly start to struggle.

This is not to say that we can accomplish anything by our own strength and determination. According to the flesh, we have nothing at our disposal but behavior modification. But the promise of the Gospel is transformation, and God asks us to contribute our choice as part of the equation. Even that can be transformed by His power. With a hesitant heart and a fleshly desire for sin, we can pray that God would *bend* our will toward His. We are always granted the grace to submit ourselves to Him. Our hearts of stone have been permanently altered and become hearts of flesh, hearts that are capable of change. It is not without difficulty, not without effort, but it is possible.

Rather than filling the void, denying our sin, or hiding our shame, we can repent, work through the process of change, and receive healing. Rather that writhing about in the darkness, we can walk toward the light of His grace and allow Him to redeem the pieces of our hearts taken captive by the enemy. We can allow Him to connect the dots, untie the knots, and free us from the falsehoods that fog our understanding of our life and circumstances. We can learn to breathe underwater.

In our own strength, we can accomplish nothing. With our own understanding, we miss most of what's going on. According to our natural ways, we encounter pain and we simply react. But God sees accurately who we are. He knows the truth about every situation. He understands the nature of man, the temptations we face, and the tactics of the enemy. He has overcome them all. He is able to take our grossest sin and give us an abundant life in return. Don't trust yourself in this life. Don't waste your pain! Submit it to God and He will bring forth life and healing. He can restore your broken heart.

Contrast the post-Egypt Israelites with Shadrach, Meshach, and Abednego in Daniel 3:8-30. After being bound and thrown into a fiery furnace, these three men were rescued by God and they walked out without a scratch. Not one hair on their heads was singed, nor did they smell of smoke. The only proof of their trial was the fact that the fire had consumed their bonds. Isn't that a beautiful picture of spiritual healing?

It's a severe mercy when God allows us to endure the flames, but in my experience, it has been worth it. The flames may have hurt my feelings, but they saved my soul. Thank God for the flames, because I don't miss my bondage. I never want to go back to Egypt. But I do want to spend the rest of my life telling you how God has led me out thus far. In the next several chapters, that's exactly what I hope to do: tell my story of God's gracious rescue. I hope to pour out my life upon these pages so that you might be encouraged, challenged, and infused with confidence that He is what we need. He is the Way out of every trial and temptation. He is the Truth that sets us free. And He is the Life that we have been longing for.

Questions for Reflection

1. *What is the difference between the kind of grace Janalee experienced in her "First Great Awakening" and her "Second Great Awakening"?*

2. *Grace does not exist to overlook sin, but to welcome us into and protect what?*

3. *What causes us to get beyond the cycle of self-loathing and self-pity?*

4. *Is there anything you are truly struggling to be free of?*

5. *Are there any thoughts or issues that have surfaced during your reading of this chapter that require some attention?*

Chapter 3

The Great Paradox

"Once God has spoken; twice I have heard this: that power belongs to God; and lovingkindness is Yours, O Lord." (Psalm 62:11-12a)

What's God Going to Do About That?

It was the wee hours of the morning when the sounds of muffled cries jolted me out of my slumber. I dragged myself out from the warmth of the covers and stumbled to my daughter's bedside where I found her sitting upright, whimpering, and clutching her blankets. She'd had another bad dream. As she told it, the house had caught on fire while we were together in her second-story bedroom. My husband broke a window and helped us all climb out to escape the smoke, but when we landed in the bushes below, we were met by malicious snakes who spat poisonous venom at us.

Poor thing! I wrapped my arms around her little frame and whispered assurances that all was well. But my best mommy kisses and cuddles offered her little comfort. Her cries only continued, so I tried to distract her with offers of a trip to the kitchen for a snack, but she refused. She was in a full-blown tizzy. I adjusted my strategy because, as you know, little ones don't understand the difference between fantasy and real life. Taking a deep breath, I gave her exactly what she needed: a good reality check. With a voice of glad confidence, I expressed my relief that it was just a dream and reminded her that we have reliable fire alarms and a sensible exit strategy. I detailed my spur-of-the-moment-very-good-plan for getting out in the case of a fire and assured her that snakes are afraid of people. Nope. She just glared at me. At that point, I became a bit offended. She'd left me with no other recourse. I hauled out the big guns and challenged her faith. Pulling on her chin until her eyes were locked onto mine, I asked her if she trusted God to take care of her. The words had barely left my mouth when she shouted, *"Mom! If a lion eats me, I'm still dead. What's God going to do about that?"* She had a point there. Feeling a bit stumped, I went back to my mommy kisses and cuddles.

Finally, she slipped back into the land of sleep and I took my exit, sulking away with my tail between my legs and a dent in my armor. "Princess-by-Day/Ruthless-Interrogator-by-Night" had really forced open a messy can of worms, and they were riddled with irony. She still believed in the benevolence of a make-believe Tooth Fairy, but she was having trouble believing that God Almighty had the power or will to protect her! Implied in her statement was the assumption that God would not or could not protect her from harm. If I wasn't mistaken, she was actually accusing Him of being irrelevant! Kids are so honest. They don't know they're supposed to keep such heresies to themselves.

She was young and her conclusions a bit impertinent, but she wasn't saying anything I wasn't already thinking. The difference between us was that I knew better than to admit it. I shared her fears and indignation but questioning the character of God didn't feel like a very safe thing to do, so I decided to file it away and move on with life. Next thing I knew, she was needling me, stirring the pot, and forcing me out of hiding.

In retrospect, it was a wonderful thing she did for me, but I'll explain all about that in the next chapter. Before we talk about me, we need to talk about us and our problem with pain. Because pain is where all our messes begin.

The Problem of Pain

This puzzle has haunted mankind throughout the ages. How can a good and powerful God allow wickedness and suffering in this world? It's the problem of pain: the great paradox. We know this isn't how things were meant to be. Things like layoffs, genocide, slander, slavery, sex trafficking, prejudice, Wall Street bailouts, natural disasters, and cellulite were not part of the original plan. But somehow, we forget about paradise lost, we're too impatient to wait for "kingdom come", and we want a reasonable explanation for the here and now. Does it really have to be this way? Certainly, a loving God would end the suffering. But He doesn't, and we all want to know why.

British Evangelical John Stott once said, *"The fact of suffering undoubtedly constitutes the single greatest challenge to the Christian faith, and has been in every generation."*[1] ABC News agrees with him. Several years ago, they put out an article entitled "Are You Angry at God?" At the time, their research revealed that 9 out of 10 people believed in the existence of God, yet most of them admitted to being angry with Him. Pain and suffering were cited as the primary cause of their resentment: *"Why does He allow babies to starve in third world countries, why does He allow bad things to happen, why does He — either actively or passively — cause so much grief?"*[2]

Trying to reconcile God's character with the wretchedness of what we experience in this life feels like a dilemma of epic proportions. Is there a way to maintain our integrity while holding to both an honest account of the human experience and a Biblical doctrine of God? Sometimes, we can chalk up our difficulties to the natural order of things, because some ills are so common to man that they make sense. The flu is contagious. Jobs can be hard to find. Our parents get old. Financial difficulties plague the rich and the poor. Cars break down. Parking spots are not manna from heaven. And eventually, we're all going to look and feel our age. We can find some logic in these things, a reasonable connection between cause and consequence, even though they may hurt our feelings. But sometimes, we feel like life, and perhaps God Himself, are against us. Our hardships can be so shocking and intense that they knock us off our feet. Life-altering storms can hit when they are nowhere on the radar screen. We can pray about situations that go from bad to worse. We can head down a path lit by faith in God's gracious leading, and our yellow brick road can turn into the valley of the shadow of death. Sometimes life's troubles are more than a little disappointing. They are unexpected, violating, and personal. There are things that don't make sense, things that don't fit with the story of our lives, things that threaten to undo us, things which we've done nothing to cause and only He could have foreseen or prevented. So, if God is personally involved in our lives, and He is supremely good and supremely powerful, why doesn't He do something about those kinds of things?

In *The Problem of Pain*, C.S. Lewis writes, *"Try to exclude the possibility of suffering which the order of nature and the existence of free-wills involve, and you find that you have excluded life itself."*[3] I suppose if God always rescued His people like He does in the Sunday School stories, He would be easy to trust. I'm certain that we would all feel better if we could expect delicate treatment from the One who presides over the universe. I'm equally sure that Christianity would have a greater market appeal if its converts were a bit more respectable and prosperous. But a few years on planet Earth eliminates those notions. My daughter had figured that one out. And even though the God of the Bible claims to be supremely good and powerful, the Gospel does not promise us immediate sanctification, gratification, prosperity, or safety in *this* life. Bear in mind the stories of the saints. They are not always pretty. Joseph went to jail as an innocent man. Hosea had to marry a prostitute and serve as a visual aid for the nation of Israel. Moses spent most of his years wandering in the desert. Jeremiah cried his life away. Most of the prophets were persecuted and murdered. All but one of the disciples died for their faith. In the past century, more believers have died for their faith than in the rest of history combined.

Listen to what Paul says in 2 Corinthians 1:8-9.

> *For we do not want you to be unaware, brethren, of our affliction which came to us in Asia, that we were burdened excessively, beyond our strength, so that we despaired even of life; indeed, we had the sentence of death within ourselves so that we would not trust in ourselves, but in God who raises the dead...*

(Review 2 Corinthians 11:23-28 for a fuller account of his tribulations.) If Paul is speaking truthfully, then his circumstances were more than he could stomach, and he wasn't just being dramatic. He despaired of life because it was more than he could bear. This unsavory idea tends to polarize people, as we see in John 6:52-58. Jesus was speaking to the masses when He announced that those who want eternal life must eat of His flesh and drink of His blood. Most people weren't looking for that kind of Messiah. When it came to His miracles, they were all in, but when He explained the costs of salvation and discipleship, most just walked away.

Like the Jews who walked away from their Messiah, we can walk away from our God if we think the cost outweighs the benefits. He didn't work for us. He failed us. He was too rigid or too distant or too powerless. What are we supposed to believe about Him in light of what's happening in this world...in light of what is happening to us?

<u>*Questions for Reflection*</u>

1. *How do we know that this life isn't what it was meant to be?*

2. *Have the struggles and difficulties of your life caused you to feel angry with God, to question where He is, or to doubt His care for you?*

3. *What have you done with those doubts and negative feelings?*

A Little Wager

Nowhere do we see this struggle more clearly in Scripture than in the story of Job. Living in the time of the patriarchs, Job had no knowledge of the law, and we have no record of prophets in that day. Nevertheless, he knew and worshipped God. He was a righteous man and Scripture tells us that God was well-pleased with him. No one could point a finger at him, not even Satan, which is why he was so viciously targeted. With God's permission, Satan set him up and Job was handed a season of suffering so severe that it caused a scandalous debate over the character of God.

In the opening scene from the heavenly realm, God the Father bragged on Job to both the heavenly host and to Satan himself. The father of lies and lover of evil hated to see such a blameless and upright man enjoying favor with the Almighty. Quite likely, he was equally aggravated to see God receiving genuine and faithful worship, and that from a mere mortal. So, when God pointed Job out as an object lesson on righteousness, Satan countered by cynically accusing Him of buying Job's affections. He claimed that God had purchased Job's loyalty through material blessing and ease. He asserted that God had blessed Job and his whole household and had placed a hedge of protection around him. However, should God's favor be removed, Job would fold, forget his loyalties, and curse God to His face. Satan's main assertion was – and is – that God is not inherently worthy of our praise and he hoped to use Job to prove it. For some reason, God agreed to the challenge. In one afternoon, Job's happy little life fell apart. He lost his children, his flocks, his servants, and his livelihood. Yet, *"Through all this Job did not sin nor did he blame God"* (Job 1:22).

The story does not end there. In Chapter 2 we return to the same scene in heaven. The Almighty said to Satan, *"Have you considered My servant Job? For there is no one like him on the earth, a blameless and upright man fearing God and turning away from evil. And he still holds fast his integrity, although you incited Me against him to ruin him without cause"* (2:3). Again, Satan challenged God and asked Him to raise the stakes, alleging that Job would crumble should enough pressure be applied. He argued that if Job's body were also afflicted, he would curse God. And our good God could have put a stop to things right then and there, but He didn't. He could have given Satan a dose of his own medicine and poured some righteous wrath on him instead, but He didn't. For reasons we do not know, and probably wouldn't understand, God decided to continue to play along. Satan was given more leash. You know the story. Poor Job experienced an all-out assault.

Job's deep and dire anguish caused everyone around him to wrestle with the great paradox, and they came to very different conclusions. Job's wife, grieving their immense losses, gave way to cynicism. Feeling hopeless and betrayed by the God they had served so faithfully she joined the enemy's cause and taunted Job's integrity. *"Do you still hold fast your integrity? Curse God and die!"* (2:9). Observing the customary days of 'shiva', Job's friends sat silently in the presence of his suffering for a week, but they could take no more. To protect God's character, or perhaps their own self-righteous skin, they "spoke the truth in love." They asserted that God is just, and only punishes the wicked. In other words, they assumed that Job was harboring some hidden and grievous sins. *"Think now, who that was innocent ever perished? Or where were the upright cut off? As I have seen, those who plow iniquity and sow trouble reap the same"* (4:7-8). *"If you return to the Almighty, you will be restored; if you remove unrighteousness far from your tent..."* (22:23). Job, on the other hand, agreed that God was punishing him, but he claimed to have a clear conscience:

> *I am accounted wicked, why then should I toil in vain? ... For He is not a man as I am that I may answer Him, that we may go to court together. There is no umpire between us, who may lay his hand upon us both.* (Job 9:29, 32-33)

Theological Quagmires

It is no small task to apprehend a right concept of God in light of what we experience on this ball of dust. Few of us avoid the tendency to deny parts of Him, to harden ourselves against Him, to misrepresent Him, although we do it in different ways (Heb. 3:7-11; Mark 6:52, Mark 8:17-18; Rev. 3:15-16). Job's wife turned to cynicism and urged him to join her in rejecting God. His friends clung to false securities, believing God is the Grand Master of the karma game. And Job made himself out to be a martyr…and he kinda was.

Let's begin with Job's friends. Sometimes, witnessing the anguish of another person is all it takes to ruffle our feathers. Our theology of God can become so fragile, so circumstantial, that even a little sympathy rattles us. We too easily find ourselves scrambling for something to hang onto. Job's friends wanted to believe that God blesses the faithful and punishes the sinful, because they needed a formula that would give them a sense of fairness and – let's be honest – control. In a bit of desperation, they wanted to capture the situation into a manageable box. But things like God, sin, and suffering cannot be contained in a box of our making. They cannot be dissected in the laboratory of our minds. They cannot be managed or manipulated.

Let's take a brief look at some of the quagmires they found themselves in.

Sinners in the Hands of an Angry God?

"If iniquity is in your hand, put it far away, do not let wickedness reside in your tents. Surely then you will lift up your face without blemish; you will be secure and will not fear.…Your life will be brighter than the noonday" (Job 11:14-15). It's easy to feel some frustration with Job's friends because what they did was both hurtful and misinformed, but it's also pretty common and not entirely baseless. Men and women of all faiths and in every stage of history have ascribed atrocities and disasters to the wrathful hand of God upon unrepentant sinners. The Haitian earthquake of 2009 was blamed on a pact with the Devil. Hurricane Katrina, which devastated New Orleans in 2005, was blamed on sexual sin and abortion. The 2011 earthquake that struck Japan was blamed on national egoism. Even non-natural atrocities such as the Holocaust and the American Civil War have been ascribed to God's judgment upon sinful people.

There's no arguing with the fact that we are sinful, that sin produces consequences, and that God Himself is the judge of mankind. Biblical accounts of disasters, disease, and wars ordained by God on an individual and national scale are seen in both the Old and the New Testament. In fact, the beginning and end of the canon are marked by judgment. The global flood recorded in Genesis 6 is probably the most well-known account of God's judgment upon the earth, and the book of Revelation tells us that more is sure to come. On a smaller scale, we have the prophetic books which detail God's displeasure and eventual punishment of the sins of Israel and the surrounding nations. And in the New Testament, even after the atoning death of Christ, we read of both suffering and judgment due to sin.

In the book of Acts, we read of two accounts of divine judgment. One took place within the early church. Ananias and Sapphira, a married couple, chose to lie in order to promote themselves (Acts 5). Later, King Herod was smitten by God when he arrogantly embraced the worship of the people (Acts 12). In both of these cases, God's judgment was fatal, immediate, and focused only upon individuals. It should be mentioned that in these cases of divine fury, God was quite determined to receive full credit.

In the book of James, we find that sin can be the cause for suffering and sickness. James ends his letter with practical advice, including the following.

> *Is anyone among you sick? Then he must call for the elders of the church and they are to pray over him, anointing him with oil in the name of the Lord; and the prayer offered in faith will restore the one who is sick, and the Lord will raise him up, and if he has committed sins, they will be forgiven him. Therefore, confess your sins to one another, and pray for one another so that you may be healed. The effective prayer of a righteous man can accomplish much.* (James 5:14-16)

Of course, we cannot assume that all sickness, personal or otherwise, is caused by sin, but we must include it as a possibility.

Sometimes we suffer not because of divine anger or for purification of sin, but for a divine cause. John 9 tells the story of a blind man healed by Jesus. When his disciples asked Jesus if the man was blind because of his own sin or the sin of his parents, Jesus said, *"It was neither that this man sinned, nor his parents; but it was in order that the works of God might be displayed in him"* (John 9:3). Sometimes, our suffering is a divine appointment to be used for God's glory. We are as clay in the hands of the Potter. Both our design and our brokenness are utilized to manifest His brilliance (2 Cor. 4:7-12, Rom. 9:20-24, Jer. 18:6). Interestingly enough, God also shows mercy to display His glory (Gen. 6, Ezek. 39:21-25, Jer. 6). Thus, we know that God will vindicate Himself, but He will not always do so with judgment.

Finally, in Job's case, we are told that he was afflicted not because of his sin, but because of Satan's wicked agenda. Even though Job was a man and therefore also a sinner, God was pleased with Him. He told Satan, *"You incited Me against him to ruin him without cause"* (Job 2:3). Without cause! Sometimes we suffer at the hand of the enemy, but without guilt or sinful cause. Let us be cautious. Suffering is certain, but the causes are not always so clear.

Questions for Reflection

1. *Do you agree that things like God and sin cannot be managed or manipulated? Why or why not?*

2. *Janalee argues that suffering is certain, but the causes of suffering are often unclear. Are there times when the causes of suffering are clear?*

3. *"The gospel does not promise us immediate sanctification, gratification, prosperity, or safety in this life." Do you agree with this statement? Why or why not?*

Curse God and Die?

This brings us to Job's wife. She played a small role in the story, but her pain was enormous, and her comments were significant. Thus she must not be overlooked. We all know the sinking ache of losing our keys, our phone, or our wallet. But what about losing your children, your livelihood, and all your possessions in a day? Not to diminish her material losses, for they were terrible, but consider the fact that losing a child is about the most difficult thing a parent can experience, and she lost every single one. She brought flowers and tears to at least ten graves! In that particular culture and time, children were a woman's everything: her identity, her purpose, her value, and her future. It's not farfetched to suppose that she felt lost to all that she had been living for. Therefore, she says, *"Do you still hold fast your integrity? Curse God and die!"* (Job 2:9).

It's quite possible that her advice to Job was the projection of her own death wish. Even so, there's something darker than hopelessness in her words. It wasn't just death that she spoke of. She mocked Job for his integrity and challenged him to curse God. That does add a different dimension to her death wish, does it not? I want to speak tenderly because her pain was very real and very raw, but she allowed her heart to move from questioning God to resentfully rejecting Him. In fact, her word choice sounds hauntingly similar to what Satan twice predicted. *"Put forth Your hand now, and touch his bone and his flesh; he will curse You to Your face"* (Job 1:11 and 2:5).

If even only for that moment, she sided with the enemy and tried to incite Job to do the same. She offered him the forbidden fruit. Job's response to her might appear harsh, but it was better than taking a bite and it was probably what she needed to hear. Based on what we know of the rest of the story, it's likely that she received it. *"You speak as one of the foolish women speaks. Shall we indeed accept good from God and not accept adversity?"* (2:10). Women do not take a liking to comparisons, especially when they are on the losing end of the stick, but perhaps Job was speaking boldly and not harshly? Perhaps he was trying to pull her out of the fog and show her just how misguided and out of character her words were. In so doing, he also reminded her of the truth that she had once embraced. Their status and wealth were not simply fruits of their own labor and intellectual pursuits, but that they had been blessed by Jehovah Jireh, and He was good and right to also withhold that blessing. In either case, to Him Job declared his allegiance.

The fact that Job's wife struggled with cynical despair, doubts, and anger with God is neither unusual nor alarming in itself. We will all face those moments. In her book *On Asking God Why*, Elisabeth Elliot says that she faced a similar fork in the road when her missionary husband, Jim Elliot, was speared to death by Auca Indians: *"Jim's death required me to deny God or believe Him, to trust Him or renounce Him. The lesson is the same for all of us. The contexts differ."*[4] Our doubts, anger, and hopelessness must be brought out of the shadows and into the light, which must begin by admitting them to God, but not end there. We must also wrestle within a safe and gracious community of allies who will fight for us and earnestly pursue our healing. It is essential that we humble ourselves to this process and offer this to each other, because the alternative can be dangerous.

Why?

At times, Job's language appears to be contradictory, rash, and even incoherent. He vacillates between anger and fear, self-hatred and self-righteousness, hope and despondence. It isn't realistic to expect much more from those who are in crisis. During a crisis or trauma, our ability to reason and logically process information is compromised. Quite aptly, he points this out when he says, *"Do you intend to reprove my words, when the words of one in despair belong to the wind?"* (6:26). His friends confused his temporary deductions and gut-wrenching emotions for absolute conclusions. Therefore, they attempted to loosen his grip on weak branches that were sure to break and shorten his fall by providing answers that only God can give.

Not only was he in emotional shock and great physical pain, but he had the added mental anguish of an uncertain standing before his God. The ground was shaking beneath his feet and he became a little desperate for answers. As one commentator put it:

> *Job desperately tries to solve the mystery behind his suffering. He struggles on his own, looking for clues. None appear. Job prays expectantly. God will surely speedily intervene in his life — heal him of his disease, explain to him what in the world is going on. But nothing happens. The horribly painful disease reduces Job's strength. He grows weaker and weaker. He becomes more confused…. Life has gone crazy for Job, and he has been locked up in the padded cell of his own mind.*[5]

Of the 42 chapters in the book, Job spent about 21 lamenting his anguish, contemplating the nature of the universe, and demanding a hearing before God. Simply put, he wanted some answers (Job 13:3, 13:15, 13:22, 23:3-4, 23:7). And who can blame him? Our first response to grief and hurt is usually the question *"Why?"* We aren't wrong for taking it to God. Job is proof of that and he's not the only example. There are 163 questions recorded in the book of Psalms, and most of them are born of pain. *"And my soul is greatly dismayed; But You, O Lord — how long?"* (Ps. 6:3). *"Why have You forgotten me? Why do I go mourning because of the oppression of the enemy?"* (Ps. 42:9). We have a humble God who does not demand silent submission and untested loyalty. In love, He seeks to win us, not to subdue us.

Nonetheless, our demands for understanding can be misleading. Sometimes, we assume that we would have peace and comfort if we could just make sense of it all. But things like sin and suffering are inherently illogical. They were not part of God's original design or His created order; thus they have no purpose or higher meaning in and of themselves. They are the maddening, chaotic anarchists that were welcomed into this world when we rebelled against God. He does choose to use them for His purposes. He is able to cause good to come from them, and He does so seamlessly. But let us not assume that there is wisdom or insight to be drawn from within these things themselves.

Stasi Eldredge writes, *"In cases of suffering, you can have understanding or you can have Jesus. If you insist on understanding, you usually lose both."*[6] She makes a good point. Nowhere in Scripture are we warned against airing our questions and doubts before God. Maintaining our spiritual integrity requires us to keep short accounts with the Lover of our Souls. Hence, we are free to walk into those murky waters and disclose the betrayal we feel. But let's not put down roots. If we linger too long, if we cling more to our need for answers than we cling to our need for God, our doubts can lead to disbelief and our questions can turn into accusations. Let us not keep the sting of betrayal and deny His arms of comfort.

God's holiness is not so delicate as to become easily tarnished or broken by the queries of His people. And questioning Him is not necessarily disrespectful of His authority or justice. But Job did cross a line. Based on what we read of God's response, Job was more certain of his own righteousness than he was of God's justice. God asks, *"Will you really annul My judgment? Will you condemn Me that you may be justified?"* (40:8) *"Who is this that darkens counsel by words without knowledge?"* (38:2)

"Will the faultfinder contend with the Almighty?" (40:2) During his inquisition, Job made his righteousness the constant and God's justice the variable. He upheld God's sovereignty and power but denied His goodness. In the end, He accused God of being unfair.

Fix It!

After being thrown into a freefall, it was only natural for Job to grasp for anything that might hold his weight. I suppose it was just as natural for his friends to do the same. Quite understandably, they succumbed to the most control-grasping, pride-feeding, formula-making response of all. They tried to fix it by offering him their very best speculations and exhortations. Most assuredly, they cared for their dear friend and ran to his side out of genuine compassion, but pride and self-preservation compromised their good intentions. Apart from Elihu, their priorities were misaligned, and their counsel misguided.

We have so much to learn from this! Most importantly, I'd like to propose that we consider our preparation, our motivation, and our methodology prior to sitting in the ash heap with someone who is suffering. Are we willing to step into the uncomfortable and engage the unpredictable? Are we able to enter into the world of their suffering with a gracious, humble, and tender spirit? Are we surrendered to a caring process, or are we driven to produce results? Are we resolved to be slow to speak and slow to become angry? Are we committed to embrace the vulnerability of empathy without trying to correct them or fix their circumstances?

Let us not underestimate the powerful simplicity of our prayers, reflective listening, and quiet presence. To offer a safe and unrefined space for the hurting is a soothing grace. Perhaps we see this most vividly in the Psalms. The Psalmists expressed every conceivable emotion, including both doubt and anger.

> *The Psalms show the heart not only how to speak but listen. If emotions are the language of the soul, then the book of Psalms gives us the grammar and syntax, teaching us how to wrestle, inviting us to rage, question, and vent anger in such a way as to move up and out of despair. The Psalms wrap nouns and verbs around our pain better than any other book.*[7]

In summary, I would suggest that it is most often our job to walk alongside and God's job to rescue, restore, and re-establish. *"He brought me up out of the pit of destruction, out of the miry clay, and He set my feet upon a rock making my footsteps firm"* (Ps. 40:2). Remember dear friends, our God is near the brokenhearted and ready to save, yet even He is reluctant to speak. *"God's not quick to give advice. He's not even real quick to give us answers, but He will give Himself…and when you're hurting, you don't stop the bleeding with answers."*[8]

Questions for Reflection

1. ***"Our doubts, our anger, and the daggers of the enemy must be brought out of the shadows and into the light, which must begin by admitting them to God, but not end there." What else should we do with them?***

2. ***Do you agree that sin and suffering are inherently illogical, without inherent purpose and meaning? If so, why do you think we so commonly try to discern the "whys" of our suffering?***

3. ***What are we to offer to those who are suffering? What have you needed from others during your times of difficulty?***

Where Were You?

Despite the fact that some of Job's arguments were disrespectful and his wife's comments were alarming, no rebuke is recorded for either blasphemy or rebellion. But to Job's friends, the Lord said this: *"My wrath is kindled against you…because you have not spoken of Me what is right as My servant Job has"* (42:7). It was this misrepresentation that most offended Him. Therefore, He interrupted their debate and spoke for Himself.

From out of a whirlwind, God demanded answers. *"Where were you when I laid the foundation of the earth?"* (38:4). For the next several chapters, He went on to connect what Job could see of creation to all that Job could not see: a wise and attentive ruler of the micro and the macro world. He gave Job a little more context, which changed everything. In response, Job said this:

> *I know that You can do all things, and that no purpose of Yours can be thwarted…Therefore, I have declared that which I did not understand, things too wonderful for me, which I did not know…I have heard of You by the hearing of the ear; but now my eye sees You; therefore I retract, and I repent in dust and ashes.* (Job 42:2-6)

God did not find it necessary to give Job the backstory. He did not explain Himself, although as we've discussed, He told Satan that He had ruined Job without cause. He didn't blame Satan for sabotage, murder, and harassment. He didn't detail His good intentions, His plans to prosper Job and return to him two-fold all that he had lost. Those things were all relevant, and they were included in the story for our benefit, but they were only circumstantial. As monumental as the specifics might seem, God exists outside of all things fleeting and temporary. He is the ultimate, unchanging reality, and so it was more understanding of Him that Job most needed. As is so often the case with those who anguish the most, Job was given an experiential knowledge of God that surpassed the wretchedness of his suffering. What he knew intellectually was moved into the conviction of his heart: "*I have heard of You by the hearing of the ear; but now my eye sees You*" (Job 42:5).

There is a sense in which we could end the discussion right here. Job has taught us that we can take our doubts and questions to God, knowing that He will show up. Those who seek shall find. Those who ask shall receive. It's comforting to know that we can cry out to God in the midst of crisis, and He will both walk with us and reveal more of Himself to us.

But when you're in the midst of a whirlwind, it can be hard to hear. Perhaps we shouldn't wait until then to ask the tough questions. It might be wise to tackle things before they get stirred up. So, let's keep going. Perhaps we can sort some things out ahead of time.

Context is King

I met Sandrine in college and instantly fell in love with her intellect, her passion for God, and her insatiable desire to learn. After twenty-five years, she still mesmerizes me with her wealth of knowledge, her lovely French accent, and her hilarious use of English idioms. Here are some of my favorites:

No way! You're pulling my legs off!

The proof is in the cookies.

God is not a 'vendle' machine.

Her husband has carpool tunnel.

We won by a landslam.

It's time to bury the ashes.

He's like a bull in Chinatown.

There's too many hoops and loops to jump through.

She's trying to teach an old monkey new tricks.

Your guess is as good as mine, but mine is better than yours.

Idioms are tricky. We kinda know what they mean and we know when to use them, but the words themselves don't always make sense. This is because we sit outside of the historical and cultural context in which they were contrived.

This is exactly what Job and his friends were trying to do; make sense of things for which they did not have the full context. When we read the narratives in Scripture, we often forget that the characters in those stories didn't know all that we know today. They did not know the end of the story or even their place within it. We have the completed canon and thus a much fuller context. And context changes everything! It is the greater truth that, when kept in the forefront of our minds, gives us perspective, patience, and peace when life knocks us off our feet.

Job didn't seem to need the fuller context of his situation, but we know that he was stuck in the crosshairs of a battle that began in eternity past. Long before Job was born, Satan enjoyed privileged standing in the heavenlies, but his arrogance led him to stir up a revolt against the Father. Not content to play second fiddle, he rose against God with one third of the angels and asserted himself as the worthy, supreme ruler. There was war in paradise. Satan lost the battle and was banished, but he maintained his arrogance even in defeat (Isaiah 14, Ezekiel 28, Luke 10:18). John Eldredge describes this well in his book, *Epic*.

> *Satan mounted his rebellion through the power of an idea: God is holding out on us. After their insurrection was squelched, and they [Satan and his demons] were hurled from the high walls of heaven, that question lingers like smoke from a forest fire: Is God truly good?...Yes, God and his angels won. Through force of arms. But power is not the same thing as goodness...His own heart has been called into question.[9]*

Banished from heaven, Satan went on to wage war against mankind, propagating the same lie. *God is not worthy of our worship. He cannot be trusted.* Satan convinced Eve that God was holding out on her and therefore she deserved better. He planted seeds of doubt and pride. She had no pain to provoke, so he created a false sense of pain. He questioned God's word, His will, and His good intentions toward her. Then he lied to her and told her that she was meant to be so much more — she was meant to be like God — which she already was! After seeing that the fruit was good for food, she was undone. Together, Adam and Eve joined the serpent, taking the beautiful gift of choice and employing it to accomplish their infamous rebellion (Gen. 3). There was nothing logical about it. Like all sin, it was irrational, insane unbelief. The results have been devastating.

Since that time, Satan has continued in his outrage and rebellion against the Father, while the mayhem created by the sin of Adam and Eve has only fed his campaign against God's goodness (Rev. 12). We are told that the whole earth is within his grasp, for a time (John 12:31, John 16:11). He's been put on a long leash, *for a time*. Look around you. This is his kingdom. During his short rule on planet earth, Satan has capitalized on the flesh to incite war, empower zealous crusades, delude cult leaders and their followers, and anesthetize weak Christians. He has delighted in every natural disaster, disease, and swollen-bellied child. It's ironic that he has built his kingdom upon the lie that God is not good when clearly, he rules his kingdom with domination, deceit, destruction, and death (John 10:10, Is. 14:20). Were it not for God's restraining hand, His people, and the ever-present witness creation provides of His glory, we would be utterly destroyed.

Knowing that the entire force of hell, the flesh, and the world system are bent upon the distortion of a true knowledge of God should give us some better footing in this life. For a little while longer, men will continue in their rebellion and the enemy, knowing his time is short, will wage war. All nations will rise up together with one voice and rage against their Maker. But rest assured, the reckoning will come. The day of redemption awaits. One day, all will behold God as He is. The dark clouds of sin and death will roll back like a scroll and we will behold Him face to face.

> *Turn to Me and be saved, all the ends of the earth; for I am God, and there is no other. I have sworn by Myself, the word has gone forth from My mouth in righteousness and will not turn back, that to Me every knee will bow, every tongue will swear allegiance. They will say of Me, "Only in the LORD are righteousness and strength." Men will come to Him, and all who were angry at Him will be put to shame. In the LORD all the offspring of Israel will be justified and will glory.* (Is. 45:22-25)

Blessed are the Unoffended

Like Job, John the Baptist wasn't privy to the whole story. Just like Job, he was persecuted for the sake of righteousness. And he had a lot of questions. His hard and faithful ministry was brought to an abrupt end as he sat in the chains and stench of a prison cell. He had long believed that the kingdom of God was coming, that the promises were being fulfilled, and that everything was about to change. Ever since that day at the Jordan, he believed that Jesus was the man to make it all happen (John 1:29-34). But as he stared at those prison walls, he began to wonder because jail wasn't the kind of change he had anticipated.

It wasn't that John had expected to share the spotlight with Jesus. He surrendered his calling months earlier by sending his disciples to follow Jesus, saying, *"He must increase, but I must decrease"* (John 3:30). No, he wasn't the kind of man interested in his own glory. His only passion was the Kingdom! And that was the sticking point. If Jesus was the Messiah, then why wasn't He doing something about Roman oppression? Why was He allowing His cousin, His forerunner, to rot in prison? That certainly wasn't how John had thought things were going to end. And if Jesus wasn't the Messiah, John still had a job to finish. With all the false prophets and false Messiahs of Israel's history, he simply had to know. So he sent his disciples to Jesus with a question: *"Are You the Expected One, or do we look for someone else?"* (Luke 7:19).

Jesus' answer was gracious and penetrating to the heart, as always. He told the disciples to return to John and report what they had seen and heard: *"the blind receive sight, the lame walk, the lepers are cleansed, and the deaf hear, the dead are raised up, the poor have the gospel preached to them. Blessed is he who does not take offense at Me"* (Luke 7:22-23).

First, He answered by clarifying something. Yes, He was the Messiah, and He was bringing the kingdom of God to mankind. He was the fulfillment of Isaiah 61 – He was the life and light of men who rescues, heals, and restores. But His ministry wasn't going to end with an earthly rule – not yet. He wasn't going to sit on an earthly throne and overthrow Roman oppression. He had his eyes set upon a much bigger prize: the salvation of men from every tongue, tribe, and nation. Therefore, He was going to lay down His life and delay the earthly kingdom, for a time. For a time, He would sacrifice His ultimate destiny and desires, so that more could be brought into His kingdom. He asks all who love Him, all who have already been welcomed in, to do the same! The short-sighted and self-righteous experience Jesus as the *"stone of stumbling"* and *"rock of offense"* (Rom. 9:33, 1 Peter 2:6-8). But blessed are those who are willing to lay aside their small stories and join Him in the larger story He is telling.

Twofold Triumph

Indeed, what shall we do with Christ? If we are to believe that a good God should spare us from the brutal tragedies of this life, then how do we explain the cross? If anyone truly deserved a life free of suffering — life as it was meant to be — it was the God-Man. But instead, Jesus willingly left His post in heaven, laid aside His glory, and stepped into a weak and vulnerable body of flesh. The Messiah deserved to be worshipped, to be treated with honor and respect, to rule with authority and power. But when He was placed by the Holy Spirit into Mary's womb, He chose to live a life and die a death He did not deserve. And in so doing, as a final appeal to us, He definitively settled the enemy's cynical disregard for God's goodness and power.

God is Infinite Wisdom, and Power, and Goodness — and

*LOVE; but if this idea is too vast for your human faculties —
if your mind loses itself in its overwhelming infinitude, fix it on
Him who condescended to take our nature upon Him, who was
raised to Heaven even in His glorified human body, in whom the
fullness of the Godhead shines.*[10]

When He selected a fleshly frame for Himself, He didn't choose
beauty[11]. When He selected His earthly parents, he chose two poor,
unknown Jews. During His brief years of ministry, He was reliant upon
the generosity of friends for his daily needs[12]. His body knew hunger,
cold, and sickness, and he became familiar with every temptation
known to man[13]. Being the Creator and Knower of all things, He was
often misunderstood, mischaracterized, and even slandered by the
creatures He loved and desired to save[14]. Even his own family doubted
Him[15]. When the time came to fulfill His final purpose on earth and
surrender His life to death — a gruesome death only fit for the worst
of criminals — He felt abandonment and dread so intense that He
sweated drops of blood[16]. And in that hour, He was betrayed, deserted,
and denied by His closest friends[17]. Out of obedience to the Father and
for the love of the world, He accepted fabricated accusations, a corrupt
trial, counterfeit condemnation, and the full cup of hell's fury[18]. And
in the moment of His greatest travail, when all the sins of our fathers'
fathers and our children's children were heaped upon His shoulders,
His Father looked away[19].

Thus Elijah returned, sat down at the Sabbath table, took hold of
the cup of suffering, and drank full the pungent poison. An innocent
man, humbled deity, betrayed leader, and abandoned friend laid down
His life and endured the height of injustice, sabotage, and cruelty. It
was the most outrageous crime of human history — our darkest hour.
His deity did not spare Him the bitterness of shame and agony. For
this reason, He was also mocked[20]. But, in all this, He overcame.

Through His death and resurrection, Christ defeated Satan on two
counts. First, He silenced all doubts regarding the goodness of the
Father. It was Christ's choice *"for the joy set before Him"* to humble
Himself, take on our fleshly weaknesses, and lay down His life[21]. But it
was also according to the Father's will, who *"so loved the world that He
sent His son"* (John 3:16). In this, His love, He proved His supreme
goodness. The highest form of goodness is love, and the highest form
of love is self-sacrifice. *"We know love by this, that He laid down His life for*

us" (1 John 3:16). Paul repeats this idea in the book of Romans.

> *For while we were still helpless, at the right time Christ died for the ungodly. For one will hardly die for a righteous man; though perhaps for the good man someone would dare even to die. But God demonstrates His own love toward us, in that while we were yet sinners, Christ died for us.* (Rom. 5:6-8)

All things in heaven, on earth, and under the earth witnessed the unthinkable. The great self-sustaining and self-sufficient Father sacrificed His beloved Son for those whom He had condemned to death. He chose mercy over justice to protect the possibility of love. The cross proves His kind intentions toward us.

In a paramount display of His goodness, Jesus chose to give up His life. But a supremely good God is of no use to us unless He is also supremely powerful. And so, it is the resurrection that proves His power. Jesus overcame evil with good. He descended into hell, ascended into heaven, and captured the keys of sin and death[22]. He swallowed up in total victory the authority granted to our enemy, and restored unto us the promise of all that awaits us now and in eternity. His life and death prove His love, but His resurrection and ascension prove His power to reign over all that the Fall stole from us.

It all boils down to this. While we remain in a body of flesh and are surrounded by a world still reeling from the Fall, we can be confident that the best is yet to come. If history's most grievous suffering resulted in unparalleled victory — if the greatest evil committed by mankind resulted in the greatest good for mankind — can we not believe Him when He promises to make good on our *"light and momentary afflictions"* (2 Cor. 4:17)? He will cause all things to become beautiful and good (Rom. 8:28, Rev. 21:5). If I may be so bold as to say it, He will make it up to us in the end. *"THINGS WHICH EYE HAS NOT SEEN AND EAR HAS NOT HEARD, and which HAVE NOT ENTERED THE HEART OF MAN, all that God has prepared for those who love Him"* (1 Cor. 2:9). Our story does not end with suffering. He is restoring the kingdom and has promised us a happily ever after.

Conclusion

Dear ones, this isn't how things were meant to be. Each and every day produces more proof that something has gone terribly wrong.

Indeed it has, but that something is not God. No one mourns sin and its devastation more than He does. Consider: why has He taken such pains to instruct us on holy living? Certainly, it's not to earn His approval, but to save us from ourselves and keep us from the grip of the enemy. Consider what He instructs us — empowers us — to do. He tells fathers to treat their children with gentleness and to live in an understanding manner with their wives. He tells wives to treat their husbands with loving respect, and children to honor and obey their parents. He tells us as members of His body to submit to one another in love, to cover a multitude of sins with grace, and to speak the truth with sincere concern. And as we interact with the world, we are to fight for justice, live at peace with all men wherever possible, respect those in authority, and work diligently as unto the Lord. Why? He has done all things with lavish generosity and fervent pleadings that we would become like Him, perfect in word and deed. Only, He has stopped short of transgressing upon the boundaries of human choice. What more could he do to create a world that reflects His blameless character, except force Himself upon us? Would we trust Him then?

The days are evil and we must live wisely (Eph. 5:15-16). But too often, just like Eve and Job, we rarely identify the work of the enemy, we don't understand the stakes, and we join the campaign against God. If we don't understand that we are living in a war, if we don't have a humble opinion of ourselves and a good amount of respect for our enemy, we are likely to blame God rather than run to Him in our time of need. If only we would accept His invitation and allow Him to speak to us, guide us, and comfort us in the midst of the ache. He always provides for us a path to Himself, where our hopes are secure. He is the only way to survive this world, prepare for the next, and keep our hearts out of trouble.

Questions for Reflection

1. How did God bring Job to a place of repentance and peace?

2. What is the greater context in which we are living?

3. *What does it mean that the entire force of hell and the world system is bent upon the distortion of a true knowledge of God? Can you think of some current examples of this?*

4. *In what way did Christ choose mercy over justice? Why?*

5. *Is it easier for you to trust in God's goodness or His power? What difference does it make to believe that He is both supremely good and supremely powerful?*

Chapter 4

Divine Dissonance

"Behold, You desire truth in the innermost being, and in the hidden part You will make me know wisdom." (Psalm 51:6)

Irreverent Inquiries

As I left my daughter's room and began the descent downstairs, her words rang in my ears. *"If a lion eats me, I'm still dead. What's God gonna do about that?"* There was something about her statement that weakened me, like a sack of potatoes had just been thrown upon my heart. And it grew heavier with each step. By the time my toes hit the cold floor, I felt like my heart did too. I could vaguely make out the words of a heated conversation going on inside me. If I went back to bed and ignored this inner controversy, I feared the matter would be settled without me. Refusing to be sidelined by my own soul, I put the kettle on for tea and prepared for a long night.

I sat down on the living room couch and grabbed a warm blanket. Immediately the day's events settled upon me and my thoughts ran to the phone call we had received that morning. It was a courtesy call to inform my husband that he had not been selected for a particular job he had applied for. After four interviews and weeks of anxious waiting, it was a resounding, *"Not you, buddy."* We had been so hopeful. It was a job prospect that had energized him and caused him to dream again. He had done research on the organization, had wrestled with the vision statement, and had carefully detailed a map for future expansion. He really wanted that job, and he hadn't gotten excited about anything like that in a long time. A few years of hard work without reward, a few hazardous alliances, and the treacherous assault of a friend would knock the wind out of anyone. All of these had done a number on our finances, our family, and our faith. But this job prospect had the potential to reroute our detours and set us back on the road to recovery. So when the phone call came in, our hearts sank. The thick fog of confusion, hurt, and exhaustion that had been held at bay in anticipation of good news became a choking reality. And it certainly didn't help when they said they had chosen the candidate God had directed them to choose. It only personalized the sting of rejection. Not only did we get eaten by that proverbial "lion," but God had hand-picked the prey and it was us!

In the harsh light of our trials, believing that God is good and trusting that He would fight for us had become very complicated. Typically, that can mean only one thing. When simple things become too complicated, there's usually a story. And where there's a story, there's probably a wound. And where there is a wound, we're likely to be harboring some unsightly spiritual bondage. So, I decided to drag my angst-filled doubt into the light and get a good look at it. I nestled into the couch, grabbed hold of the blanket as if it channeled courage, and gave my heart a chance to speak up. I asked myself a dangerous question and listened without editing my answers. *Is God worthy of my trust?*

Progressive Revelation

I do realize it was disrespectful and perhaps foolhardy to challenge the character of God. I was asking a question that has only one correct answer, and we all know what it is! God has already spoken for Himself and has authoritatively informed us of His good character and intentions. He wants to be known and has gone to great lengths to progressively reveal Himself throughout the ages. His supremacy, power, and goodness are on full display, clearly seen by all who would choose to take a glance.

First, He has illustrated for all mankind His divinity, His power, and His nature through the natural world, otherwise known as *General Revelation.* The fact that creation has become subject to futility does not diminish the glory He infused into it. Romans 1:20 tells us, *"For since the creation of the world His invisible attributes, His eternal power and divine nature, have been clearly seen, being understood through what has been made, so that they are without excuse."* Take note that this passage is not suggesting that God has proven to us through creation that He exists, but that He has proven *who He is.* Think about all that you have learned of Him by observing a thunderstorm, studying the animal kingdom, taking an anatomy course, or looking through a microscope. Not only is His majesty seen through His creation, but so is His heart. The same God who created the sun, moon and stars also created babies and the breasts that nourish them. *"Come to think of it,"* writes John Eldredge, *"He is the wellspring of everything that has ever romanced your heart. The thundering strength of a waterfall, the delicacy of a flower, the stirring capacity of music, the richness of wine. The masculine and the feminine that fill all creation come from the same heart."*[1]

In addition to this illustrative lesson on who God is through the natural world, we have also been granted knowledge of God's nature, work, and purposes through *Special Revelation*. This includes dreams, visions, prophecy and the inspired and inerrant Word of God (Heb. 1:1, 2 Tim. 3:16-17). Because God is a relational being, He desires to communicate with those He loves, and He has done so in many ways throughout history. Having a completed canon of scripture gives us a clearer lens to interpret these communications, therefore all forms of special revelation must come under the authority of the Scriptures. Within the written Word of God, we find answers to questions nature cannot reveal, who we are, where we came from, how we are to live, and what we are to live for. Tethered to these realities is a progressive disclosure of the personhood of God. He reveals more and more of Himself through the story He tells in human history.

> *What we think we see in the beginning is only a dim reality compared with what we will see and understand at the end...But what is more wonderful is for us, who now sit in a still more favored viewpoint, to look first in the account of Genesis and see that which God starts with as a miniature in Abraham's family unfold into grand magnitude in the book of Revelation.*[2]

It is through the Scriptures, *Special Revelation*, that we find a conclusive display of God through His Son, the Christ. This is known as the *Ultimate Revelation* of God. *"God, after He spoke long ago to the fathers in the prophets in many portions and in many ways, in these last days has spoken to us in His Son, whom He appointed heir of all things, through whom also He made the world"* (Heb. 1:1-2). Christ spent 33 years upon this earth, as recorded in history and in Scripture, and walked among us so that we would know Him. He said, *"He who has seen Me has seen the Father"* (John 14:9). And what He did to display the Father was magnificent! He healed the sick and handicapped, rescued the adulteress, resisted the religious oppressors, blessed the children, fed the masses, spoke good news to the lost, and in due course, He laid down His life for us all. He not only revealed a heart of compassion, love, and mercy, but He also brought to man the kingdom of God, a place of wholeness.

Just before His death and resurrection, Christ shared the Passover with His disciples and told them, *"I have many more things to say to you, but you cannot bear them now"* (John 16:12). And so, after His ascension, He sent His Spirit as a seal of our salvation, a Counselor and Life-Giver to those who belong to Him, so that His revelation would reach into our souls, enlighten our hearts, and display His manifold wisdom to the world. Indeed, our spiritual gifts are nothing less than the very imprint of God. The fruit produced through us is the manifestation of His life and power within us.

In summary, God has gone to great lengths to display His character for all humanity to see. Everything He created, everything He did, everything He said, and everything He empowers us to do, points to His good character. So the correct answer to my question was a resounding *YES, God is good and trustworthy*! Any reservations regarding God's character would be irreverent and seemingly irrelevant as well. But I wasn't looking for the right answer. I already knew that in my head. I was asking because I had a feeling that my heart was not in agreement!

Questions for Reflection

1. *Have you ever asked yourself the question, "Is God worthy of my trust?" What would be your answer, and why?*

2. *What are the differences between General, Special, and Ultimate Revelation?*

3. *Why are all three forms of revelation necessary?*

The Heart Thinks

The heart is far more complex than we have come to believe. It's certainly more than fluffy emotions and whimsical fantasies. The intellect is objective in nature, gathering facts and ideas. The head makes observations and creates categories for information, but the heart is subjective. The heart has an ability to perceive and process what the intellect cannot. In his book *Waking the Dead*, John Eldredge writes, *"The mind stands detached, but it is with the heart that we experience and respond to all of life…The heart lives in the far more bloody and magnificent realities of living and dying and loving and hating."*[3]

The heart is powerful and influential! It is the core of our physical and spiritual life, the innermost part of man; the primal, moldable hub that connects and in fact controls all other parts. For this reason, it is the heart that God cares most about. In 1 Samuel 16:7, we read that God prioritizes the heart: *"God sees not as man sees, for man looks at the outward appearance, but the LORD looks at the heart."* And in Proverbs 4:23 we are directed to tend to it with care: *"Watch over your heart with all diligence, for from it flow the springs of life."* The heart is central.

If we take a look at the word *heart* in the Bible (NASB), we will find it used 726 times to describe so much more than we would expect. Consider the following uses:

Our hidden thoughts.

- *Why are you reasoning about these things in your hearts?* (Mark 2:8)

- *For the Word of God is living and active and sharper than any two-edged sword, and piercing as far as the division of soul and spirit, of both joints and marrow, and able to judge the thoughts and intentions of the heart.* (Heb. 4:12)

Our will.

- *Let each one do just as he has purposed in his heart…* (2 Cor. 9:7)

Our desires.

- *Therefore, God gave them over in the lusts of their hearts…* (Rom. 1:24)

- *Brethren, my heart's desire and my prayer to God for them is for their salvation.* (Rom. 10:1)

Our feelings.

- *Reproach has broken my heart and I am so sick.* (Ps. 69:20)

- *Therefore, my heart is glad and my glory rejoices; my flesh also will dwell securely.* (Ps. 16:9)

Our conscience.

- *In that they show the work of the Law written in their hearts, their conscience bearing witness and their thoughts alternately accusing or else defending them.* (Rom. 2:15)

- *We shall know by this that we are of the truth, and shall assure our heart before Him in whatever our heart condemns us…* (1 John 3:19-20)

Our character.

- *No one who has a haughty look and an arrogant heart will I endure.* (Ps. 101:5)

- *For judgment will again be righteous, and all the upright in heart will follow it.* (Ps. 94:15)

Our spiritual response to God.

- *For with the heart a person believes, resulting in righteousness, and with the mouth he confesses, resulting in salvation.* (Rom. 10:10)

- *HE HAS BLINDED THEIR EYES AND HE HARDENED THEIR HEART, SO THAT THEY WOULD NOT SEE WITH THEIR EYES AND PERCEIVE WITH THEIR HEART, AND BE CONVERTED AND I HEAL THEM.* (John 12:40)

The place of spiritual life or death.

- *The heart is more deceitful than all else and is desperately sick; who can understand it?* (Jer. 17:9)

- *Now He who establishes us with you in Christ and anointed us is God, who also sealed us and gave us the Spirit in our hearts as a pledge.* (2 Cor. 1:21-22)

- *…that Christ may dwell in your hearts through faith.* (Eph. 3:17)

For the believer, the heart holds more promise than the "*more deceitful than all else and desperately sick*" indictment. It is capable of the lowest and the highest of conditions. As such, it sits at the very root of our sin problems, our spiritual battle, and our sanctification. While it's the place where Satan does most of his damage, it's also the place of our renewal and rebirth, where God restores us in wholeness and produces a new life of holiness.

The thinking function of the heart, sometimes referred to as the *mind*, is vital to this process of sanctification. It serves as a rudder that sets the course for our defilement and our deliverance. For this reason, Paul admonishes us in Romans 12:2, *"Do not be conformed to this world, but be transformed by the renewal of your mind..."* I'd like to suggest that he's not speaking of the intellect, but of the eyes of the heart.

The most common use of the word *heart* in Scripture is referring to thought. If we take a look at the New Testament alone, we see the Greek word *nous* (G3563) translated as *mind* 24 times. Strong's Concordance defines this word as *"reason in the narrower sense, as the capacity for spiritual truth, the higher powers of the soul, the faculty of perceiving divine things, or recognizing goodness and of hating evil."*[4] In other words, the heart has a mind of its own. It is best understood as the seat of reflection. It keeps a running log of our life experiences and it arrives at its own interpretations and conclusions, whether we are aware of them or not, whether we would consciously agree with them or not. According to Proverbs 23:7, these thoughts of the heart carry more weight than our intellect. They are a conclusive report on our personhood: *"For as he thinks within himself, so he is."* In this way, the heart is the place of our deepest contemplation, which determines not only how we choose to behave and believe, but *who we are*.

Although it's a bit of a wild card, the heart does not operate autonomously. It is informed by both the Spirit and the flesh. Our position in Christ is secure and the Holy Spirit indwells us as the seal of our approval before God, but in our flesh dwells no good thing, and therefore our heart is forever battling between these two realities. This is the nature of our struggle onward toward sanctification. Whatever the mind of the heart chooses to focus upon will be its master. In this way, the heart must choose daily whom it will serve. According to the apostle Paul, we may choose to take our thoughts captive and make them obedient to Christ (2 Cor. 10:5) or we may choose to set our thoughts upon the desires of the flesh (Rom. 7:25).

1 Corinthians 2:16 says we have the mind of Christ. That's an

amazing reality, but it's a positional reality just like being welcomed into a relationship with Christ at the point of salvation is a positional reality. The relationship is available to us, but we must choose whether or not we will enter in and actualize it. In the same way, the mind of Christ is available to us, but we must choose to silence the many other voices and focus upon the still small voice of God. We must sit at His feet as Mary did and set aside the distractions so that we can hear from Him, enter into His rest, and know the freedom that comes from a loyalty to One.

In this area, secular science is catching up with biblical truth. Recently, scientists have concluded that our subconscious thoughts control most of our lives. Stem cell biologist Dr. Bruce Lipton has been quoted as saying,

> *The function of the mind is to create coherence between our beliefs and the reality we experience…What that means is that your mind will adjust the body's biology and behavior to fit with your beliefs….Most people don't even acknowledge that their subconscious mind is at play, when the fact is that the subconscious mind is a million times more powerful than the conscious mind and that we operate 95 to 99 percent of our lives from subconscious programs.[5]*

Because the heart is where our spiritual battle and sanctification takes place, it stands to reason that the heart is the truest measurement of our spiritual formation. Sadly, we often prefer the more manageable externals of our intellect and behavior. I suppose it is our fleshly default to ignore the heart and try to get by on lesser things. Service, strategies, programs, and knowledge are good things, but lesser things for sure. They are life-giving and eternally fruitful when and only when they are accomplished as we abide in the love of Christ. And abiding can only be done through the heart. Therefore, our heart is our lifeline to God and God is our lifeline to everything else.

The Heart Speaks

It was for this reason that I asked myself the question, *Is God worthy of my trust?* I knew the correct answer and wanted to feel a firm confidence in it, but a very familiar ache in my soul indicated that I might need to give my heart a chance to speak up. So I invited God into the conversation and asked Him to expose my hidden thoughts and intentions. I wanted to know what I was harboring against Him and why. What was it that felt so familiar about our current situation? When had I felt like this before?

More eagerly than I'd like to admit, the answers came back as a gut punch. No words came to my mind, but my entire countenance fell as I remembered a time of confusion and difficulty within my family of origin. When I was a teenager, my father lost his job. In the months that followed, he took a job several hours away from home, and we saw very little of him. After months of separation and mounting responsibilities, my mom began to crumble under the weight of living like a single mom. She experienced a physical and emotional breakdown. Suddenly finding ourselves without parental involvement and oversight, my siblings and I felt isolated and afraid. Of course, we didn't know how to identify those feelings, let alone talk about them. We busied ourselves with friends and school activities, but the numbing losses and confusion were too disorienting for me to ignore.

In an attempt to reconnect, my mother went to visit my father and sent my siblings off to stay with friends. I refused to leave the comforts of home and was allowed to stay home alone. That very first night, I woke up from a frightening dream and couldn't get back to sleep. Normally, I would sneak into my parents' bedroom and sleep on the floor, but that would have offered me little comfort in an empty house, so I tried to pray myself back to sleep.

When my prayers seemed to bounce off the ceiling, fear, loneliness, and anger welled up inside me and found their way out through tears. In that moment of vulnerability, I began to reconsider my position on things such as sin and suffering. It occurred to me that some of the Bible verses I'd memorized as a child might not be as reliable as I wanted them to be. I wanted to trust in God's love and care for me, but there were too many conflicting stories in Scripture and a growing number of examples in my own life where He didn't appear to care at all. My confidence in His goodness was shaken and with it came the realization that anything could happen to me in this crazy life. There are no guarantees. In fact, God could unleash all the powers of hell against me without compromising His character or His Word. Isn't that what happened to Job? So, why would I trust in His sweet little promises when there was plenty of evidence to prove they weren't entirely true?

At some point before sunrise, I embraced a series of lies as my new reality, and spiritual bondage was born within me. I came to the sad conclusion that I was indeed helpless and alone in a world much too large and too cold for me to bear; that God was powerful and sovereign, but not loving or good, and definitely not worthy of my trust. Even though I knew the truth, my heart fully embraced these lies.

I chalked up that little dialogue to theological musing or maybe just a rough night. On a conscious level, I had no idea what I had done or the impact it would have. Unfortunately, it opened the door for more deception, other forms of bondage, and a decreased sense of intimacy with God. In effect, it sent me into a downward spiral that lasted for nearly two decades.

John Eldredge describes this well in his book *The Sacred Romance*:

> *Embedded in our stories, deep down in our heart, in a place so well guarded that they have rarely if ever been exposed to the light of day, are other grief-laden and often angry questions: "God, why did you allow this to happen to me? Why did you make me like this? What will you allow to happen next?" In the secret places of our heart, we believe God is the One who did not protect us from these things or even the One who perpetrated them upon us. Our questions about him make us begin to live with a deep apprehension that clings anxiously to the depths of our hearts. "Do you really care for me, God?" This is the question that has ship- wrecked many of our hearts, leaving them grounded on reefs of pain and doubt, no longer free to accompany us on spiritual pilgrimage.[6]*

Questions for Reflection

1. ***What distinctions are drawn between the brain, the heart, and the mind?***

2. ***What does it mean that "the heart thinks"?***

3. *"Anything can happen in this life. We have no guarantees. In fact, God could unleash all the powers of hell against me without compromising either His character or His Word." Is this a true statement? Why or why not?*

Opportune Times

Each of us has a similar story of a specific time in our childhood when we realized the world wasn't good and safe. Those who were responsible to protect us, including God, didn't come through. And thus, we came to the sad conclusions that they couldn't be trusted, that we were alone, and we had to find a way to make life work on our own. In essence, we adopted an orphan mentality.

I remember the exact moment this happened for our curly-topped son. He was five years old and didn't appreciate the limits I was placing on his sugar consumption. I said, *"No"* to a sugar and jelly sandwich, *"No"* to a grilled marshmallow tortilla, and *"No"* to an ice-cream smoothie. Unwilling to live under such tyranny, he gathered up his favorite worldly goods, stuffed them in his spiderman backpack and defiantly announced that he'd had enough. *"I'm moving in with grandma to live the way I want."* Grandma lived 2 houses away, so I let him go and walked him back home after dinner.

In a general sense, we have many such defining moments in our lives because life provides us with many painful events. And pain sets the stage upon which the battle for our heart is played out. As we discussed in the last chapter, pain is that force which demands a reaction from us. It is a change agent. At those fork-in-the-road moments, if we don't bring God into the conversation and allow Him to speak for Himself, the void will be filled by another voice: our flesh, the enemy, or both. Often, the greatest damage is done by the things we choose to believe as a result of painful situations. C.S. Lewis faced this temptation in the aftermath of his wife's death:

> *Not that I am (I think) in much danger of ceasing to believe in God. The real danger is of coming to believe such dreadful things about Him. The conclusion I dread is not "So there's no God after all," but "So this is what God's really like. Deceive yourself*

no longer. [7]

Even though I wouldn't have described this time in my history as terribly painful or traumatic, the instability of it all rendered me weak enough to fall for the enemy's false "soulutions". He is keenly aware of our weaknesses and eagerly awaits *"opportune times"* when we are most vulnerable (Luke 4:13). Was it not when Job was at his lowest that the enemy spoke through his wife, *"Curse God and die"* (Job 2:9)? Was it not in the hunger and loneliness of the wilderness that Satan came to tempt Jesus (Matt. 4:1-11)? Was it not during David's time of distress that his *"strong enemy"* confronted him (Ps. 18:17-18)? Don't think that the Devil won't kick you when you're down. The work of Satan and his legions is a very sticky subject with a history of rabbit holes, heresies, and formulaic simplifications, but his plunder is legendary. John 10:10 says that Satan *only* comes to steal, kill, and destroy. One of his primary means of accomplishing this is to propagate an inadequate and distorted view of God. The contortions are endless, but if we follow the breadcrumbs of our sin and dysfunction back far enough, we will always find a nest of sulfurous deceptions aimed at God's good character. *"In one way or another, every problem we have in this world is the fruit of deception — the result of believing something that simply isn't true."* [8]

Having said all this, pain is not our only liability. Human pride produces an equally advantageous opportunity for the enemy. As we discussed in chapter 2, we come at this life from a limited point of reference. This is not morally bad, but it can be hazardous. Too easily the enemy rouses our pride by convincing us that our perspective and subsequent conclusions are right, good, and even authoritative. Case in point: not too long ago, the known world was convinced that the sun revolved around the earth. Observations made from a limited point of reference led to faulty conclusions. The mere suggestion that man was not the center of the universe created an uproar. When we fail to accept that ours is not the most reliable point of reference; when we place ourselves at the center of the universe, we are more likely to make wrong and often maligning assumptions about the character of God. We must humble ourselves to the realization that our observations about this life and about God come from a small and compromised perspective. More succinctly, we must consider ourselves with sober judgement and conduct ourselves in accordance with faith rather than sight (Rom. 12:3 and 2 Cor. 5:7).

Regardless of how we get there, a darkened understanding of God will certainly distort our relationship with Him, but the destruction doesn't stop there. It will also distort our sense of self, our relationship with others, and our worldview. As Hannah Whitall Smith says in her book *The Unselfishness of God*, "*It is of course evident that everything in one's religious life depends on the sort of God one worships. The character of the worshiper must necessarily be molded by the character of the object worshipped.*"[9] We will treat others, and ourselves, the way we think God treats us. We will expect of others and ourselves what we think God expects of us. We will view others the way we think God views us. There's no way to extract our relationship with God out of the rest of our life. If your relationship with God is lacking, then so is your relationship with your spouse, your children, your parents, your church family, your friends, and your co-workers or boss. *If your eye is clear, your whole body will be full of light. But if your eye is bad, your whole body will be full of darkness. If therefore the light that is in you is darkness, how great is the darkness!*" (Matt. 6:22-23).

Et Tu, Brute?

Journalist Edward R. Murrow once said, "*Some truths are so naked that we feel sorry for them and we cover them up, at least a little bit.*"[10] Here's a bit of naked truth: we are deceived. We are all prone to contradictions, heresies, hypocrisy, and falsehoods. And it's the result of choices we have made, even if we made them subconsciously. In the words of John Owen, "*There are traitors in our hearts, ready to take part, to close, and side with every temptation, and to give up all to them.*"[11] Owen speaks of something the writers of Scripture knew only too well. We can believe in Christ for the greatness of salvation and still struggle to trust Him with our sick child, our faltering marriage, our dead-end job, and our insecurities. Much like the father who brought his demon-possessed son to Jesus, we believe and yet we struggle to believe: "*I do believe; help my unbelief*" (Mark 9:24).

The heart is divided. King David knew it. A man after God's own heart (Acts 13:22), he asked the Lord in Psalm 86:11, "*…Unite my heart to fear Your name.*" Paul knew it. He proved his loyalty to Christ and the Gospel in all that he suffered, yet he admitted in the book of Romans, "*For I joyfully concur with the law of God in the inner man, but I see a different law in the members of my body, waging war against the law of my mind and making* *me a prisoner of the law of sin which is in my members"* (Rom. 7:22-23). And James, the brother of Jesus, knew it as well and warned the believers who had fled Jerusalem of it. Even though they had risked life and limb for the Gospel and continued to do so, they harbored some skepticism. *"But he must ask in faith without any doubting, for the one who doubts is like the surf of the sea, driven and tossed by the wind. For that person ought not to expect that he will receive anything from the Lord, being a double-minded man, unstable in all his ways."* (James 1:6-8).

Few of us would deny our duplicity, but we are too blinded by familiarity to recognize it.

> *If I tempted you, you would know it. If I accused you, you would know it. But if I deceived you, you wouldn't know it. If you knew you were being deceived, then you would no longer be deceived. Eve was deceived and she believed a lie. Deception has been the primary strategy of Satan from the beginning.*[12]

We cannot see our enemy, but he knows us and our weaknesses, and he watches for the best opportunities to captivate us with his version of reality. In the story I told of my youth, I thought I was wrestling with the ideas of sin, suffering, and God's promises. I thought I was having a theological debate with myself, and so I threw up no resistance. In reality, my fear and loneliness were being manipulated by dark forces, and I all too willingly agreed with their lying accusations against God's Word and character. As Neil Anderson reminds us, *"The spiritual battle for our minds does not operate according to the laws of nature, which we can comprehend. There are no physical barriers that can confine or restrict the movements of Satan."*[13]

Of course, we know that Biblical truth interprets our experience and not vice versa, but sometimes the pain of life blinds us. Sometimes we think we have the corner on life and justice. Sometimes, we're too young and unaware to know what we're up against. We began making decisions about the world, about life, about ourselves, and about God long before we understood things like the Gospel, God's sovereignty, and grace. How do you explain the concept of an inner dialogue to a 5-year old? When was the last time you went back and corrected the misunderstandings of your childhood?

> *You see, we don't really develop our core convictions so much as they develop within us, when we are young. Down deep in the*

innermost parts they form, down in deep water, like the shifting of the continental plates. Certainly, we'd reject the more disabling beliefs if we could; but they form when we are vulnerable, without our really knowing it, like a handprint in wet cement, and over time the cement hardens and there you have it.[14]

Divine Dissonance

Psychologists believe we will do just about anything to avoid opposition to our worldview once it has become established. In fact, it's such a well-known phenomenon that they've got a name for it. *Cognitive dissonance* is defined as the "*mental conflict that occurs when beliefs or assumptions are contradicted by new information.*"[15] The concept was introduced by the psychologist Leon Festinger (1919–1989) in the late 1950s. He and later researchers showed that, when confronted with challenging new information, most people seek to preserve their current understanding of the world by rejecting, explaining away, or avoiding the new information – or by convincing themselves that no conflict really exists. Frantz Fanon says,

> *Sometimes people hold a core belief that is very strong. When they are presented with evidence that works against that belief, the new evidence cannot be accepted. It would create a feeling that is extremely uncomfortable, called cognitive dissonance. And because it is important to protect the core belief, they will rationalize, ignore, and even deny anything that doesn't fit in with the core belief.*[16]

We all have conflicts between our knowledge and our beliefs, between our head and our heart, but we tend to rationalize, minimize, and deny their existence. We may declare God's grace upon our lives, but our perfectionism contradicts such claims. We may praise God for His goodness and profess our trust in Him, but our attractively packaged contingency plans prove otherwise. Fortunately, God's love is both compassionate and fierce. He isn't afraid to inflict pain so that He might also heal. The pain of our lives can be commandeered by the enemy to lure us into some tragic "soulutions", but God has a way of redeeming painful experiences and making them useful. Here's a little-known secret: our worst fears, chief frustrations, and deepest sorrows position us for the greatest growth and freedom. The same sadness, anger, and anxiety that opened the door for the bondage you're in right now, is also the blinking exit sign that will lead you out. Familiar pain is a red flag, indicating that there are holes in our heart preventing us from experiencing God's life and love in their fullness. According to C.S. Lewis, "*We can ignore pleasure. But pain insists upon being attended to. God whispers to us in our pleasures, speaks in our conscience, but shouts in our pains; it's his megaphone to rouse a deaf world.*"[17] Dislodging the falsehoods and implanting the truth of God requires a crisis of faith that only God can provide. He uses the presence of pain to reorient us toward the heart, because that is what He's after.

Consider the way that Jesus three times drew Peter back to the shame of his betrayal. He was not reproaching him. He was bringing him back to a painful wound and a wrong choice, so that He could restore him. From that very place He also commissioned him (Luke 22:31-32, John 21:7-19). This is Divine Dissonance: the One whom we assault and slander brings us back to the place of our pain, so that we may see our choices through His eyes. There, He identifies our sin and the invitation we once rejected. Just as Jesus did with Peter, He recovers what was lost and restores dignity and honor where there was shame. He faithfully and gently brings us back to our greatest failures, for our good.

> *Divinely interrupting our lives is not an extraordinary event. Supernaturally showing up, speaking into the heart, and creating a longing for Himself—this is His realm. He speaks to us. He leads us. He heals us. He presses into us with his manifest presence as we reach out to him.*[18]

Without any specific context, the Holy Spirit may confer with our spirit to confirm the presence of sin, such as a lie. But if there is also a wound that needs to be healed, He will often reveal to us the root of sin as it took place within our experience. He invites us back into those tender memories so that He can heal both our wounding *and* our sin. If we do not allow the Spirit of God into this process and bounce our conclusions against the wall of His Word, our unresolved hurts and unanswered questions will become our entire reference point. Unless we allow Him to convene with our inner man, we will unintentionally forsake His truth for a cocktail mixed of our own limited understanding and the enemy's deceitful distortions. We must agree that whatever tool God chooses to use, it is His good pleasure to expose us and cure us, not to condemn us. Romans 8:1-2 tells us that there is no condemnation for those who are in Christ Jesus because He has set us free from the law of sin and death. We are promised in the book of 1 John that if we repent of our sin, He is faithful and just to forgive us and to cleanse us from all unrighteousness. In all this, He is indeed the Author and Perfecter of our salvation (see Heb. 12:2).

So much of our sanctification is found in this very process of walking with God through the hidden recesses of the heart, allowing Him to shed His light into the darkened corners. Because God created man for fellowship, for closeness, for a vibrant and real relationship, we should not be surprised that it is within – and only within - the wild and safe movements of that relationship that we find life, truth, and healing. *"For in Him we live and move and exist"* (Acts 17:28).

Questions for Reflection

1. ***What does it mean that "our heart is our lifeline to God and God is our lifeline to everything else"? Do you agree with this statement?***

2. ***What are "opportune times"? Can you think of any of these moments in your own life?***

3. ***What are the similarities and differences between cognitive dissonance and divine dissonance?***

4. ***What do you think of the statement, "Our worst fears, chief frustrations, and deepest sorrows position us for the greatest growth and freedom"?***

Unite My Heart

Just as Jesus brought Peter back to his pain, so He did with me. Through a difficult season in my adult life, He brought me back to the false reality that I had created as a young woman. I cannot see the spirit world, or my sin, but the Holy Spirit who dwells within me *"reveals mysteries from the darkness and brings the deep darkness into light"* (Job 12:22). My faithful Companion and Counselor showed me the madness within my heart: a list of angry indictments against Him. *He abandoned me and I am left to fend for myself. He doesn't really care about me, doesn't have compassion toward me, and will not fight for me. I am alone.*

I had plenty of evidence to support my conclusions, but the fact that I saw myself as an orphan and was disappointed with a supremely good and powerful God was proof enough that I was somehow deceived. And the Holy Spirit within me confirmed it. *"The Spirit Himself testifies with our spirit that we are children of God"* (Rom. 8:16). Yet acknowledging the truth, no matter how earnestly we do it, does not remove the lie. We have divided hearts; therefore, we can believe a lie and the truth at the same time. We must remove the lie with repentance, then replace it with truth. While our conscience condemns us for our inconsistencies, only repentance can rid of us of our mental blocks. Even though these lies were logical to me, I renounced them as lies out of faith that His Word is true. I repented for believing them, for rebelling against God and rejecting Him.

Going before the Father in repentance was not enough either. It did plow up some tough ground in my heart, creating some soft soil for God to plant good truthful seeds, but it did not heal the wound. I still felt the ache from the devastation that those years brought upon my family. In the aftermath of what seemed to be a mild earthquake, my family moved to another state, leaving my older sister behind to attend college. But being reunited with my father did not improve the situation. A series of shockwaves rippled through our lives; deception, addiction, adultery, and divorce. Many years later, the tremors still continue. I had to ask Him. *What happened? Where were you? What am I to believe about all this?*

In response, He brought me to a story found in 1 Kings 18-19. Elijah served as a prophet of God in the northern kingdom of Israel during the evil reign of King Ahab. In this particular passage, Elijah was instructed to host a showdown between Baal and his prophets and the God of Israel. At God's bidding, Elijah set up the competition with the odds clearly in Baal's favor. When Baal didn't come through, despite the pleadings and self-flagellations of his prophets, Elijah called down fire from heaven and the glory of God won the day. Then, he had the prophets of Baal rounded up and he slaughtered every one of them. As if that wasn't a full day's work, he witnessed the miraculous return of rain and he outran King Ahab, who was riding in his chariot with quite a head start!

Here's the most gripping part of the story. When Ahab reported to his wife, Jezebel, all that had happened, she issued Elijah a death threat and he ran for his life. We would expect our fearless prophet to be full of valor and come back with a brazen rebuttal, but the text tells us that he was afraid! He went more than a day's journey, then sheltered himself under a juniper tree and prayed for death. Instead, he was sent on a pilgrimage to Mt. Horeb, the mountain of God. At the same mountain where God had met with Moses, He asked Elijah what he was doing there. Elijah responded by saying, *"I have been very zealous for the Lord, the God of hosts; for the sons of Israel have forsaken Your covenant, torn down Your altars and killed Your prophets with the sword. And I alone am left; and they seek my life, to take it away"* (1 Kings 19:10).

At this, God displayed His power to Elijah as He passed by. 1 Kings 19:11-13 says,

> *And a great and strong wind was rending the mountains and breaking in pieces the rocks before the Lord; but the Lord was not in the wind. And after the wind an earthquake, but the Lord was not in the earthquake. And after the earthquake a fire, but the Lord was not in the fire; and after the fire a sound of a gentle blowing.*

It was in the gentle blowing that God revealed Himself to Elijah, who immediately covered himself with his mantle. The Lord asked Elijah a second time, *"What are you doing here?"* (19:13), and Elijah responded as he had before. Their conversation concluded when the Lord sent Elijah back to work, declared a series of judgments against the idolatrous nation of Israel, assigned him an assistant and successor, and informed him that there were 7,000 other faithful followers who had not bent the knee to Baal.

James 5:17 says that Elijah was a man with a nature just like ours. Just as we do, he became fearful and discouraged. He had some wrong assumptions, and he allowed his heart to slip into the abyss of doubt and disbelief. He ran away, but God came after him! In the same way, God went looking for Adam in the garden: *"Where are you?"* (Gen. 3:9) He pursued Hagar into the wilderness: *"What is the matter?"* (Gen 21:9-

20). He intercepted Paul on the road to Damascus: *"Why are you persecuting me?"* (Acts 9:4). Because He first loved us (1 John 4:19), He will leave the ninety-nine to find His lost, weary, and headstrong sheep (Luke 15:4).

> *So long as we imagine that it is we who have to look for God, then we must often lose heart. But it is the other way about: he is looking for us. And so, we can afford to recognize that very often we are not looking for God; far from it, we are in full flight from him, in high rebellion against him. And he knows that and has taken it into account. He has followed us into our own darkness; there where we thought finally to escape him, we run straight into his arms.*[19]

It occurred to me that this is what He was doing for me. He came looking for me. After years of running, He found me in the wilderness and brought me to His mountain. He let me taste afresh His power and His presence, and He drew me out with a hushed whisper: *"Why don't you trust me?"* I reminded Him of all that had happened, and I allowed myself to dwell in the pain long enough to give Him a full accounting of it. Then, He did something unexpected. He offered me His hand and asked me to walk with Him for the rest of the journey. He asked if I would be willing to choose differently this time and trust Him to be faithful. He assured me that I wouldn't be alone and that the story wasn't over yet. God is not in a hurry. He is gracious enough to train our hearts through new experiences. I accepted His offer, believing it would be another lesson in breathing underwater, that I would *"see the goodness of the Lord in the land of the living"* (Ps. 27:13).

Then, just as He did with Elijah, He sent me back to work. Literally. Within six weeks, I was a working mom, and my husband had a tuition-free grant to return to school. We weren't out of the woods yet, but we weren't lost anymore, and I knew we weren't alone. I won't tell you that the journey from there was easy. It was painful, and familiar pain is the worst, but we must revisit the pain in order to find restoration. What I can say is that, for the first time in my life, I set my heart upon trusting Him to walk the road with me. I was willing to span the distance between what I wanted to believe and what I was experiencing with a thread of faith. Although it began as a thin and brittle thread, it grew stronger over time. And I discovered along the way that God is far greater than the pain.

Conclusion

Let us not underestimate our capacity to become deceived. *"Take care, brethren, lest there should be in any one of you an evil, unbelieving heart, in falling away from the living God"* (Heb. 3:12). We would be wise to pay attention on those days when our guard is down, and our inner world is revealed. Let's not chalk it up to a bad day, edit ourselves, or stuff the ugly thoughts and feelings that arise. Instead, let us take every thought captive to the obedience of Christ. Consider the Psalms. The Holy Spirit inspired writers of the Psalms to give a full rendering of their thoughts and feelings. They often do as we are instructed to do in Psalm 62:8. *"Pour out your heart before Him."* But consider what they do at the end of each chapter. Who do they point to? They take their questions, doubts, anger, and hurt to God. They do not allow their pain, doubts, and fears to take root. They lay them at His feet and allow God to answer for Himself. They admit to God what is in their hearts, while submitting to Him their emotions, their loyalty, and their expectations. That is purposeful, not disrespectful!

The heart cannot be tamed, cannot be managed, but it can be surrendered and transformed. The heart can be divided, but only God knows us intimately from the inside out and can disclose to us our duality. The eyes of our hearts must be opened by the Holy Spirit for us to understand truth. So invite Him in! We must allow the Holy Spirit, the lover of our souls, to dialogue with us. Then we can join Him as He leads the battle between the truth and the lies, hope and despair, faithfulness and idolatry, love and hate. The next time life throws you a painful season, don't just survive it. Throw your whole heart into it!

> *Where can I go from Your Spirit? Or where can I flee from Your presence? If I ascend to heaven, You are there. If I make my bed in Sheol, behold, You are there. If I take the wings of the dawn, if I dwell in the remotest part of the sea, even there Your hand will lead me, and Your right hand will lay hold of me. If I say, "Surely the darkness will overwhelm me, and the light around me will be night," even the darkness is not dark to You, and the night is as bright as the day. Darkness and light are alike to You.* (Ps. 139:7-12)

Questions for Reflection

1. *How do we remove lies and replace them with truth?*

2. *Can you describe a time when you, like Elijah, triumphed over adversaries and then ran and hid?*

3. *What does it mean that, "God's not in a hurry. He is gracious enough to train our hearts through new experiences"?*

4. *How can we "throw our whole heart" into a painful season?*

Chapter 5

Mirrored Realities

Sunday Morning Shenanigans

I opened my eyes to welcome the day and found that my bedroom door had been closed, which wasn't a sign of good things to come. It meant only one thing: the children were up and didn't want me to know it. So, I threw off the covers and walked into the kitchen to pour myself a cup of courage and assess the damage. I took a few sips and rubbed the sleep out of my eyes, then walked over to the living room and took a deep breath. I'd neglected to put on my glasses but could still make out the light mist of cereal and milk covering the floor. Fortunately, it had been mopped up in a few areas by the clean laundry I had folded the night before. Front and center was a makeshift fort, comprised of couch seats, exercise mats, and blankets. *"Wow! Girls you've accomplished a lot this morning."* Two very delighted little girls peered out from under a blanket and asked if I liked their castle. I smiled weakly and asked them where they had put their brother who, judging from the scent in the air, was in dire need of a diaper change. *"Oh, he's in the dungeon."*

About that time, my husband came bolting out of our bedroom and announced the time. We had only 45 minutes to change a dirty diaper, clean up the living room, take showers, and dress everyone for Sunday morning church. Our usual departure time put us at the service approximately 7 minutes late, so there was no time to spare. In a slight panic, I chugged the remaining coffee in my cup and went on a rampage. Wishing I was one of those organized mothers who sets out clothes the night before, I grabbed the cleanest-looking clothes from the folded laundry and tossed them to the girls while the two-year-old went into the shower with Daddy. I tried to return some order to the living room, but the girls demanded that their castle become a permanent fixture and my husband yelled orders from the shower that I stop cleaning and get ready. I can't explain how, but we managed to get ready with a few seconds to spare. After a quick panty and shoe check, we headed to the car. But when we arrived at the church building, we discovered an empty parking lot. And that's when we realized that we had forgotten daylight savings time!

Clean faces, combed hair, and dirt-free clothes don't last long, especially when you have an hour to kill and only a playground with which to do it. After our children landed in every bare spot and mud puddle they could possibly find, we brushed them off and headed into the building to find our seats. As the music began, I took a good look around and tried to convince myself that I was just as poised and put-together as every other woman in the room, but the pine straw stuck in my son's hair told a different tale. As if that wasn't enough, our oldest daughter was standing on the chair next to me while triumphantly singing at the very top of her lungs. She was almost in tune and usually got the words right, but tried to hit those high notes and fell just a hair shy. I wasn't the only one to notice. Several people in front of us turned to see what was wrong with her. One little boy looked to be particularly offended, but I told myself he was just jealous because his mom wouldn't let him stand on his chair. I aimed a very nice smile in his direction and tugged at my daughter's hand, then shot a glare at my husband that said, *People like us shouldn't breed!*

My Big, Fat Identity Crisis

As we headed home that afternoon, I couldn't let it go. I felt so exposed. I berated myself for all the ways I should have done better. I should have prepared the night before. I should have gotten up earlier, or perhaps even later. I should have put the darn laundry away! But would it have made a difference? Even with the best of preparations, I have always managed to miss calm-cool-and-collected by a long shot. Try as I may to be vanilla sweet, benignly innocent, and vaguely disconnected, I think too hard, say too much, laugh too loud, and cry too easily. I've always been far too inquisitive to feel at home with small talk, way too idealistic to feign diplomacy, much too accident-prone to appear poised, and clearly too passionate to keep my mouth shut. The struggle is real and it runs deep: an insatiable need to feel adequate and acceptable and an incessant voice of shame that won't be sidelined. By the time we got home, I was ready to crawl into a hole.

Arguably, the Bible says a lot about our new identity in Christ, offering me ample reason to feel secure and free. But too often the truth of God's love and acceptance has fallen cold on my heart while the menacing monster of insecurity has breathed hot on my neck. And if I had seen this monster face to face, looked it in the eye, and seen its soul, I'd like to assume I would have taken it down by now. But such clarity has evaded me. I feel as if I've been circling for years, waiting for the storm to pass so that I can land on steadfast ground. But the storm rages and illumination has only come as brief lightning strikes. Such moments of brilliance have enabled me to identify and dodge some of the swirling shadows, but there's been no miraculous quieting of the storm for me. On this side of eternity, that might be as good as it gets. I'd like to be more steadfast, with an internal compass that reads true north and guides me safely past the pitfalls of self-doubt and insecurity. I pray for such a day of deliverance, but this particular battle might just accompany me to the gates of glory.

Rather than expound on my bird's-eye view of who we are in Christ and how we obtain victory over the darkness that plagues our peace, I'd like to share some of what I have seen and experienced from close range encounters over the last decade or so. What we see at close range certainly isn't as objective as what we see from a distance, so forgive me if my anecdotes fail your credibility test, but sometimes we need to see things up close and personal to understand their living, breathing realities. Get comfy and settle in for a few stories and reflections I've been collecting. I promise to honestly pass along the grace that has been granted to me thus far. And I pray that God will grant you a few flashes of illumination, making His truth astonishingly personal and transformative.

"My Delight"

Just after my journey of emotional and spiritual healing began, a friend gave me a challenging assignment. I was to write a letter. Not just any letter, but a letter to me by God. In other words, I was to ask God what He had to say to me about me, and write it down – without editing, without fact checking. It's not that I doubted God would communicate with me. I knew He would. As one of His sheep, I am afforded the awesome opportunity to hear His voice (John 10:27). I was afraid of what He would say. I felt safe asking Him to replace my lies with truth, safe asking Him to set me straight, but the idea of putting my whole self before God Almighty and asking for a general assessment sounded like the makings of a really bad day. It felt like the dream where you arrive at work and realize you forgot your presentation, your boss's birthday, or your pants. We are all going to stand before Him and give an account for our lives one day, but I was in no hurry. For this people-pleasing middle child, asking anyone that kind of question was dangerous. But, I did it. And when my pen met paper, I got the shock of my life.

> *Beloved, trust in me and I will give you strength. I will give you Myself. I desire you, all of you, and you need Me. As a deer pants for water, long for Me. I don't want your obedience, but your whole heart, broken and restored. I have given you a new name, born of Myself. You are "My Delight." You are lovely and delicate as a morning flower that opens to the sun…so bloom in Me. Take delight in My warmth. Bask in My love. Delight in Me, that I may delight in you. Rest in Me, release to My embrace, and let Me speak tenderly to you.*

I look back at it now and I'm just as stunned as I was then. He wrote me a psalm, a lovely piece of poetry, and He gave me a new name. He bestowed upon me a new identity. Any woman would blush at such lavish love and affection, but not me. I would have preferred that He had given me a task list rather than a love letter. I didn't trust His kindness. Not yet. The only thing I trusted was what I could secure by my own merit. I wanted to know how to earn His love, because I didn't believe He would give it freely. I had so much to learn and this was the invitation, albeit unappreciated. As God would have it, that very day, I began to discover my identity in Him.

Questions for Reflection

1. ***What does your internal dialogue sound like? How does it impact your emotions, your motivations, and your relationships?***

2. ***Biblically speaking, how do we know that our identity is in Christ? What kind of difference should that make in our lives?***

3. Would you be willing to let God "write" you a letter?

Bamboozled by the Three-Ring Circus

Quiet solitude is a most delightful thing. It gives the soul room to breathe and the mind a chance to unwind and recalibrate. The still, small voice of God can be hard to hear amidst the clamor of our daily lives, but His whispers ring out in the hushed moments. Mother Teresa said, *"We need to find God, and He cannot be found in noise and restlessness. God is the friend of silence. See how nature – trees, flowers, grass –grows in silence; see the stars, the moon and the sun, how they move in silence...We need silence to be able to touch souls."*[1]

For most of my life, I dreaded silence. Sitting in stillness was filled with trepidation for me, because every attempt to taste a bit of its sweetness was disturbed by an unwelcome antagonist. Lovely little things like lying in bed too long, sitting on the front porch swing at dusk, or hiding away with a good book were ruined by the invading voice of shame. Its fierce accusations and relentless indecency chased me out of bed each morning and nipped at my heels until it was finally drowned out by sleep at night.

It would come out of nowhere. I'd be enjoying the warmth of my morning shower and a painful memory would streak across my mind with the emotional impact of a freight train. Later, I'd be folding clothes on the couch and a moment of failure would flash before me with a humiliating tagline. Even benign memories were returned to me with a demeaning tone, and future events were confirmed as fiascos before they even took place. Most crippling were the accusations that pegged me as a dismal disgrace. Stasi Eldredge describes it well: *"I am not enough, and I am too much at the same time. Not pretty enough, not thin enough, not kind enough, not gracious enough, not disciplined enough. But too emotional, too needy, too sensitive, too strong, too opinionated, too messy."*[2]

In her famous TED talk, "Listening to Shame," Brené Brown calls this the *"warm wash of shame."*

> *For women, shame is do it all, do it perfectly, and never let them see you sweat...Shame, for women, is this web of unobtainable, conflicting, competing expectations about who we're supposed to*

be. And it's a straitjacket. For men, shame is not a bunch of competing, conflicting expectations. Shame is one: do not be perceived as what? Weak.[3]

We all know the voice of shame. It comes at us from every direction and it attacks us in our most vulnerable place: our identity. John Eldredge says, *"The deepest arrows we've known are lodged in the places of our self-identity and no amount of positive thinking or self-affirmation will remove them."*[4]

One of the reasons we cannot seem to escape its slanderous harassment is because shame is woven into the fabric of our sin nature.

One of the tragic implications of this event [the Fall] is that man lost his secure status with God and began to struggle with feelings of arrogance, inadequacy, and despair, valuing the opinions of others more than the truth of God. This robbed man of his true self-worth and put him on a continual, but fruitless, search for significance through his success and the approval of others.[5]

Sin created a dread-filled sense of isolation and chaos in each of us. It set in motion a works orientation and gave birth to a distorted sense of worth and performance-based, codependent relationships. Insecurity became the norm, and we became driven by our fear of rejection and isolation. According to our fallen flesh, we must strive to earn our worth and compete for love and acceptance. Coming from our flesh, shame drives us to perform, then mocks us in our exhaustion.

Our world system reinforces these shame-based inclinations of the flesh. Its raging system of work and fear reduces all men to commodities. According to the world, we are not inherently valuable as image-bearers, we are not *equal*, and survival of the fittest is a reality. How contrary are Jesus' words to us on this! He tells us to live in the world, but not to become defined by it (John 17:14-19). As citizens of a heavenly kingdom, we are to pledge allegiance to an entirely different set of values and definitions, and that includes the value we place upon ourselves as image-bearers of God. Unfortunately, the world's shaming mantra is louder and more familiar to us. Too often, we agree to its terms and attempt to play the game, using the resources of this world to gain approval and the validation that we could somehow prove our merit.

The ringleader of this circus manipulates the world and our flesh to distort the truth of who God is and who He has made us to be. We see this first in the Garden. Satan cast doubt upon the character of God, directly challenging the truth of what He had said to Adam and Eve. We know this. His primary tool is deception, and his primary target is God. But look carefully at what he did next. He enticed Eve with pride and assaulted her identity at the very same time! *"In the day you eat from it, your eyes will be opened and you will be like God"* (Gen. 3:5). As if she wasn't already? Did she not know that she had been created in the image of God, that she displayed Him and His glory to the world? The enemy deceived her and tempted her to covet something she already possessed! *This* is what he does to us every day.

John Eldredge says, *"The story of your life is the story of the long and brutal assault on your heart by the one that knows what you can become and fears it."*[6] There is a strategy and a theme to the disappointments we've endured, the wounds we've received, and the lies we've believed. They are all aimed at our uniqueness, our calling, our true identity and hidden glory. The enemy targets those places within us where God has placed the manifestation of Himself. In those treasured places, he levies his assault. He lies to us, accuses us, shames us, deceives us, tempts us, distracts us, and intimidates us so that we would forget who we are, forget who God is, and fail to fully walk in the calling for which we were designed! The enemy doesn't have the final word. He does not have the authority to snuff out our rights as children of God. What has been broken can be repaired, and what has been lost can be recovered.

This was an eye-opener for me. As part of my lesson on spiritual bondage, I began to realize that I needed to apply grace to the voice in my head, and I also needed to take up arms against the enemy, because he was trying to shame me into making devastating agreements that would put distance between me and God. He masqueraded as the Holy Spirit by "convicting" me of sin with a voice of condemnation. The messages I received were so harsh and confusing that I didn't even know what to repent for. He also masqueraded as my flesh and showered me with temptations, wicked thoughts, and feelings that I could not repent away. After wasting much time and energy looking under every rock in my soul and finding nothing, I was left demoralized and directionless.

The fog lifted when the Holy Spirit made it clear to me that I was entertaining the voice of the enemy. I learned that when the Holy Spirit convicts us of sin, we know exactly what we did wrong and how to make it right. I learned to take my thoughts captive and test the spirits. When I became aware of a thought or feeling that didn't line up with God's word and character, I asked God where it came from and how I should deal with it. Perhaps I would have some repenting to do, and perhaps a great deal of work in allowing God to bring all of the pieces to light. But sometimes, I simply needed to rebuke the enemy and cover the situation with truth and life and love. There was no longer a need to spin my wheels on conviction that wasn't from God or on sin that wasn't mine.

Questions for Reflection

1. ***Do you agree that shame affects men and women differently? How do you experience shame?***

2. ***How do the flesh, the world, and the Devil assault us with shame?***

3. ***How can we distinguish between the condemnation that comes from the enemy and conviction that comes from the Holy Spirit?***

Game Face

Everyone has a game face. When the pressure is on and we want to avoid rejection or gain approval, we slip on a little mask and carry out a little façade. Sometimes, who we are isn't what people want, so we learn how to adapt. We play the part and no one is the wiser. We don a little "Proverbs 31 Meets Miss America", "Devoted Daddy", or "Holy and Hopeful" and sail through intimidating situations with ease. Whether it's saccharine sweetness, superhuman strength, or effortless efficiency that's needed, we find a way to fake it till we make it, and we feel protected from indecent exposure and the haunting shadow of failure. Unfortunately, it takes a lot of endurance and patience to keep it up. Eventually, my cheeks would cramp up from smiling so much, my stomach would ache from sucking it in, and I'd always find myself falling into the deadly trap of transparency.

> *Whether our false positive is appearance, marriage, money making, position, education, or notoriety, it only works enough to keep us seduced and distracted, and we never get to the real issues. Even if we could make everybody believe we were "Every Woman" (or "Every Man"), we ourselves would know better. Self-doubt would devour us. In one way or another and sooner or later, we'll give ourselves away.*[7]

John Eldredge writes, *"What we are doing in this costume ball of life is looking to avoid exposure while at the same time trying to offer something that will bring us glory."*[8] To be honest, there are some temporary benefits, but it's an incredibly damaging game. Every time I've put on one of those masks and pretended to be someone I'm not, it felt like a betrayal. I was rejecting myself, and it hurt. It was suffocating. Every bit of validation and acceptance I received from others while playing these little roles only intensified my self-loathing. And it intensified my sense of isolation as well, because we cannot truly connect with others and enjoy intimacy with them while living out of our false identity.

Something remarkable happened to change all that for me. I was visiting with a friend when it all came pouring out. I described what it was like to feel like a failure of a woman who couldn't meet anyone's expectations. I acknowledged the shame that gnawed away at me day and night, hounding me, hedging me in like a vicious abuser. I didn't make it look prettier than it was. I didn't hide the hurt and anger that was swelling up inside of me, begging for release. The choking tears came and I didn't stop them. I needed help and I sincerely hoped there was some to be had.

My wise friend challenged me to take a critical look at my assumptions. Specifically, I was to name every single thing I thought I had to be and do in order to be "okay" or to be loved. And in reverse, I was to name the negative traits that disqualified me from receiving them. With both lists, I was to identify any lies I was believing as well as any false expectations I had attached to my sense of significance. I was to call them out and reject them. Then, I was to ask God to reveal to me His truth: His expectations of me. It wasn't easy and my defenses were high, but I took on the task full speed ahead.

It's amazing what you can discover when you allow yourself to ponder deep and hard questions. What did I think I had to do and be? That was an easy one and one my heart readily divulged. Perfect! Thin and beautiful. Gracious and diplomatic. Happy and agreeable. Smart and well-spoken. Organized. Well-prepared, and very much put together. It came out in a rush of exasperated exhaustion: the unforgiving demands I had placed upon myself. And I had plenty of evidence to prove the direct correlation between the successful accomplishment of these things and wonderful rewards like respect, admiration, and friendship. Unfortunately, I always walked into the room feeling anything but those things.

And what of the negative traits? What disqualified me from the love and acceptance I craved? Once provoked, the accusing litany came pouring out and couldn't be stopped or silenced by the shame that held it captive. Weak and vulnerable. Flighty and irrational. Pushy and opinionated. Unorganized. Undisciplined. Unpredictable. Wouldn't you know it, I had many memories of direct and indirect "feedback" from others to indicate that my self-assessment was correct. I suppose it wasn't much of a leap for me to conclude that I actually deserved every bit of rejection, criticism, and indifference I'd ever received.

Striving to get what I needed by way of behavior modification wasn't working very well. And I needed to free myself from the obligation to perform for others. So, by faith, I rejected this litany of lies and asked God for the truth. And do you know what happened? He answered me. In my spirit, He answered every claim. As I worked through each item on my list, He gently spoke to my heart, reminding me that I was His idea, that my design was according to His very specific plan and purposes. He released me from the need to hide and pretend. He encouraged me to be comfortable with vulnerability, because that was how He designed me to experience grace. He encouraged me to embrace my brokenness and to be attentive to the brokenness of others, because that was how He designed me to show love. We laughed together as He reminded me that He doesn't play by the rules either. He rarely meets the expectations of others. And I didn't need to be afraid when others didn't understand or approve. In fact, sometimes He had put me front and center with my inquisitive, unconventional self, just to stir the pot.

As I sat at my bedside that night I was overcome with relief and awe. My God stole the keys from my captors and rescued me out of my prison because He loved me. Nothing was clearer to me than this. He loved me. It was an answer to Paul's prayer for the Ephesians: *"...that you, being rooted and grounded in love, may be able to comprehend with all the saints what is the breadth and length and height and depth, and to know the love of Christ which surpasses knowledge, that you may be filled up to all the fullness of God"* (Eph. 3:18-19). Love that surpasses knowledge. Love that fills us up. Love that strengthens us in our spirit. Love that grounds us, that gives us rooted security. Now, that kind of love can set us free from comparison and the fear that drives us (1 John 4:18).

I want to be very careful how I say this, but it does need to be said. There is a comprehension that surpasses knowledge. What the Bible said about me did not ring true before that night. I am not challenging the authority or inerrancy of Scripture. Even though I knew my Bible, the truth of God's love for me simply bounced off as if my heart was too hard to absorb it. I could not bring its truth into the vault of my identity. It wasn't until God revealed to me the many false expectations I had of myself, and I began to reject them and renounce the voices of shame, that I could embrace the truths of God. What had been lovely and unobtainable words on a page took on life when they were spoken to my heart.

That night, as I laid my head on my pillow and listened to the beating of my heart so swollen with gratitude. But I had one last question. Who am I? He responded with this: *"That's exactly what I'm showing you."*

<u>Questions for Reflection</u>

1. ***What expectations do you try to meet in order to secure love and acceptance? What are the things you think you need to be and do in order to be "okay" or to be loved? Name the negative traits that disqualify you from receiving them.***

2. ***How would you describe your game face? When do you usually use it? What are the results?***

3. What would it look like to let go of your game face?

Green-Eyed Monsters

When I see another person who has something I don't have, who has accomplished something I long to have accomplished, who appears in a way I long to appear, who is able to do things I cannot seem to do, I can go down the road to self-abasement – but sometimes I don't. Sometimes, my honest-to-goodness real reaction is just bitter green-eyed jealousy. It's ugly, but true. I've often wanted to have and be what I see in every other woman. I wanted to feel put together and poised and very much in control. From my vantage point, I've always been the one hanging on by a thread, and it has made me shamefully mad.

James speaks of this very thing, and he says it comes from the love of the world.

> *For where jealousy and selfish ambition exist, there is disorder and every evil thing…What is the source of quarrels and conflicts among you? Is not the source your pleasures that wage war in your members? You lust and do not have; so you commit murder. You are envious and cannot obtain; so you fight and quarrel. You do not have because you do not ask. You ask and do not receive, because you ask with wrong motives, so that you may spend it on your pleasures. You adulteresses, do you not know that friendship with the world is hostility toward God? (James 3:16, 4:1-4a)*

What James says here is hard to accept. He calls a group of believers immoral because they were fighting with one another - not because they were zealous for God, but because they were selfish. He rips away their justifications and points to the personal desires that motivate their behavior: the desire to get even, to be right, to be admired, to look good, to be validated. Remember Cain and Abel? King David and Uriah's wife? Ananias and Sapphira? Joseph and his brothers? Each of their stories began with jealousy and selfish ambition. In their greedy desires, they determined to steal, lie, kill, and destroy.

This lesson hit home one day when I observed a conflict between my two daughters. They were probably about three and five at the time, playing in the living room with dolls. You've seen it a thousand times. The oldest wanted what the younger one had and proceeded to beg, bribe, and whine in attempts to get it. Reveling in the momentary pleasures of power, the younger daughter emphatically refused and went on to display her superior use of the toy. What followed was like a wrestling match gone bad. The situation was not going to resolve itself, so I marched into the living room to address it. In my very best preschool language, I explained the foolishness of their little skirmish. There was no need to fight over toys. They had more toys than they knew what to do with. *"Don't we give you what you need?"* Just about then, I felt a tap on my shoulder and a little whisper to my heart. *"I give you what you need."*

Just like my daughters, I was so consumed with what I thought I needed from this world that I was willing to beg, manipulate, and fight to get it. *"Do you not know that friendship with the world is hostility toward God?"* (James 4:3). Perhaps I needed to reckon with the fact that my discontentment was with God. Was He not able to meet my needs?

> *Ask, and it will be given to you; seek, and you will find; knock, and it will be opened to you. For everyone who asks receives, and he who seeks finds, and to him who knocks it will be opened. Or what man is there among you who, when his son asks for a loaf, will give him a stone? Or if he asks for a fish, he will not give him a snake, will he? If you then, being evil, know how to give good gifts to your children, how much more will your Father who is in heaven give what is good to those who ask Him!* (Matt. 7:7-11)

Sometimes we just want more. And because we don't recognize our need for the living water that satisfies our thirst, we go running to the nearest spigot. We need more love, more grace, more reassurance, more intimacy with the Father; but instead, we compete with others to be more beautiful, more successful, more secure, more admired, more respectable. Isn't that where Eve went wrong? She wanted more, so she reached for something that wasn't hers. What would have happened if she took her desire to God? Would He have denied her? Would He have given her a stone (Matt. 7:9)? He is a good father who delights to meet our needs. And unlike everything else in this created world, He is not finite. He is infinite, without limitation, which means that His love, His favor, His notice, His grace, and His purposes are freely available for all of us. You do not need to compete for a seat at His table, because there is a seat with your name on it. *"You prepare a table before me in the presence of my enemies; You have anointed my head with oil; my cup overflows. Surely goodness and lovingkindness will follow me all the days of my life, and I will dwell in the house of the LORD forever"* (Ps. 23:5-6).

Questions for Reflection

1. **"Sometimes we just want more. And because we don't recognize our need for the living water that satisfies our thirst, we go running to the nearest spigot." Have you ever been in a place where you realized you wanted more? How did you respond to that desire?**

2. **What is the "more" you want?**

Don't Let Your Mess Define You

Winter was dragging on a bit too long one year. The girls and I were weary from the cold and eager for a change of scenery, so I gathered them up and we flew out to visit my mom and step-dad. In a way, I was running away from the stress and uncertainty of our life back home. A series of unfortunate events had propelled my husband into the lonely world of self-employment, while I was unexpectedly expecting our third child and slugging my way through a long season of emotional and spiritual healing. As with many couples, my concern was our family life and his concern was our livelihood. While he was desperately trying to reinvent himself, redeem his manhood, and get us back on track financially, I was trying to expose every area of dysfunction in him and in our marriage in order to secure a healthier, happier home for our new baby. Quite naturally, the tensions were mounting. We both felt isolated and desperate, but neither of us had the emotional energy, the time, or the perspective to offer the other. When it was decided that I would spend a few weeks with my mom, we were both relieved. Being the beneficiary of my mommy's nurturing care sounded like a dream vacation for me, and my husband was looking forward to the opportunity to push through, uninterrupted, and get some work done!

In most ways, it was a lovely visit. Home-cooked meals without peanut butter, tuna, or beans, fun outings for the children, new maternity clothes for me, and the comfort of a listening ear. Graciously, my mom took care of me and eased my burden. But that's not why God sent me on a trip back home. There was one thing I expected from my mom that she was not able to deliver. She had always been my cheerleader, always believed the best of me, and always assured me, as only a mom can, that all would be well. But my sweet mom was too concerned for me and my growing family to offer those things. Instead, she asked careful questions, she mentioned a few unfavorable observations, and she delivered one or two gentle criticisms. And just like that, I stopped sleeping…again.

What was I to do? I didn't know how to get myself together and be a better mom or tell my husband how to be a better provider for our family. I wanted an action plan, but couldn't see a viable way out of our circumstances and couldn't produce more resources with which to rise above them. After several anxious days and sleepless nights, I was spent. It was the wee hours of the morning as I sat on her couch, head in hands. She stepped out of her bedroom and sat with me, asking what she could do. I asked her to pray for me. She bowed her weary head on my behalf, pleading with God to spare me from what she had suffered as a young wife and mom, begging Him to rescue me from the mess my life had become. And in that very moment, I understood where my anxiety was coming from and why God had put us on that plane.

First, while it was certainly true that my mom suffered as a wife and a mom and she was rightly concerned that I was headed down the same path, I could no longer live in the fear of following in her footsteps. Secondly, our circumstances were quite bleak, and we were in need of rescue, but it was not a necessary leap that God was disappointed in us, that He was punishing us, or that we deserved it. In that moment, I understood that neither my mom's circumstances nor our circumstances defined me.

I was so relieved by this revelation that I slept restfully the rest of the night and got up the next morning determined to go home and finish out that very difficult season knowing that God was with us and had our lives in His capable hands. I could rest in that knowledge and stop carrying the heavy burden of shame and anxiety.

Questions for Reflection

1. **In what ways have you been tempted to let your circumstances define you?**

2. **If our circumstances don't define us, then what are we to do with them?**

Don't Take it to Heart

After the real estate market crashed in 2008, we were forced to start over again. My husband received a grant to go back to school, and so it was up to me to bring in some income. I had been a stay-at-home mom since my first child was born and much preferred it that way, but life doesn't always work out the way we want it to. My mom and step-dad graciously agreed to relocate near us and manage our two little girls and one bundle of a boy so that I could rejoin the rat race. I discovered, all too quickly, that it was indeed an infestation. Although it was a relatively short season, it was very intense. I enjoyed the work, but the smiling lies, the lucrative betrayals, and the covetous pursuit of dominance were more than I could take. I doggie-paddled for a few years until my husband was settled in a new career, and then resigned. By that time, I was water-logged and slightly delirious. Certainly, I was relieved to be able to return home where I could pursue the things that truly mattered to me, but I was so confused about what had happened in my job and what it said about me. Without any real closure, I said a few goodbyes, turned in my keys, and left.

I drove home in a puddle of angry tears. I hated that place for what it had done to me and what I had allowed it to take from me. I had given up all my time and energy; nights, weekends, holidays, and several of my children's school events. What good had that done? Who had benefited from those sacrifices? Certainly not my family! I barely saw my kids and when I did, I was too tired and distracted to do them any good. Would they even want me back home again?

I will tell you honestly what happened next, but please don't follow my example. It's not advisable to demand answers from the Creator of the Universe and the One who holds the keys of life and death. But I make these mistakes so you don't have to! I took my guilt and anger and threw it at God. After all, I had been content to stay at home, but this was His idea, His provision for us. *What did I do to deserve such hateful behavior? Didn't I do a good job? Why didn't You defend me? If that was all necessary, what was I supposed to learn? How am I supposed to make this up to my children?*

About that time, something extraordinary happened. The cleansing waters of relief washed over me, and I realized that it was truly over. No more juggling work and family responsibilities. No more walking on eggshells trying to meet expectations without compromising my integrity. No more posturing and politicking. The weighty burden I had been carrying was completely lifted. The oppressive fog, the knot in my stomach, the pounding in my head, the tension in my jaw…gone. I was free.

Right then and there, I started a list of all the things I wanted to do with my newfound freedom:

1. Go eat lunch with my kids at school
2. Join a gym
3. Paint the living room
4. Clean and re-organize my kitchen cabinets
5. Buy a pair of sensible shoes
6. Finish writing this book

Then another extraordinary thing happened. God asked me a question. "*What damage was done to you?*" Now that was a good question, one that I was only too eager to answer. The victim in me had a list a mile long that I had memorized for such an opportunity. My feelings, for starters. My feelings were deeply wounded. Those were not nice people! And my dreams, the ones that included appreciation, validation, enjoying the fruits of my labor, a raise? Totally dashed. And what about my self-esteem? I had been lied to, lied about, falsely accused, under-paid, and undermined. Who walks away from that kind of abuse unharmed?

When I heard my answers, I was embarrassed at my short-sighted selfishness. First, I had experienced many injustices, but I had taken all of them too personally. The things that happen to us in this fallen, disappointing world, even the attacks on our character and personhood, are not about us. They do not define us, do not change our status as children of the King, and certainty cannot alter our eternal destiny (Rom. 8:31-39).

Second, my struggle indicated just how much power and influence I'd given away. To get along and get by, I had submitted myself to the priorities, definitions, and values of those unworthy of such deference. *"For am I now seeking the favor of people, or of God? Or am I striving to please. people?"* (Gal. 1:10).

Third, I had forgotten why God had placed me there to begin with. It wasn't for my advancement or fulfillment. My family did need the salary it provided, but as with all other work and relationships we find ourselves in, my purpose was for the world — the messy, lost, broken world. I had wasted so much time and energy nursing my bruises, when those around me were mortally wounded. Dead people smell, but I carried about the aroma of Christ! Instead of complaining about the stench, I should have been more focused on petitioning the Father to raise the dead. I was fighting the wrong battle: fighting to protect my flesh, when I should have been putting it to death. Moreover, I should have been fighting for those whom He had entrusted to me during that time. So much drama over something that had to die anyway!

And even though all those truths resonated with me, the hurt was still too present to allow them to settle into my heart. Healing was needed before the soil of my heart could receive what God wanted to teach me. Transformation of the mind must often accompany the healing of the soul.

As I continued the long drive home, God brought a very old memory to my mind. At the age of five or six, I was participating in our church's worship service with my family when a family friend came over to me and knelt at my feet. He had tears streaming down his face as he explained that God had given him a dream the night before and there was a message in it for me. I remember nothing of the dream, except that it scared me, but his conclusion was surprisingly encouraging. *"You are important to God. He has a special purpose for your life."*

Feeling remarkably unseen and insignificant at that time in my life, I went home reveling in the idea that I was indeed special and my life had meaning. Unfortunately, God's message was hijacked by the enemy. Instead of receiving the life-giving truth of God's unconditional love and resting in His sovereign design, I embraced the bondage of a performance trap. The gift became an obligation. Somehow, I concluded that there was nothing inherently special about me. Therefore, if I wanted to be loved, respected, or valued, I had to prove myself. I had to be the best: the most gifted, most spiritual, most used by God. And these burdensome marching orders were immediately followed by condescending accusations. *"Who do you think you are, trying to be better than everyone else?! Everyone is special to God!"* I was lured into the trap by pride, and shame bolted the door behind me.

Why had God brought this particular memory to mind? Because I was caught in that very same trap once again. In my pride, I had chased after the praise of man. By the grace of God, I failed to achieve it. I was clearly not the best, not the most important, and not the most respected. And shame just stood there mocking me. Not only had I failed to gain favor with men, but I had failed as a Christian to love them.

Healing often begins with repentance. So I confessed my idolatry and renounced it. Then I took a stand against the seeds of pride and shame that had enticed me and abused me over the years. Having done this, I felt much relief, but one question lingered in my mind. Why had that family friend come to me with that message – and who sent him? Was his message from God and I missed the blessing, or was he sent by my enemy to confirm the lies I was believing?

When I took these questions to my Father, He responded with this: *"I delivered that message to you, not because it isn't true of everyone else, but because you needed to hear it. And I always give you what you need."*

Questions for Reflection

1. *Have you had similar struggles in your place of employment? Why do you think God placed you where He did?*

2. *In your experience, has the transformation of your mind accompanied the healing of your soul? If not, are there areas where this might be needed?*

Perfectly Equipped

I was preparing to teach a small lesson at my church some time ago and was truly struggling through it. There was no question that God had opened the door for me to do the teaching, but I couldn't shake my anxiety and confusion. There were so many different ways to approach the material and I couldn't decide which path to choose, because I didn't know who would be there and what they would need to hear. In other words, because I didn't know who my audience was, I couldn't prepare my case against their criticisms. I was actually trying to bullet-proof my lesson, which made it pretty impossible to make any progress. Because God is God and it was His idea for me anyway, He was faithful to give me a lesson, and I delivered it with all the grace available to me at the time. The overall response was good, and I felt relieved that I had done what He asked me to do. But, as I reviewed the night in my mind over the next few days, the sincere questions and comments that were posed by my friends, by women I like and have a great deal of respect for, began to take on a critical tone. I replayed that tape in my mind and each time it was worse than the time before. This continued until I began to doubt that I should ever teach again. My sounding-board husband finally put his foot down and chastised me for my madness. I saw what I was doing and knew it was unhealthy and unwarranted, but still couldn't seem to understand or remedy the situation.

Then I received a text from my brother, and what followed set the stage for my deliverance. It seems that my father had fallen ill while visiting with him and his family, and so all my siblings were included in several days of group text communication. I chimed in to ask a few questions, but mostly observed, feeling a vague and familiar sense of rejection. Then I began to connect the dots.

You see, my family of origin is chock-a-block full of engineering brains; people who think like engineers, people who are engineers, and people who marry engineers. In some cases, the engineers married other engineers. And they are darling people, but there's no denying that intelligence is often lauded and empirical evidence is a condition for credibility in that world. Emotions are not often acknowledged or trusted. In fact, those who display too much emotion, those who can't keep up in a battle of trivia, and those who can't hold their own in a theological or political debate are often considered to be intellectually inferior.

I'm not being critical of engineers or their brains. I truly enjoy people who desire to figure things out, and I appreciate their methodical approach to problem solving. It's refreshing and even grounding for me, so much so that I married one such man and bore him two children with the same predisposition. But I'm as far away from that brain as you can get. I'm an intuitive feeler, an abstract and random thinker for whom logic is optional and facts are irrelevant.

You can imagine where I'm going here. As the pain of rejection swelled within me, God showed me a series of lies that I had bought into as a child. Among the most impactful were these three:

- I believed that I was an outsider and always would be. There was no point trying to fit in, because I would always end up being found out and rejected.
- I believed that if I wanted to be heard, I had to prove my case with evidence that would be perceived as credible, because I had no credibility of my own. And, unfortunately, evidence always eluded me.
- Because of these things, I believed that I wasn't as intelligent and worthy of respect as those who were more practically minded.

I had received these messages from my family of origin over 20 years before this event and, quite obviously, they had stuck. I had seen signs of them at every turn, and had many times asked God to reveal the root issue(s) but had no understanding until He decided to show me on that particular day. I rejected these beliefs as lies and then began to ask God for His thoughts on the matter. *Do you think I'm intelligent? Why do I always feel like I'm missing something?* His answer wasn't what I wanted, but it was exactly what I needed. *"I have perfectly equipped you for your calling."*

A good look at Scripture proves that God isn't defined by our failures, limitations, or dysfunctions, and at no point in history have they gotten in His way. Rahab was a harlot. Ruth was a widow and a Moabite. King David was an adulterer, liar, and murderer. Paul was a first-century Nazi. We can't be too limited, because Lazarus was dead, and God still managed to use him! Despite their complications and difficulties, when God infused His grace and power into their hearts, these people became beautiful ambassadors of grace. He breathes life into our mortal flesh, and we are defined by that interaction! He gladly shares with us a reflection of His identity and glory, but He will not allow Himself to be defined by our limitations. He will never be codependent with us.

But there's more. God is displayed through our weaknesses! Yet He is also revealed through the fingerprint of glory He stamped upon each of us. Our uniqueness makes part of His manifold wisdom known, according to Paul in Ephesians 3. The way God reveals Himself to each of us, the way He exemplifies Himself through us, and the way we connect with Him is unique. It displays just a portion of who He is for all to see. The body of Christ is like a kaleidoscope of God's personhood. Who I am matters, and what God reveals to me and demonstrates through me matters. It's not complete, but it isn't intended to be! Only God Himself is complete. Only He has all wisdom, all truth, all love, all understanding. My individuality and yours are pieces of His manifold wisdom and reflections of His glory. As we in His body are fitted together with Christ as our cornerstone, we will create a brilliant expression of God Himself.

Questions for Reflection

1. *What does it mean that God "gladly shares with us a reflection of His identity and glory, but He will not allow Himself to be defined by our limitations. He will never be codependent with us"?*

2. *"My individuality and yours are pieces of His manifold wisdom and reflections of His glory." Is this a true statement? Why or why not?*

Go Big or Go Home

Faith in who God says He is and faith in who He says we are is not our normal frame of reference. Doubt, shame, and pride are. When God came to Abraham with promises for a child, he considered his physical limitations and doubted God. Sarah laughed (Gen. 17-18:15). Abraham and Sarah both decided to take matters into their own hands and used Hagar to bring about God's work. In doing so, they brought upon themselves great sorrow and discord. Moses had reason to believe he had a great calling upon his life when God rescued him from the Nile and grew him up under Pharaoh's nose. But he too took matters into his own hands and murdered an Egyptian. Later, when God sent him to stand before Pharaoh and rescue the Israelites, he remembered his failures, considered his slow tongue, and tried to shirk his calling (Ex. 3). When the angel of the Lord appeared to Gideon and commissioned him to defeat the Midianites, Gideon questioned God's faithfulness. Undeterred, the Lord commissioned him again, but he considered his poor lineage and requested that someone more worthy be called. He went on to test God a total of three more times before finally stepping out in obedience (Judg. 6:11-24).

We are no different. Shame-based self-abasement will not cure our pride or empower us to be who we are in Christ. Arrogance and self-glorification will not cure our insecurity. Shame says we are worthless, and it is a lie. Pride says we are God, and it is a lie. The truth and cure for this pendulum of insanity is found in God. If we want to grow up as His children, embrace our identity in Him, and walk in truth, we must allow God to change our references. What we need is a larger view of Him.

The bulk of our sanctification revolves around this process of discovering who we are in light of who God is. Who we are and who He is are mirrored realities. As He reveals more of Himself to us, we will have a clearer grasp of who we are, producing both humility and a sense of self-worth. It begins with the majesty of God and ends with our grateful receiving of it. As John Piper says,

> *Nobody stands on the edge of the Alps or the Rockies or the Grand Canyon in order to go there to feel better about ourselves. Do you know why you go there? Because you were written to be satisfied with splendor, not self. You were created and a law*

written on your heart to be infinitely, eternally, fully, joyfully satisfied in a grand splendor, not a great self.[9]

True satisfaction is found in beholding the glory of Him, and yet the natural outcome of this will also be the glorious unfolding of who we are. As we allow Him to remove the layers of sin and falsehood from our hearts, our fleshly glories fade and the brilliance of our eternal glory shines through. The truest thing about us isn't sin and failure, but the glory and delight of God. *"But we all, with unveiled face, beholding as in a mirror the glory of the Lord, are being transformed into the same image from glory to glory, just as from the Lord, the Spirit"* (2 Cor. 3:18). After all, our story didn't begin with the sin of Genesis 3. It began in Genesis 1 with glory. And to glory it is returning.

Questions for Reflection

1.   What is meant by the statement, "Who we are and who He is are mirrored realities"?

2.   Why is it that the truest thing about us is glory and the delight of God rather than sin and failure?

Identity is Bestowed

Contrary to what our individualistic society tells us, identity is not something we draw out of our inner self. We can't construct our identity from where we live, what we do, or what we have. Our identity doesn't even come from our function, our preferences, our personality, or our dreams and desires. While these things reflect our individuality, they cannot grant us an identity. Identity is something we receive. *"For better or for worse,"* John Eldredge writes, *"identity is bestowed."*[10] Such an idea is questionable, if not offensive, to those infatuated with self-determination, but it is true nonetheless.

The creator determines the identity of that which is created. That which is created lacks the authority to determine its own identity, value, function, or worth. Romans 9:20 says, *"On the contrary, who are you, O man, who answers back to God? The thing molded will not say to the molder, 'Why did you make me like this,' will it? Or does not the potter have a right over the clay, to make from the same lump one vessel for honorable use and another for common use?"* Let that sink in for a minute.

What God says of us carries the weight of authority and truth we can't find anywhere else. Hebrews 6:13 says, *"For when God made the promise to Abraham, since He could swear by no one greater, He swore by Himself..."* There is no truth or authority more credible than God's. So, when God calls us forgiven, loved, holy, sanctified, and friend, we don't need a second opinion.

If we don't take great comfort in what God says about us, our problem might not be self-esteem, but God-esteem. We may have an authority problem first and an identity problem second. For example, if we esteem the opinion of our father, our spouse, or our boss more than the opinion of God, then we have denied our Creator His rightful position of authority and replaced Him with a member of creation. This is the slimy pit of creature worship described in Romans chapter 1. *"For they exchanged the truth of God for falsehood, and worshiped and served the creature rather than the Creator, who is blessed forever."* (Rom. 1:25).

Our hearts were created for worship. If we do not bow to God, we will bow to His creation and that never ends well. Created things do not possess enough authority to bestow identity, to infuse us with power, or to direct us with purpose. All idols disappoint. Consequently, when we reject God and bow to idols, an identity crisis is sure to follow! Our truest self can only be found and expressed in right relationship with God. Therefore, aligning ourselves with the truth and under the authority of God might just be the quickest way to improve our sense of self.

This hard truth settled upon me softly while I was attending a women's conference in the mountains of Colorado. Our precious community group surprised me with travel arrangements and a warm seat at the event as a gift of love and an investment in my healing journey. It was a godsend and an unexpected blessing.

As we neared the end of the retreat, we were instructed to find a lonely place and ask God what gift He had for us. The answer was to be drawn or written down in letter form. It was a sweet assignment, but not one that came easily. I sat in silence for quite some time, thinking that my time would be better spent on a nap. My spiritual muscles were tired, my emotional tank was so full it hurt, and I missed home. I didn't need a gift.

I contemplated my options while my mind wandered over the events of the previous 10 years. A distinct pattern of divine goodness emerged so I pulled out my pen to scribble a list of all the ways God had rescued me with His grace, brought healing to my heart, and restored my relationships. A bit astonished at the mercy He had poured out over me and my family and not sure if I had ever properly thanked Him, praised Him for His mighty work, I took the opportunity and wrote Him a little thank-you note. Overwhelmed by His compassion and kindness, I concluded that a gift was quite unnecessary. I lacked for nothing. My cup was full and overflowing and so I finished my time with this. *"My heart is satisfied, Lord. What more could I ask for? Is there even more to be had?"* Unbeknownst to me, that was the question He'd been waiting for. You can imagine my surprise when He responded with this:

> *These are but small things I've given to you, tokens of My love, to woo your heart, to show you I can be trusted. Now, you know that I am good. But I'm not satisfied, even though you may think you are. I've been intentional, waiting for the right time to ask you a question…Will you be mine?*

I was undone. For ten years He had been patiently and persistently pursuing me, proving His love for me over and over again. And here He was once more, most ardently and tenderly offering me an identity born of love, born of Himself, and the most intimate form of belonging. *"Will you be mine?"*

This God of ours uses His authority to draw us close to His heart; to protect, pursue, and heal rather than demand and demean. He extends Himself to us with this outlandish love and unashamedly asks for love in return. Why would we pacify Him with duty and pretense when we could fall in love?

> *"I will betroth you to Me forever; Yes, I will betroth you to Me in righteousness and in justice, In favor and in compassion, And I will betroth you to Me in faithfulness. Then you will know the Lord"* (Hosea 2:19-20).

<u>Questions for Reflection</u>

1. *"Identity is not something we draw out of our inner self. We can't construct our identity from where we live, what we do, or what we have. Our identity doesn't even come from our function, our preferences, our personality, or our dreams and desires." Do you agree with this? Why or why not?*

2. *Why does idolatry leave us empty?*

3. *How is our God-bestowed identity a form of belonging?*

Chapter 6

Pardon the Parish

Note to the Reader: In this chapter, "Church" refers to the universal body of Christ and "church" refers to a local place of worship.

Salsa and Sedition

We were newlyweds living off part-time jobs and leftover pizza while renting a tiny little duplex apartment from a sweet elderly couple who knew what simple beginnings were like. I don't recall their names, but I'll never forget the way he held her hand and opened doors for her as if she was as delightful to him as she had been more than six decades before. Every time I saw them, I couldn't help but smile and wonder if God would grace us with a lifetime of love like that.

As graduates of a Bible college, we assumed that God would place us in ministry, but the specific path remained unclear. So we took grad classes and flexed our muscles with late-night debates over the purpose of the Church and the missions mandate. Soon, we were given an opportunity to explore the implementation of these ideologies. One sunny fall afternoon, my husband came home from a class beaming with excitement. Evidently, one of his essays had caught his professor's attention. He commended David for his clear writing style and noteworthy understanding of the course content and went on to explain his need for a ghostwriter for the books he was writing about his work indigenous church planting movements worldwide.

After several more conversations and a few team meetings, we received an offer to ghostwrite a series of books while serving with a church planting team in Europe. For David, it was as obvious as the nose on his face. He had left the mission field to attend Bible college, and he fully intended to return. I was less than eager, but certainly wasn't admitting it at the time. It only made sense to grab hold of such an opportunity. I had just completed a master's degree in intercultural studies, so I guessed I needed to use it. And those commendable papers were not authored by my dear husband alone. We had burned the midnight oil together, debating every idea and battling through the wording of each paragraph. This opportunity seemed to be a perfect fit for our gifting, training, and desires. We signed on. And just like that, the "nestling in" phase was over, and we were off and running.

Being young college grads far from home, we had few local connections from which to raise support, so a couple from our church welcomed us into their home, enabling us to save funds for the adventure ahead. Gladly, we moved out of our tiny duplex, gave away our garage sale treasures, and settled into their spare bedroom.

The next six months were filled with more problems than preparations. My parents had separated during my last semester of grad school and they were on their way toward divorce, something I never thought would happen. I begged God to intervene and stop it. Nonetheless, it became finalized, sending shock waves through our family and community of friends. They divorced after 29 years of marriage. Then our generous friends, whose spare room we were using, revealed that a nasty addiction from the past had returned with a vengeance and they were facing a medical and marital crisis. Our presence likely agitated an already sensitive situation; thus, we were overstaying our welcome. As for us, we were busy dashing each other's dreams and needling each other's deepest wounds. Regardless of that fact, we still hadn't figured out how to make a budget, schedule our week, or have a fair argument, but we were making plans to live together, work together, and join a gospel revolution 4,000 miles away.

Such uncertainty and instability was more than our fragile beginnings could bear. We fought constantly and couldn't seem to resolve our conflicts, probably because neither of us knew why we were fighting at all. I began to voice my doubts and fears regarding going overseas. In his young zeal, my husband attempted to counter my doubts with promises of a supportive and intimate mission community, but his idealism only fueled my resistance, and vice versa. It didn't take long for my reservations to turn into outright refusal. And since my every reluctance was met by further insistence, I suggested he pull a William Carey[1] and go alone. When it was all said and done, my extremely disappointed husband withdrew our application and we sheepishly moved out of our friends' home.

After a thorny first year of marriage, we fit the sum total of our worldly goods into a Nissan Sentra and moved into a second-story condo. It felt massive compared to that spare bedroom, but not big enough to engulf the growing divide between us. I remember sitting on the living room floor as we ate a meager dinner of salsa and chips around our lovely Step Reebok/dining table. There weren't many safe topics of conversation to choose from, and we weren't wise enough to stick with them anyway. That particular night, the chosen topic was selecting a new home church. David spoke of his ideals and I spoke of my resentments and doubts. He threw out suggestions and I shot them down. He reminded me of our shared convictions, and I recoiled like a wounded animal. When it became clear that escape was not an option, I went on the attack. With a bitter resolve, I announced that I didn't want to go to church anymore. And I didn't stop there. I went on to detail every negative thought I had about Church, Christians, and even God. I unloaded some very harsh, irreverent things that I was surprised to hear come out of my mouth. But I wasn't sorry. For me, it was a long-awaited exhale. For my poor young husband, it felt like a volcanic eruption.

He let out a defeated sigh, looked at me with finality, and said, *"Based on Scripture, I can't offer you any comfort for your salvation."* Then he got up and went to bed, resigned to live with a cold-hearted wife who did not share his passion for Church and missions and would not support his dreams. He had lived far from God his whole life and come to Christ as an adult, never looking back. His wife, the one who came to Christ as a small child and grew up in the Church, was indistinguishable from a non-believer.

Isn't It Ironic?

What's funny about my sudden disdain for God and the Church is that I had always been one of those annoyingly good, straight-laced, "religious" girls with the perfect Christian family. In fact, it was my identity. Sadly, it was also a lie. As with all false identities, I had to convince myself and others that it was true in order to feel okay.

In reality, mine was not the perfect family, and I wasn't so good and strait-laced either. It surely wasn't for lack of trying. I did well in school, never got in trouble, never stole or drank or did drugs, and never rebelled against my parents – at least not outwardly. But I was a wide-eyed dreamer, a boy-crazed romantic, and a boundary-less people-pleaser with a deep well of insecurities. Who I was in the midst of all that mess was a far cry from the girl I longed to be.

As for my family, here's the backstory. My parents came to Christ shortly after I was born. One of my aunts had sent my mom a Bible, and she read the book of John. Intrigued, she began watching the 700 Club with Pat Robertson, and subsequently surrendered her heart to God. Hers was a radical conversion indeed. She fell in love with Jesus and poured herself into a relationship with Him. My sweetest childhood memories include sitting next to her as she worshipped in church, watching her read her Bible as we played, and waking to hear her praying over me as I slept. She was passionate, eager to learn, and ready to serve. And serve she did. She and my father did some amazing things together. They helped start a Christian school, ran a youth group, taught Precept Bible studies, and took in needy children. They held leadership positions in every church we attended and, from what everyone could see, they sought to honor God in all they did and had. But there was a lot that everyone couldn't see. A reckless and destructive undercurrent ran through their marriage. And it grew more and more menacing with time.

Things began to unravel when I was in high school. It became harder and harder for my parents to conceal or manage their problems. The summer before my junior year, my dad lost his job and decided to take a new one hours away. He stayed in a hotel during the week and came home on weekends. Sadly, we saw him less and less as time went by. My mom worked feverishly to pick up the slack and hang onto her distant husband, but the added stress and increasing dysfunction were too much for her. Within 6 months, she had exhausted herself and suffered a breakdown. My siblings and I lost ourselves in school, activities, and friends. Believe it or not, I still thought my family was healthy and normal. I didn't know where my fear, anger, and depression could be coming from except that there was something wrong with me, that I was just too undisciplined, fragile, and needy.

Something shifted in my mind the afternoon our pastor's wife paid my mom a visit. I was sitting in our upstairs landing when I saw her walking up the stairs. She had not even knocked. She simply ushered herself in and walked out onto the sun porch where my mom had been hiding. About an hour later, she emerged and descended the stairs, leaving just as silently as she had come. Shortly thereafter, my mom stepped out, sternly looked at me, and said, *"Stop watching me. I'm fine!"*

Clearly, something was wrong, and I desperately wanted to know what it was. What was happening with my family, and what was wrong with me?

Most regrettably, those I thought should have had the answers, my church community, were silent. Surely they knew that all was not well with us, but no one said a word. And the silence was killing me. I felt like I was choking, hands around my throat, surrounded by many who were capable of rescuing me, but they only watched. No one thought it was their place or responsibility to step in. I had always loved going to church and church activities, and I eagerly learned everything I could about the Bible and Christian life, but the gulf between what I understood from Scripture, what I was being taught, and what I was experiencing in life was growing wider and wider. I was coming to the conclusion that the Church wasn't the safe and true place I had been told it was. And the Gospel wasn't as powerful as they asserted.

Questions for Reflection

1. *Have you ever been in a similar place, where you felt anti-Church, anti-Christians, and maybe even anti-God?*

2. *What advice would you give to someone in a place like that?*

3. *Have you had a supportive person or community in your life during a time of difficulty? If so, what difference did that make? If not, how did the absence of support affect you?*

Burst My Bubble

I hobbled through the rest of that year, until my dad lost that job as well and found another one in a small town outside of Cleveland. I chose to move with my family, but the transition was exceedingly difficult for everyone, exponentially increasing the instability within our home. By the end of the year, I decided to go to Bible college, thinking it would be a fresh start and a safe place for my heart. I hoped to get answers to my questions and finally experience the love of God. But I was emotionally stuck, which made it pretty hard for me to successfully move into adulthood. Not long after settling into college life, I discovered that there are no safe places, especially for basket cases like myself. Geography didn't change my baggage. I lugged it with me wherever I went, and it tended to create nothing but chaos and drama.

Considering who I was at the time, I think God truly moved mountains to keep me safe and somewhat sane. Unfortunately, once again, I was surrounded by good teaching and godly people, but all I knew was truth I couldn't access; truth that contradicted everything I felt and experienced. In many ways, academia cemented the divide. Truth became an idea to debate rather than a Person to engage. And Scripture became a textbook to study and an unforgiving measuring tape to live up to.

Not knowing who I was or what I wanted to do after graduation, I enrolled in graduate school and hid myself for another year in the Christian bubble. Alas, when I returned home for Christmas break, God pierced through that bubble and I did a full face-plant on the harsh surface of reality.

I was so looking forward to my own bed, my mom's cooking, and the familiarity of home that I drove straight through the night to get there. But as soon as I put down my bags and collapsed onto my soft mattress, my mom came in with a look I didn't recognize. Without much ado, she told me that she was leaving my father, citing irreconcilable differences. They had nothing in common and she wasn't attracted to him anymore. I'm sure I asked questions and argued with her, but I can't remember any of that now. I just remember calling a friend and telling her that I felt like I'd been swallowed by a black hole. Life, as I knew it, was over. I forced myself to fall asleep and hoped I wouldn't wake up.

When the shock wore off, I switched into problem-solving mode and tried to talk her out of it. I also tried to rally my dad and get him to fight for his wife. I didn't tell him what was coming, but I watched him like a hawk, I peppered him with questions on his whereabouts, and made him buy a nice Christmas gift for her. As a Christmas present, I bought them a scrapbook and filled it with family pictures. I spent hours writing out my favorite memories of them as well as the acts of love they had shown me that I most appreciated. But it didn't work.

Even as an adult child, I wanted the security of a family home to come back to and to bring my future children back to. I didn't know who I was without my family and didn't believe I could make it in the world without them. Consequently, I determined to do everything I could to save it. My next course of action was to meet with my pastor and his wife. I told them what I understood and asked them to step in. I'm sure their intentions were honorable but involving them only caused more confusion and further alienated my mom. She sank deeper and deeper into despair. Truly, she meant what she said. She was done, and I was out of remedies.

Finally, I gathered my siblings together and told them what was happening. My sister was married with a baby several states away. My younger brother was home from college like myself. My youngest brother was a senior in high school. And then there was my "adopted" sister, a lively young lady who had joined our family several years prior. We all had jobs and some capacity to take care of ourselves, but in that moment, every one of us felt like an orphan.

Refusing to stick around and watch my family burn to the ground, I threw my hands in the air and went back to school, hiding in my dorm room until classes began again. A few days later, my mom called, pleading for my love and support. I gave her anything but. I warned her that she would lose all credibility, she would lose her kids, and she would never be able to serve in the ministry again. In her mind, there were no other options. She had hoped to leave with my support, but that was not going to happen. So, she left my father and my siblings, believing that she was leaving her faith as well. Sadly, that was exactly how the rest of us saw it: as an outright rejection of God, and marriage, and us.

Within a few weeks, she found a lawyer and wrote up papers that would lead to a divorce. At that point, as is often the case, her story changed. She accused my father of abuses and addictions. Assuming she was manipulating the truth to gain support, few believed her. Even so, the Christian friends and family members that granted credence to her accusations still concluded that reconciliation was the Biblical mandate. Letters, phone calls, and emails came pouring in adjuring her to forgive my father and reconsider her plans.

The elders of our church requested that she explain her Biblical grounds. She responded by chronicling the events of the two weeks before she left, events that had become all too typical for their life together. There was no response from the elder board, but the pastor's wife secretly tracked down my mom, who had relocated to a different city. She told my mom that she believed her and had pleaded with her husband to act, but he would not touch the situation. He had found the letter my mom composed to be too incriminating, so he destroyed it. He then instructed the elders to cut off all contact with my mom. One called her anyway and assured her that he knew a woman wouldn't leave her husband after 29 years without cause. Still, there was nothing he could, or would, do. A week later, my father was given an opportunity to repent before the entire congregation for failing to love my mom as he ought, and they started a new Sunday school class, "Loving Your Wife."

Two previous pastors contacted my mom as well. One had been very dear to us. We were family friends, spending many Sunday afternoons and even enjoying a few trips and vacations together. When he heard the news of my parents, he sent my mom a letter urging her to lay aside her "evil plan" to divorce and instead spend a weekend at his home with my father to discuss reconciliation. She declined. The second pastor asked her how long the abuses and addictions had gone on, concerned that he had failed to detect it in the years he had served as our pastor. Kudos to him for asking, but she had only just scratched the surface of the life she had lived for 29 years. She didn't know what she didn't know, so she alleviated his conscience. Neither one took the time to find out what had happened. Neither one offered support, intervention, or assistance.

She Got What She Deserved?

The twelve months after my mom left are a blur. In January, she moved out and found an apartment in a neighboring town. In May, she moved to South Carolina and secured an apartment an hour from me and five minutes from her sister. Also in May, David and I got engaged and I graduated from grad school. In August, we got married and settled into that sweet little duplex apartment. In October, despite many prayers and pleadings, my parents' divorce became finalized. And because life just rolls on, one month later, we were signed up to be church planting and book writing missionaries in Europe.

That Thanksgiving was our first holiday without a family home, so my siblings and I decided to get together at my grandma's house (my father's mother) where we had celebrated many holidays. Unfortunately, the joys of being together were forced and short-lived. The morning after we arrived, we got a call from my aunt. My mother had been admitted to the hospital and was suffering from a severe physical and psychological breakdown, her third one. My aunt said there was nothing we could do, so *"Have a Happy Thanksgiving!"* We sat in the living room stumped for words. Bless her heart, grandma always had something to say. *"She got what she deserved."* I felt sick.

The next morning, my dad invited me to breakfast, and I did my best to let him know I wasn't going to play the game anymore. *"Dad, why can't we talk about problems in our family? Why can't we say we're sorry? Why can't we be open about difficult things? Why is it that NO ONE said a word after that phone call yesterday? Why didn't we stop and pray for the woman who loved us and sacrificed herself for us, for YOU, the last 29 years?"* He looked at me blankly, then reprimanded me for not eating enough and losing too much weight.

It was a long drive back home and my heart was blistered from the tug-of-war. Which is more important to God: the institution of marriage, or the health and safety of those within it? Clearly, it wasn't possible for my mom to have both, and perhaps she would be left with neither. I wasn't exactly sure what she had experienced in her marriage with my dad, but I was beginning to think she had covered it up for far too long. Whether or not he was guilty of all she had accused him of, it was painfully obvious that he didn't love her and wasn't going to fight for her. Either way, I was discovering that my life had been a lie.

It took weeks before Mom got out of the hospital and could see us. We sat on folding chairs in her tiny apartment and I noticed how petite and fragile she had become. I looked at her hands and saw that her wedding rings were gone, as was the ruby and diamond band I had picked out for her that Christmas. When she admitted that she had pawned them, my face felt hot and I couldn't hold back the angry tears that began to fall. Before I could tell her that I was going to buy them back, that they were symbols of my family, my legacy, my fight for her, she said something that squeezed the air right out of my lungs.

"You betrayed me!" She shook with fury and gripped the sides of her chair. The words burned into me and I wanted to argue. I wanted to remind her that I was the child. I was trying to be faithful to what she had taught me. I had believed her all the times she told me that Dad loved us and was a good and godly man. I believed her when she said that God hates divorce. I believed her when she said that it was our job to do the right thing and God would take care of the rest. Was she not the one who had lied, had betrayed all of us? What was the truth anyway? Was I to believe her version of the truth when she had it all together, or when she was falling apart?

Instead, I said nothing. It would have been cruel to contend with her. She was barely able to sit in front of me, barely willing to live. As I looked at her shaking and stammering, a flood of memories came back to me. She was such a patient mom, no matter what mischief I had caused. Whether it was picking her rose petals and baking them in my mud pies, cleaning her new couch with Vaseline, shampooing the carpet with water and baby powder, or setting the house on fire during a game of hide and seek, she laughed more than she scolded and gave more hugs than spankings. But she certainly wasn't afraid to pick a fight when necessary. I entered the world as a preemie with the odds stacked against me and was going downhill fast when she refused to follow the doctor's strict orders regarding parental contact and formula feeding. She kidnapped me from the hospital and quite literally nursed me back to health. And I wasn't the only one she fought for. She took in neglected children, fed them, clothed them, and made sure they saw a doctor. She was fierce and fearless in the way she loved and sacrificed for others. Looking at her then, frail and defeated, I was afraid I had lost that mother forever.

She was released into her sister's care and stayed with her for a year. During that time, with her sister's help, she attended a support group for abused women, found a therapist, found a psychiatrist who prescribed medication for her, and began quilting as a therapeutic hobby. She also gathered the courage to attend her sister's church. She expected to have to answer for herself as a divorced woman, so she met with the pastor and explained her questionable status. Presuming she may want to remarry someday, which she eventually did, he listened to her story and then took it upon himself to determine whether he would be able to officiate her future wedding in good conscience. To his credit, he did his homework. He read her journals and made phone calls to her previous friends to see if they could validate her story. When he was satisfied with the information he had obtained, he came to her with his conclusion. He was convinced that God had gotten her out of her marriage, and he advised her to never go back. She was free to go on with her life as best she could.

Between a Rock and a Hard Place

As the year with her sister ended, it became clear that Mom was still unable to care for herself or keep a job. With no other family nearby, the responsibility was placed squarely on our shoulders. And this brings us back to the beginning. About the time David and I were eating salsa and chips around that Step Reebok, arguing about which church we should attend, Mom was packing up her things and heading our way.

I must have sat on the floor for hours, listening to the ticking of the clock, trying to make heads or tails of it all. I knew the things I'd said to my husband were wrong, but so was most of what I saw happening around me at the time. Why did I have to play nice when my husband was throwing temper tantrums, my parents had gone off the deep end, and our closest friends were keeping dark secrets? My heart was heavy with rage and hurt over so much more than I understood at the time. I wanted God to speak into my pain and confusion, but He was silent. I wanted the church to step in and help us, but they had offered nothing. Exhaustion finally won out, and I fell asleep with my husband's words still ringing in my ears: *"Based on Scripture, I can't offer you any comfort for your salvation."*

It seemed like minutes later when I woke up in a cold sweat and a puddle of tears. I had dreamed that I was hovering over hell and the emptiness was calling to me. It felt real and terrifying. I wondered if it was God's way of warning me. Was my husband right? Was I allowing my anger and confusion, my messed-up life, to drag me away to hell? How was it possible to belong to Jesus and be so hardened and cynical? Where were the people who had struggled through such things and overcome? I didn't know anyone who was struggling the way I was. I didn't know anyone who could show me the way out. And those conversations weren't being had anywhere I looked.

I was grief-stricken from the relationships that had been lost, whiplashed from the trust that had been betrayed, and thoroughly displaced in my worldview. I couldn't trust myself or my parents anymore. They had lived a lie and I had defended it. I couldn't trust my husband. I was too broken to care about his dreams, and he was too lost in his dreams to care about my brokenness. I couldn't trust the Church. Instead of using their authority and influence to bring healing, they had stood by for too long. When they finally did step in, it was to use their authority to alienate and condemn. I was not who I thought I was or wanted to be. My family wasn't what I thought it was and never would be. Marriage wasn't turning out to be what I had hoped it would be. And the Church wasn't what I had been taught it was or what I needed it to be. I was so very disappointed in all of us.

Charging the Church

In the face of every complaint and every grievance, you've made it clear that the real issue is that I'm either sinful, heretical, immoral, foolish, unenlightened, selfish, consumerist or ignorant…Maybe it's me, but me is all I'm capable of being right now, and that's where I was really hoping you would meet me.…Even if we are the woman in adultery, or the doubting follower, or the rebellious prodigal, or the demon-riddled young man, we can't be anything else right now in this moment; and in this moment, we need a Church big enough, and tough enough, and loving enough; not just for us as we might one day be then, but for us as we are, now.[2]

According to Scripture, the universal Church, the bride of Christ, is empowered and protected by the Holy Spirit. She carries the charge of the Gospel, and she is the tangible Kingdom of God on earth until He returns. He has granted the Church authority and power to propel the Gospel and to wage war against the kingdom of darkness.

This was precisely my problem. Because of what it was given, I expected the Church to carry more weight, not only in the areas of doctrine and prescriptive truth, but in compassion, in strength, and in wisdom. Specifically, I expected the Church to be able to bear up under the burden of my family's brokenness, discern the reality of the situation as well as the will of the Lord, and fiercely fight for us. I had hoped the Church would come alongside me and help me understand my own brokenness, show me how to walk out the Spirit-led transformation promised in Scripture. And most recently, I had hoped that the church that matched us and married us would have discipled us through the blazing fury of our new and faltering marriage, but they stood by and silently watched the show instead. There's no question, we were the problem. But wasn't that why we needed to be shown how to span the distance between the truths of God, the promises of His Word, and our experience of them? Instead, it appeared that the Church had become a place of legalistic demands, lofty promises, and a powerless gospel. For all these reasons and more, I assigned the Church most of the blame for the mess we were in.

I was in full rebellion against all authority, doubting the heart of God, distancing myself from my family, resenting my husband, and reviling the Church. Completely stuck, I was bouncing between my desire to throw it all away, and reminding myself of what Peter said to Jesus: *"Lord, to whom shall we go? You have words of eternal life"* (John 6:68). I knew with absolute certainty that I couldn't deny Jesus Christ as my Savior and Lord. I believed the Bible to be inspired, reliable, and authoritative. I believed the creeds of our faith. I believed in the necessity of a daily walk with God. Without a doubt, I wanted to be on "Team Jesus." I just wished there was a way to do it while avoiding any affiliation with His bride and body, the Church. And that is putting it lightly, my friends. A little diplomacy is a good idea when you're taking a swing at God's bride! He has made His unconditional favor for the Church quite clear, despite her abuses of power and misapplications of truth. How then could I oppose the Church or leave it, and maintain my life in Christ? I guess I felt the same way about the Church that my mom had felt about her marriage. Trapped, abused, and plumb worn out. It wasn't what it was intended to be, wasn't a safe place, and didn't even feel like a true place. But I feared walking out would be apostasy.

A week after my mom moved in, David and I ran into an old college acquaintance. He was about ten years our senior, with a lovely English accent, a warm heart, and a passion for the marginalized. He was preparing to launch a church for Gen-Xers and was looking for a team to join him. A church for the skeptics, cynics, and rebels? Now that was something I could get behind. We jumped at the opportunity. Had he been a fly on the wall in our living room the week before, he may have taken pity on me and invited me to attend his church, but he never would have asked for my participation on the leadership team. Maybe he saw me for who and what I was at the time, but he humbly and graciously made room for me anyway. Looking back, I believe that this church was what God used to protect me from myself. It kept me in a safe faith community until I was ready for the work of healing that would come years later. We went to church weekly, led small groups, discipled college students, and even attended meetings with leaders from other churches. I played nice. I didn't leave the Church and didn't stop serving, but I did rage against it in my heart. I didn't go anywhere, but I was running.

Questions for Reflection

1. *Janalee confronted her dad with some of her frustrations with their family. What kinds of frustrations have you had with your own family of origin? What have you done with these frustrations?*

2. *What did it mean for Janalee's husband to say, "Based on Scripture, I can't offer you any comfort for your salvation"? Was he right? What counsel would you have given to him?*

3. *What should be our response when the Church fails to measure up to what it should do or what we need it to do?*

A Three-Hour Tour

When I think about my years of running, I can't get away from the story of Jonah. One of the most famous Old Testament prophets, he was called by God to deliver a message of repentance to his enemies, the wicked people of Nineveh. Instead of packing his bags for a trip to Sin City, he refused and ran the other way. Surely, he knew he couldn't run from God, but he boarded a ship headed for Tarshish anyway. Of course, God caught up with him, and when He did, He made His presence known. He brought upon that ship such a great storm that even the heathen crew identified it as a supernatural event. They drew straws to assign the blame and Jonah was found out. He admitted his guilt, but rather than repent, he instructed the crew to throw him overboard. With reluctance, they prayed for pardon and then tossed the prophet into the angry sea where God directed a fish to swallow him whole.

In classic rebel style, Jonah waited until he was in the grip of death before crying out to God for mercy. Mr. Pouty Pants sat in "time out", surrounded with digestive fluids, half-chewed breakfasts, and a diminishing air supply for up to three days before reconsidering his position. Finally, he humbled himself and agreed to obey. *"While I was fainting away, I remembered the Lord and my prayer came to You into Your holy temple…But I will sacrifice to You with a voice of thanksgiving. That which I have vowed I will pay."* (Jonah 2:7,9).

The fish brought him to the shores of Nineveh and spit him out. Jonah entered the city and delivered God's message of judgment. Surprisingly, he got a better response than most prophets do. The people repented in hopes that God would *"…turn and relent, and withdraw His burning anger"* (Jonah 3:9). Even the ruler of Nineveh tore his royal robes, put on sackcloth, sat in ashes, and declared a nationwide renouncing of evil.

Oddly enough, Jonah became indignant with God over the matter. He had humbled himself in the belly of the fish and had fulfilled his vow to obey, but something was still amiss in his heart.

> *Please, LORD, was not this what I said while I was still in my own country? Therefore, in order to forestall this, I fled to Tarshish, for I knew that You are a gracious and compassionate God, slow to anger and abundant in lovingkindness, and one who relents concerning calamity. Therefore now, O LORD, please take my life from me, for death is better to me than life.* (Jonah 4:2-3)

He ran away again, this time to the east of the city, where he sat in languish and fury. In response, God provided a vine to protect Jonah from the scorching sun and wind, but then sent a worm to eat it, causing it to wither. And Jonah begged God for death. The book ends with this final rebuke: *"You had compassion on the plant for which you did not work and which you did not cause to grow, which came up overnight and perished overnight. Should I not have compassion on Nineveh, the great city...?"* (Jonah 4:11).

It's almost unbelievable how devastated Jonah was by God's pardon of Nineveh. Perhaps it was for that very reason that our Lord sent him to Nineveh. Jonah was the man for the job because he had a strong sense of justice and an even larger dose of bitterness. He who sees everything, and judges rightly went after Jonah and exposed his heart. Indeed, our good God went to great lengths to hem him in, to show him his callousness, and to compel him with the offer of redemption. For that reason, Jonah is an unusual book of prophecy. Unlike others, it seems to focus upon God's message to the prophet rather than to the people for whom the prophet was sent. While the Gentile city repented, it was the prophet of God who continued in sin! But God was not finished with Jonah. The probability that he wrote the book himself gives us reason to believe he did eventually have a change of heart. I hope to hear the rest of that story someday. If Jesus is taking reservations for the wedding feast, I call the seat next to Jonah.

Good Reason

To appreciate Jonah's position, it's important to consider a few points of context. First, let's not overlook the fact that God was asking Jonah to pay a visit to the Assyrians, who had done unspeakable things to his people. He was called to deliver a message of mercy to the most barbaric people in history, to a people who considered torture a cultural pastime; to those who showed no mercy. Added to this is the fact that Old Testament prophecy foretold that Israel's demise was sure to come at their hands. While Assyria was growing in power and resources, Jonah's contemporaries, Amos, Obadiah, and Joel, were preaching imminent judgment to Israel. The handwriting was on the wall. While God was extending mercy to Israel's sworn enemies, He was also confirming the ruin of Israel. According to God's will, Jonah was sent to preach repentance to those who had already ravaged Israel and would soon return to finish them off.

Second, we can't assume that Jonah ran away because he thought he would get away with it. God's wrath toward disobedient prophets was well known (see 1 Kings 13). It's quite likely that Jonah was counting on this. Remember, the runaway prophet was found sound asleep in the hold of the ship in the middle of a torrential storm. Even the experienced, professional sailors were panicking. They knew a paranormal storm when they saw one! But Jonah didn't even flinch. He wasn't looking over his shoulder to see if God had caught up with him. And when he picked the short end of the stick, he didn't even consider repentance. He asked to be thrown overboard. It sounds like he wanted to get it over with and finalize his fatalistic expectations. We see this again after he was spared by the fish, was spit out on Assyrian soil, and delivered his message. What did he do? He stomped away. Presumably, he was resigned to God's wrath that would be poured out upon him and the Israelite people, and he refused to condone a scandalous mercy wasted on such a ferociously sinful people. Perhaps he knew better, but he was angry enough to not care. He was so angry that only death held the promise of relief. In Jonah's own words, *"I have good reason to be angry, even to death"* (Jonah 4:9). Good reason indeed. God's compassion was weighing in favor of the wrong team!

Don't Let the Sun Go Down

I relate to Jonah's struggle. In my bitterness and unbelief, I ran from God, threw myself into the deep with a death wish, and sat myself down for a good pout. I made the One who loves me, the One who is able and willing to guard me, into my opponent! I refused the vulnerability that is used to bring about transforming fruit and exchanged it for a vulnerability to the one who loves destruction. Jonah pronounces this truth: *"Those who worship worthless idols forfeit the mercy that could be theirs"* (Jonah 2:8 NET). In the worst way, I resisted and resented my Savior and His people. I was hell-bent on my own version of justice, and I deeply resented God's misplaced mercies. Even so, Jonah didn't win my writing contest because of his rebellion. His story offers me more than validation.

Let's begin with the obvious. God loves the world, and not just His chosen people, but *all* people. He loves all the people of the world and He wants us to love them too. This is the second greatest commandment. *"'YOU SHALL LOVE THE LORD YOUR GOD WITH ALL YOUR HEART, AND WITH ALL YOUR SOUL, AND WITH ALL YOUR MIND.' This is the great and foremost commandment. The second is like it, 'YOU SHALL LOVE YOUR NEIGHBOR AS YOURSELF.'"* (Matt. 22:37-39). The whole Law and the Prophets depend upon these two commandments.

Now, that's all well and good and easy and we can nod and sing "Kumbaya"… until one or two of those people God loves in this mad world does something bad: lies to our face, flirts with our spouse, bullies our kid, steals our promotion, or disappoints our needs and expectations. Then, to protect our love, we must forgive them before bitterness kills it. And suddenly love isn't simple anymore. That's because forgiveness isn't simple at all.

Reasoning according to our flesh, most of us would agree with Jonah that forgiveness is scandalously unfair and unjust. Our natural instincts tell us that forgiveness is an entirely insensitive and oppositional thing to ask of someone who has been wronged. As C.S. Lewis wrote in *Mere Christianity*:

> *Everyone says forgiveness is a lovely idea, until they have something to forgive, as we had during the war. And then, to mention the subject at all is to be greeted with howls of anger. It is not that people think this too high and difficult a virtue: it is that they think it hateful and contemptible. 'That sort of talk makes them sick,' they say. And half of you already want to ask me, 'I wonder how you'd feel about forgiving the Gestapo if you were a Pole or a Jew?*[8]

Indeed, forgiveness seems to be a ridiculously weak response to the brutality we face every day. How can something as benevolent and defenseless as forgiveness combat the ferocious threats that assault us? How can it protect us when we're in the ring with a repeat offender? It certainly doesn't compare to the power-rush of bitterness. Anger and hardness of heart are entirely more enticing than fear, vulnerability, and weakness. Vindication, retaliation, and superiority hold far more promise of protection than being a doormat. But, as with all sin, the initial benefits pale in comparison to the long-term consequences. I'd like to point out three:

1. For sure, bitterness feels empowering and anger does feel better than weakness, but it's also numbing. It toughens up our softness and puts walls around our vulnerability. We can't selectively numb ourselves from emotions. To numb ourselves to pain and sadness or fear is also to numb ourselves to love, joy, and peace. The reason for this is simple anatomy. Our emotions originate in the heart, and the heart is the dwelling place of God. It is through the heart that we hear from God, receive from God, and abide with Him.

Therefore, numbing the heart is akin to quenching the Spirit of God.

2. In all honesty, it doesn't work anyway. When we choose bitterness in order to avoid the stinging pain we feel after being offended or victimized, it does work temporarily, but unfortunately, nothing can truly insulate us from pain. Even the best drug, the best food, the best book, the best sex only numbs us temporarily. When it wears off – and it always does – the pain comes back with a vengeance, and we need another fix. This is the cycle of every addiction. It kills *us*, slowly or quickly, but it does not kill the pain. It can't, because pain is a guarantee on this side of eternity. None of us will escape it. We can attempt to stop the bleeding, but we will only end up hemorrhaging from the inside.

3. In this way, unforgiveness is like a gateway sin. "*BE ANGRY, AND yet DO NOT SIN; do not let the sun go down on your anger, and do not give the devil an opportunity*" (Eph. 4:26-27). There's nothing special about anger. It's not a sin, but, as this verse indicates, it can lead to sin. Paul simply points out what we already know: anger is a symptom of a wound, and if we don't allow God to heal our wounds, they will get infected with bitterness. Decided unforgiveness compounds our bondage. Bitter people are easy to entice, easy to manipulate and deceive, easy to ensnare, and easy to shame. And it happens without any effort at all! Simply let the sun go down on your anger...a few times. That's exactly what happened to Jonah. That's exactly what happened to me.

Protecting our hearts should be motivation enough to live a life of grace and forgiveness. The threat of becoming deadened to everything good, separated from the One we most need, and rendered vulnerable to the enemy should be enough to make us throw ourselves at the feet of Jesus and surrender our litany of wrongs suffered. But there's more we need to understand. The consequences of our disobedience in this area are far graver than we may realize. According to Chester and Betsy Klystra, "*[Forgiveness] is the key to freedom. As long as unforgiveness is present, God's hand of protection, mercy, and restoration is hindered at best and stopped at worst.*"[4]

To forgive those who have sinned against us is a Biblical command issued to us with razor-sharp teeth. It's not issued with a promise, such as, "*Children, obey your parents in the Lord, for this is right... so that it may be well with you, and that you may live long on the earth"* (Eph. 6:1, 3). No, it is issued with severe warnings. Jesus taught that God's willingness to forgive us is contingent upon our willingness to forgive others: *"For if you forgive others for their transgressions, your heavenly Father will also forgive you. But if you do not forgive others, then your Father will not forgive your transgressions"* (Matt. 6:14-15). In the same sermon, He reiterates His point with this statement: *"For in the way you judge, you will be judged; and by your standard of measure, it will be measured to you"* (Matt. 7:2). This concept appears again in Mark 11:25-26: *"Whenever you stand praying, forgive, if you have anything against anyone, so that your Father who is in heaven will also forgive you your transgressions. But if you do not forgive, neither will your Father who is in heaven forgive your transgressions."* James declares the same truths in his letter: *"For judgment will be merciless to one who has shown no mercy..."*(James 2:13). Thus it would appear that the Father interacts with us, at least in this regard, in the same way we interact with others.

It is no small thing that the Lord's Prayer implies this same prickly notion: *"…and forgive us our debts, as we also have forgiven our debtors"* (Matt. 6:12). C.S. Lewis addresses this in his book *The Weight of Glory*:

> *We believe that God forgives us our sins; but also that He will not do so unless we forgive other people their sins against us. There is no doubt about the second part of this statement. It is in the Lord's Prayer; it was emphatically stated by our Lord. If you don't forgive, you will not be forgiven. No part of His teaching is clearer, and there are no exceptions to it. He doesn't say that we are to forgive other people's sins provided they are not too frightful, or provided there are extenuating circumstances, or anything of that sort. We are to forgive them all, however spiteful, however mean, however often they are repeated. If we don't, we shall be forgiven none of our own.*[5]

As if that wasn't enough, Jesus took things one step further when was doing a Q & A with His disciples. Peter asked about forgiveness. In response, Jesus told a chilling parable of a servant who owed his master money and was shown mercy, but then turned around and demanded payment from his fellow slave. Upon hearing of it, the master confronted his servant and issued to him a severe consequence.

> *You wicked slave; I forgave you all that debt because you pleaded with me. Should you not also have had mercy on your fellow slave, in the same way that I had mercy on you?"* *And his lord, moved*

with anger, handed him over to the torturers until he should repay all that was owed him. My heavenly Father will also do the same to you, if each of you does not forgive his brother from your heart. (Matt. 18:32-35)

This was what Jesus said to His disciples, not to the Pharisees or the teachers of the law. To His own chosen followers, and to us, He issued this warning. Not only will God not forgive our sins if we do not forgive the sins of others, but He will turn us over to the torment of the enemy until we return to Him in repentance. This passage is not suggesting that unforgiveness causes us to lose our salvation, but it illustrates the compounding nature of unforgiveness and sheds more light upon Paul's warnings to the believers in Ephesus and Corinth. *"Be angry, and yet do not sin; do not let the sun go down on your anger, and do not give the devil an opportunity"* (Eph. 4:26-27). *"But one whom you forgive anything, I forgive also; for indeed what I have forgiven, if I have forgiven anything, I did it for your sakes in the presence of Christ, so that no advantage would be taken of us by Satan, for we are not ignorant of his schemes"* (2 Cor. 2:10-11). Bitterness opens a door to the tormenting work of the enemy. God allows it so that we may grow weary of the pitiless barrage; that we would remember the kindness of the Lord and return to Him in repentance.

Herein lies a great secret. Forgiveness is not a virtue to be admired, nor is it weak or enabling. It is a command to be followed. But more than that, it is a sophisticated self-defense move that can keep you close to the heart of God and save your soul from the assault of the enemy. What's more, it is a gift. It is not only the gift of pardon for wrongdoers, but also the gift of healing grace from the Father for the hurting. The act of forgiving another requires that we make our way to the throne room of God, bringing with us a burden we cannot bear and injuries we cannot mend. It motivates us to run to God for help. And help He does. Jesus is our Great High Priest who experientially understands us.

For we do not have a high priest who cannot sympathize with our weaknesses, but One who has been tempted in all things as we are, yet without sin. Therefore, let us draw near with confidence to the throne of grace, so that we may receive mercy and find grace to help in time of need." (Heb. 4:15-16)

Rest assured, His kind of help is hardly a casserole dish and a get-well card. The intervention from our Great High Priest is an all-out rescue. He who created all things and holds all things together by the word of His power sees all, knows all, understands all, and can redeem all (Col. 1:17, Heb. 1:3).

Questions for Reflection

1. *"Those who worship worthless idols forfeit the mercy that could be theirs" (Jon. 2:8 NET). What does this passage mean?*

2. *"Anger and hardness of heart are entirely more enticing than fear, vulnerability, and weakness. Vindication, retaliation, and superiority hold far more promise of protection than being a doormat." Have you experienced the false empowerment of bitterness?*

3. *According to Scripture, how does God interact with us in the same ways that we interact with others?*

4. *Who are the people you need to forgive?*

Guilt by Association

Even though Scripture issues some very stern warnings about unforgiveness, the thought of turning over our rights and defenses to God can feel even more terrifying. Bitterness isn't so much rooted in what was done to us, but in Who allowed it. Bitterness says that God has betrayed us, that He was the referee who refused to call foul, and that it was on His watch that we got hurt. The bitter heart says that it is absurd for a God who was asleep at the wheel to demand our forgiveness. It says we have a right to protect ourselves. Like most spiritual bondage, the bitter heart serves an idol of self-preservation, declaring that God is not good and cannot be trusted.

It may be difficult to believe that our unforgiveness can bring to bear such grave consequences, and that such hardness can take place within the heart of a believer. But the writers of Scripture were speaking to believers when they issued their warnings. I can attest to the fact that my bitterness, despair, and callousness of heart existed right alongside a genuine desire to understand the things of God, to grow in my faith, and to walk uprightly. Several good friends have gingerly questioned if I was a genuine believer back then. They are in good company. If you recall, my husband and I had the same question. I can't look back and prove my salvation by any of my good works or good intentions, but I can testify that all of this took place as my spirit resonated with His Spirit to rein me in at times, to remind me of truth, and to lead me right where He wanted me to go. I was in an awful place, full of bitterness and bondage, but could I rescue myself? My best attempts to let it go, get over it, and do the right thing didn't work, because healing just doesn't work that way. And, rest assured, He did heal me. As only He can, He reached in and pulled out those deeply embedded, tender-to-the-touch soul splinters. They tended to surface only one at a time, but as cumbersome and consequential as my sin was, He was not in a hurry. His delight in me wasn't contingent upon my behavior or my sin. He chose to heal me for my good, not for His convenience. His healing of me was pure love, pure gift.

Heal the Broken and Release the Oppressed

It had been nearly ten years of running when the Holy Spirit of God finally intervened, and He did it in the way I had always hoped someone would. It began with the "First Great Awakening" I've described before. He invaded my life with the true Gospel of grace. I saw my own sinfulness in many areas and received forgiveness from God for myself. He invited me into the intimate relationship I had always wanted.

As an overflow of the love and kindness the Father was giving to me, I saw the need to forgive my mother. Our relationship had long been restored and she had come out on the other side of her distresses with great triumph. Nevertheless, I did blame her for hiding the truth from me, and in some ways, for neglecting me and failing to protect me. Without a doubt, I knew she had never intended to deceive us. She didn't know she was obscuring reality. She was simply living out of the worldview she had received from her own upbringing, simply trying to be obedient to her understanding of Scripture, simply doing whatever it took to make it "work." Seeing a larger view of her story and seeing the cost she had been willing to pay to live a life she thought was honoring to God made it easy for me to forgive her, and so I did. In fact, I was amazed at how fruitful her life had been and how faithfully she had lived despite her circumstances.

Shortly thereafter, I saw the need to forgive my father. There was much I didn't understand, and still don't. But for what he did, for what he neglected to do, I forgave him. Then, I chose to acquit him for the consequences I had paid for his choices, because they were lingering in my mind, reinforcing the defensive walls I had against him. Sadly, forgiving my dad did not restore the trust or relationship between us, and I needed to forgive him for the grief of those losses as well. Even so, the choice to forgive him did enable me to open the door for the possibility that God could re-establish those things in time.

Grace was given to me in such abundance that I shared it with everyone I could. Thinking it was a new idea, I explained it often and in great detail, but most people weren't impressed. Most nodded in agreement as if it were old news. Even some of my closest friends and family members stared at me blankly, suggesting they already knew of this revolutionary thing called *grace. THEY ALREADY KNEW??* Why hadn't all these enlightened people extended it to me, rescued me from the graceless pit I was in? As I scanned through my mental files of sermons, teachings, and courses I had sat through over the years, I couldn't retrieve anything pertaining to God's transforming grace for life *after* salvation. I had to wonder, were they holding out on me, or had they never experienced it themselves? Either way, my introduction to grace afforded me greater intimacy with God and enabled me to receive forgiveness for myself and to forgive my parents. But my distrust and indignation toward the Church only increased.

Soon after this, I experienced my "Second Great Awakening" which included lessons on guarding my heart, spiritual bondage, and inner healing. I discovered that I needed to pay closer attention to the thoughts that were flying around in my heart and take them captive, even resisting the accusations and manipulations of the enemy. I learned to repent, not only for my bad behavior, but for the toxic thoughts and motivations underlying them. Finally, I found the joy and freedom of keeping short accounts with God, bringing my concerns, questions, and troubles to Him and refusing to be seduced by false "soulutions". In these three things, I depended upon the intimate guidance of the Holy Spirit, which was the greatest blessing of all. As I followed His leading, truth became a Person and Scripture took on life and power! Spiritual disciplines became meaningful and the teaching and training I had been exposed to became useful.

This inner revolution was just as groundbreaking as grace, and I couldn't keep it to myself. But once again, those around me weren't impressed. Rather than apathetic nods, I got raised eyebrows, sideways glances, and demands for Biblical proof. In the eyes of many, the idea of hearing from God outside of Scripture was dangerous, and to speak of my spiritual bondage as alliances with the enemy was akin to absolving the flesh.

If you find yourself thinking the same thing, let me clarify. Nothing I received was contrary to Scripture and I didn't consider it to be equal to Scripture in authority or inerrancy. It was the application of Biblical truths, spoken to my heart as promised (John 14:26, John 16:13-15, 1 Cor. 2:10-11). While sitting at the feet of Jesus, I was given what I needed when I needed it most. In the same vein, I neither blamed the Devil for my sinful choices, nor did I deny the selfish inclinations of my flesh. My sin is always a result of my own choices, and thus it is my responsibility. However, in my estimation, the Devil and his work were thoroughly neglected in my past. Acknowledging his influence was a course correction which brought me in line with what Scripture advises, providing me with a more comprehensive battle plan for my soul (John 8:44, James 4:7, 2 Cor. 2:11).

I found these concerns to be oddly ironic since the very best solutions offered to me by others hadn't helped me at all. From my perspective, they (and the Church at large) had been focused on all the wrong things and either passively silent or smugly oppositional on the issues that had threatened to take me out emotionally and spiritually. As you might imagine, I dug my heels in even deeper. What good was the Church at all? Not only did it lack the integrity to heal the broken, but it was either impotently powerless or too self-righteous to defend the defenseless and release the captives!

In my not-so-humble opinion, this explained why my family and I had slipped through the cracks. We had bought into a system where God was silent, the heart was ignored, intimate community was improbable, if not impossible, and the enemy's role was reduced to that of a tempter. Thus, we relied upon legalism and other external pressures to control our sinful behavior. We adhered to a form of godliness, but it was devoid of power (2 Tim. 3:5).

Two Steps Forward, One Step Back

God's plans cannot be thwarted. He wasn't wringing His hands over the Church or my attitude with it. Four years after my healing journey had begun, He began a third work: reconciling me to the Church. He put us in a fellowship group where we experienced intimate community for the first time. Those in our group varied in backgrounds, ages, marital status, church affiliations, and ethnicity, but we were all a little bruised and in need of a safe place. It was through the development of these precious friendships that God began to change my negative expectations of Christians and break down my stronghold of bitterness against the Church.

For several years, we shared our stories and our lives. We learned how to wrestle through our hurts together and we learned to fight for each other. I felt a sense of acceptance and belonging. In fact, I felt so safe with these friends that I willingly and happily attended church on Sundays again. I had hugs to give and relationships to tend to. Moreover, I was finding more and more people on Sunday mornings who were just as lost and damaged as I had been, and they wanted answers! I realized that I was being set free, not only because God loves me, but because He wanted to love others through me. He expanded my borders, and I began spending time with people who craved the restoration Jesus was bringing me. It filled me with joy to share it. Walking with others on their own road to redemption became my passion.

David and I were so grateful for the warmth of fellowship and life-giving ministry that God was giving us, but He was not finished. Those very tender places of redemption became the subject of opposition and scrutiny for the leadership of our local church. They began to doubt our loyalty, question our theology, and ultimately, they dismissed our philosophy of ministry. It was suggested that we would be happier elsewhere, but we stayed. The leadership reaffirmed their position and requested conformity, but we resisted. We tried to meet with them and work things out, but it didn't go well. I am certain that my bitterness cast a shadow upon my perceptions and intensified their suspicions of us. I am equally certain that the relationships were not strong enough to sustain the mildest of conflicts. As a result, tempers flared, resentments surfaced, and we felt completely stuck. If we left, they threatened to disband our group. If we stayed, we would have to submit to their authority without their support or esteem. But that wasn't the choice I was most concerned about. The choice in front of me was much more consequential. Would I walk away from the Church altogether and try to find a sense of community with ex-church Christians? Or would I finally forgive and seek reconciliation with this thing called "church"?

Let me connect the dots. While sitting in the belly of that fish, Jonah did repent to God for his rebellion. He did obey God's command to preach repentance to the Ninevites. But there's no doubt that his heart was still running to Tarshish. And so was I. I sat in a seat on Sunday mornings and led a community group during the week, but I was railing against the Church all day long! There we were, Jonah and I, enjoying a shady spot on a hill, hoping God would rain down His wrath upon those who deserved it. In His great kindness, God provided for Jonah a vine, just as he provided for me a community group. It was sweet refreshment in the desert, a healing balm, and a priceless treasure. For a time, I forgot about my bitterness. I thought maybe the Church had changed. But then God appointed a worm to kill Jonah's dear vine and, once again, I felt defenseless as one more church used its power and authority to isolate and marginalize. In both cases, God exercised His gentle discipline so that we would come to a humble recognition of the sin we had welcomed into our souls.

I knew I had issues with the Church, but I had no idea what had become of my heart. It didn't feel like hardness, didn't feel like arrogant entitlement, although it most certainly was. It felt like a throbbing, stinging wound. Unfortunately, years of neglect had allowed infection to set in. By the time this particular conflict took place, it was so inflamed and shockingly tender to the touch that I couldn't problem-solve or act with diplomacy and tact. I could do nothing but cry and beat my breast.

My husband and I spent weeks doing an inventory of offenses, trying to lay out our case, strategize our response, and find ways to bring resolution. But neither of us could do so with a clear mind or a clear conscience. There was too much water under that bridge, and too many bridges, for that matter. Finally, the unmistakably best path became apparent to both of us. There was only one thing we could do, one choice we could make; one unilateral decision that didn't depend on anyone else. We could forgive.

There was nothing within me that *wanted* to forgive, but my flesh never wants to do what is right. My flesh wanted to pull a stunt like my daughter had pulled in elementary school. While we were eating dinner together one night, she insisted that I come to her school the next day and eat lunch with her. Noting her unusual assertiveness, I cleared my schedule. When I arrived at the school lunchroom the next day, she walked over to an unsuspecting classmate and asked him to join us. I thought it was curious that she would invite a boy to eat with us, but those thoughts were cut short when I realized she had a very specific, and not-at-all-romantic, agenda. Evidently, he had been treating her poorly, so she decided to stage an intervention! After thanking us for joining her, she launched into an interrogation that made me pity the fool boy. When she was done, she leaned back in her chair and gave me a look that said, "*Your turn Mama Bear*".

I wanted to presume upon God's justice like that and offer my two cents to boot! I wanted to lay out my case and watch Him defend us and set the Church straight for once, but He didn't. I wanted an apology and a little validation, but I got neither. Our flesh never wants to do what is right and the enemy doesn't want to lose his territory, but we always have choices, don't we? So, we chose to submit our will to the work of the Holy Spirit. We sat down together and begged God for whole-hearted obedience. We forgave the leaders who had offended us until we felt free to move forward with clean hands and hearts.

Questions for Reflection

1. **Do you agree that bitterness is rooted in a declaration that God is not good and cannot be trusted? Why or why not?**

2. *Janalee says that her bitterness didn't feel like hardness, but a throbbing, stinging wound. How can we become bitter and not know it?*

3. *"Understanding that I was loved and accepted enabled me to receive from Jesus, and together we could process the tangled web within my heart." How does feeling loved and accepted affect our willingness to change?*

4. *Why do you think their community group was so healing for Janalee?*

Guilt Trip

I chose to forgive, but it was more of a process than an event, and it was a complicated one at that. It didn't remove the hurt or negative expectations. It didn't repair relationships. There was still much work to be done. Undeniably, I had been trusting in myself and my ability to defend myself and it was time to demolish my hardness of heart and seek the Lord. Wanting to be faithful with my side of the equation, I began praying for the gift of repentance (2 Tim. 2:25). Hosea refers to this as breaking up unplowed ground.

> *Sow for yourselves righteousness, reap the fruit of unfailing love, and break up your unplowed ground; for it is time to seek the LORD, until he comes and showers righteousness on you. But you have planted wickedness, you have reaped evil, you have eaten the fruit of deception because you have depended on your own strength and on your many warriors.* (Hos. 10:12-13 NIV)

I often think better on paper, so quite naturally I began there. I spent several afternoons writing out a chart of all the churches I had ever attended and every Christian organization I had been a part of and listed all the positive and negative experiences I'd had with each one. I was careful to include the internal messages I had received: what I had come to believe about myself, about God, and about the Church as a result. My simple objective was to take an honest look at what had happened within my heart and soul all those years, and to resolve any issues I found. As I scanned through these memories, many lies and unforgiven offenses became apparent. Thus, I began the work of repenting, renouncing, and forgiving.

To my surprise, dealing with my lies was easy, but forgiveness didn't turn out to be the straightforward exercise I thought it would be. I was tempted to bypass the acknowledgement of wrongs committed and minimize their effects. In some cases, I wanted to fault myself because I was also to blame, because I might have misunderstood, or because I may have made too much of nothing. In other cases, I tried to excuse the words and actions of others because they had extenuating circumstances or good intentions. Surely, there were times when I was also to blame, when I had misunderstood, when I had made too much of unintentional transgressions, and when my offenders deserved some compassion.

But I could not be free from what I would not acknowledge. And, perhaps more importantly, I needed to honor my soul by investigating and resolving what it had kept record of. I needed to act based on my perceptions, because offenses are hidden within our perceptions. Therefore, forgiveness became an act of disciplined intention, based on my perceptions of what had transpired. Then I covered with forgiveness the consequences I had paid for these wrongs. In all this, I applied what I had learned about walking bravely with the Spirit of God as He pointed out both sin and wounding. I could not sidestep my sin or the sins of others if I wanted to move forward in freedom.

A few weeks later, I stumbled upon a blog post written by the pastor I spoke of previously, the one who had known my family the best, the one who had asked my mother to pursue reconciliation. Because that particular post wasn't very kind or generous, I decided to get a better sample. I spent the next few weeks reading what he had to say about politics, sin, theology, and marriage in hopes that my assumptions about him were wrong, not only the assumptions I was making at that very moment, but the ones I had come to years before. I sincerely anticipated that he would prove to be gracious and wise, Biblically sound and abounding in love. Try as I may, I could only see Biblically sound. Before I knew it, I had responded to one of his posts with a critical review of my own. He answered by asking for my phone number.

Twenty years had passed since we had last spoken. I had asked him to write a letter of recommendation for me when I applied for Bible college. He did so gladly and with superlatives. For that and so much more, I had great appreciation for his friendship and respect for his ministry, but I needed answers. After exchanging pleasantries and becoming a bit reacquainted, I began to ask the questions that had been lingering for decades. Had he seen what was happening in our family? Why didn't he step in *before* my mom left? Had he ever tried to teach us grace, because I had missed it entirely?

He offered his impressions of my family and asked a few questions about what had transpired. Wanting to reminisce, he pulled his wife close to the phone and detailed the happenings in their life and ministry. My resolution outweighed my affections, so I broke in with a question. *"Did you see what was happening, or not?"* With a sigh, he explained that he was too busy with the business of church, too preoccupied with the doctrinal conflicts that were taking place within the denomination, to notice that there was something amiss. However, he assured me that he was having great success with others like us. He even predicted that, had he seen it at the time, he would have addressed the problem and set us back on track. I wanted to believe him, but I was doubtful.

He ended our conversation by recounting a haunting saga of abuse within his inner circle. His voice broke as he described painful betrayals, shame-filled confessions, and the costly decisions he was being forced to make. He hoped it would prove to me that he was capable of leading the way for the broken. It did not, but it was enough. I brought the call to a close, humbled by a realization. God was, in that very moment, burning into this pastor's soul everything I would have wanted him to know and more. Because the Father loves all His children, He disciplines them so that they will grow. And I was intimately acquainted with the sting of the Father's discipline, which gave me compassion for my pastor. Knowing that God was more intent upon his sanctification and more interested in the fruit of his ministry than I was, I released him and his debt, entrusting them both to the Lord.

That conversation was a gift, but there are no prerequisites to forgiveness. We can forgive another person even if we don't agree with them. We can forgive them even when they have not repented. Unlike reconciliation, forgiveness is not dependent upon the other person or the offense. It simply requires us to forgo compensation. With our pain laid bare and the truth brought to light, it is tempting to make demands, but our response must be to relinquish our right to retaliation and let the One True Judge do what is just.

Back to the Drawing Board

Feeling much lighter in spirit and optimistic about my restored view of the Church, I decided to attend a ladies' retreat at my church. Perhaps it was foolhardy and premature, but I was determined to relish the fruits of my labor. So off I went. I smiled, took notes, and tried very hard to engage in small talk and have a good time…and I plum wore myself out in the first two hours.

There was something contrary going on under the surface and, try as I might, I couldn't bend it to my will. It was an unsettled anxiety that came out in full force during one of the break-out sessions. There were about seven of us having a pretty good discussion where everyone was respectfully and honestly contributing, but I was growing more and more uncomfortable. I didn't approach the topic from the same perspective as the rest of the group and couldn't quite keep it to myself. I tried to voice my thoughts as questions or concerns but understating my ideas didn't help. I felt misunderstood and perhaps even a little chastised and dismissed. As each woman shared, my mind began to race. *I am always misunderstood. They think my ideas are unbiblical. Why do I always make things so complicated? I knew I shouldn't have come. I don't belong here, and I don't belong in the Church.* I felt like I was caught in the middle of a debate and I wasn't quite sure which voice was my own.

I waited until our session was over, and meekly pulled one of the ladies aside to get her take on it. She listened carefully as I described what I was trying to say and how I interpreted the responses I got. Apparently, her understanding of the conversation was entirely contrary to mine, and she suggested that I pay close attention to the evening session, which was on spiritual warfare. I did as she suggested, and as I listened to the speaker describe the work and voice of the enemy, I saw that I had more work to do. My failure to forgive the Church for so long had indeed given the Devil a foothold.

When I got home, I dragged my weary self to my prayer closet and asked God to show me what I had missed, to help me uncover what I'd left undone. What remained of my root of bitterness? In response, He sent me to Hebrews chapter 12:

Therefore, since we have so great a cloud of witnesses surrounding us, let us also lay aside every encumbrance and the sin which so easily entangles us, and let us run with endurance the race that is set before us, fixing our eyes on Jesus, the author and perfecter of faith, who for the joy set before Him endured the cross, despising the shame, and has sat down at the right hand of the throne of God. (v. 1-2)

"My son, do not regard lightly the discipline of the Lord, Nor faint when you are reproved by Him; For those whom the Lord loves He disciplines, And He scourges every son whom He receives."...All discipline for the moment seems not to be joyful, but sorrowful; yet to those who have been trained by it, afterwards it yields the peaceful fruit of righteousness. (v. 5 6, 11)

Therefore, strengthen the hands that are weak and the knees that are feeble, and make straight paths for your feet, so that the limb which is lame may not be put out of joint, but rather be healed. Pursue peace with all men, and the sanctification without which no one will see the Lord. See to it that no one comes short of the grace of God; that no root of bitterness springing up causes trouble, and by it may be defiled... (v. 12-15)

When I read these verses, the Holy Spirit sliced clean through my bone and marrow to expose the "speculations" and "lofty ideas" that had been fortifying my bitterness (2 Cor. 10:3-5). Forgiving the Church for every offense I had held onto wasn't enough. Forgiveness isn't always enough. Yes, it's necessary to forgive, but there was more work to be done. There remained lies, accusations, inner vows, and unrealistic expectations embedded within my soul – utterly illogical, arrogant, and untrue. Nevertheless, they were true to me, and needed to be dislodged and disproven.

1. **The Church doesn't care about the broken and oppressed. It cannot be trusted.** At first glance, these statements appeared to be lies and so I repented for believing them. But I knew in my heart that there was something else at play. I had said these things as

accusations or judgments against the Church, and thus I needed to repent for that as well. They were not objective observations. They were not Spirit-led discernments. They were indictments, born from anger and used to rationalize my rejection of the Church and rebellion against it. These (and other) judgments against the Church were the sins that so easily entangled (Heb. 12:1), and what the KJV calls the "besetting" sins that had me by the ankles and kept me from moving forward.

There's always some truth, some evidence, to support our lies and judgments. In my experiences, churches did fail to care, defend, and protect. But to categorically assign the Church a failing grade because of those experiences was more cynicism than truth. Once I removed my lies and judgments, I could see that the Church is capable of great compassion and valor, and equally capable of great impotence. Only God is consistently good and powerful. He would parent my children perfectly. He would love my husband unconditionally. He would pastor and lead my church flawlessly, without selfishness, without pride, without the limitations of humanity. He would be able to meet every need and make every decision without hesitation. But He has given the charge to us and asks us to trust in Him while we serve each other. *"He seems to do nothing of Himself which He can possibly delegate to His creatures. He commands us to do slowly and blunderingly what He could do perfectly and in the twinkling of an eye. Creation seems to be delegation through and through."*[6]

Removing my judgments was necessary, but they rested upon a substructure of unrealistic expectations and that needed to be removed as well. Somewhere along the way, I had taken my deep well of hurts and unmet needs and combined them with a few select commands from scripture then sprinkled one or two noble pronouncements made by well-intentioned pastors and ended up with some very lofty ideals. Naturally, those firmly held hopes were swiftly disappointed, but I didn't think to amend them. Instead, I doubled down, defended them, and accused the Church with a list of unforgiving judgments.

In humility, I rescinded the idol-like status I'd given to the Church and reminded my heart that only God is *"able to do far more abundantly beyond all that we ask or think"* (Eph. 3:20). God works through the Church, but the Church is *not* God. The Church is not God! This is great news for all who will receive it.

2. ***If the Church won't care for the broken and oppressed, I will. I will never betray another hurting person.*** Out of survivor's guilt, misplaced loyalty, and fury, I made two separate vows that committed me, unconditionally, to those who were hurting. This is not what it means to *"Vindicate the weak and fatherless; Do justice to the afflicted and destitute. Rescue the weak and needy"* (Ps. 82:3-4) or to *"…seek justice…plead for the widow"* (Isa. 1:17). On the contrary, it was a personal vendetta. I picked up my mom's pain as an offense against the Church and against God and His goodness. As if it were my cross to bear and with an air of superiority, I assigned myself a savior status. In so doing, I failed to run with endurance the race set before *me* (Heb. 12:2). I took it upon myself to rescue all those who had tripped or fallen behind. Most assuredly, this was a false cross, and thus I had to lay it down.

As with all vows, I had assigned to myself responsibilities and abilities that belong to Jesus alone. He is the only Healer in this race, the only Hero. Edward Smith speaks of this in his book *Healing Life's Deepest Hurts:*

> *When we seek to find resolution or restitution from those who were responsible for our original wounding or look to others later in life to fill these vacuums, we will always be disappointed. Only truth from the Holy Spirit, spoken softly and gently, can calm the raging waves of our painful past.*[7]

Not only were these vows a false cross, but they were a hindrance to God's work in others. When we fall because of our own sinful obstacles, it is God who disciplines us unto repentance and obedience. Failure and discipline have a purpose, and I had to allow others to experience both. Of course, I may encourage, pray for and with, offer truth, fight for, defend, stand in the gap, and share my story of God's grace and healing. But I cannot fail to run my own race, and I cannot stop and carry others through theirs. I must run beside, keeping my eyes on Jesus. *"Let us run with endurance the race that is set before us, fixing our eyes on Jesus, the author and perfecter of faith"* (Heb. 12:2).

I suppose it goes without saying that my self-determined path to rescue broken humanity had a shelf life. Hurting people often have unrealistic expectations, inexhaustible needs, unhealthy boundaries, and misplaced desires. (It takes one to know one.) Their demands are infinite, but I am finite. All the skills, tools, and gifting in the world can't make up for the fact that I am, and always will be, human. On this side of eternity, that makes me deeply inadequate. My insight is limited, my solutions are limited, and my empathy is limited. The pressure is off, though, because God can use me, but I am NOT God! This too is great news for all who will receive it.

3. ***I'm alone.*** Underneath it all, at the very center of my web, were feelings of abandonment. I felt abandoned by my family and abandoned by the Church. This was the source of my hurt, the gaping wound that gave the enemy easy access to me. It nipped at my heels in the little things and battered me bruised in the big ones. Either way, the message I came to believe was the same. *I am alone.*

The writer of Hebrews refers to this as a "lame limb", the injury I had failed to take to God for healing. "*Therefore, strengthen the hands that are weak and the knees that are feeble, and make straight paths for your feet, so that the limb which is lame may not be put out of joint, but rather be healed*" (Heb. 12:12). I had tried to protect myself from the pain of abandonment with anger, but then let the sun go down upon it too many times. Before I knew it, my "limb" became dislocated by sinful bondage.

These feelings of abandonment and isolation, and the lies attached to them, were coming from so many different places and times within my heart and story. *I am alone.* This was the message that preceded all the others and laid the foundation for everything else. No wonder it took years to untangle! Hiding behind all the anger and debate, posing, and postulating was a frightened little girl just wanting to feel safe, a confused teenager craving the security of something tangible and constant, a desperate college student aching for love and belonging, and a cynical young woman running from the sadness. God peeled away the layers and revealed my fragmented soul, born out of self-sufficiency and manipulated by the enemy.

Stasi Eldredge captures it perfectly:

You see, we all pretty much handle our brokenness in the same way – we mishandle it. It hurts too much to go there. So, we shut the door to that room in our hearts, and we throw away the key…But that does not bring healing…Usually it orphans the little girl in that room, leaves her to fend for herself. The best thing we can do is to let Jesus come in, open the door and invite Him in to find us in those hurting places.[8]

Jesus cares! When I turned my gaze to Him, I found Him standing at the door knocking (Rev. 3:20). In my younger years, I only knew Him as my Savior and, evidently, there were parts of me that still saw Him that way. As an adult, my perception had been changed by His humble pursuit of me and His unashamed vulnerability. It was the adult in me then, the one who knew the lovely personhood of Jesus, that opened the door and invited Him into those shattered places. On behalf of my younger self, I asked my Father, my Friend, and my Comforter to gather the broken places within my heart and bind them back together with His love. I relinquished my protective grip and asked Him to re-parent those young places and grow me up.

Gladly, I can report that this very important work was in the capable hands of the only One who could carry the burden of my pain and pay the enormity of debts owed to me. Only He could bear up under the weight of my grief and redeem what had been lost. This is, in fact, one of the "Yes and Amen" promises we can hold Him to (2 Cor. 1:20).

Then I will make up to you for the years that the swarming locust has eaten, the creeping locust, the stripping locust and the gnawing locust, My great army which I sent among you. You will have plenty to eat and be satisfied and praise the name of the Lord your God, who has dealt wondrously with you; then My people will never be put to shame. (Joel 2:25-26)

Conclusion

I quite relate to Paul. I was once a vile offender, a crusader against God's people – but I was shown mercy. In God's abundant grace, He chose me as His instrument to display His great patience and kind intention toward sinners.

> *I thank Christ Jesus our Lord, who has strengthened me, because He considered me faithful, putting me into service, even though I was formerly a blasphemer and a persecutor and a violent aggressor. Yet I was shown mercy because I acted ignorantly in unbelief; and the grace of our Lord was more than abundant, with the faith and love which are found in Christ Jesus. It is a trustworthy statement, deserving full acceptance, that Christ Jesus came into the world to save sinners, among whom I am foremost of all. Yet for this reason I found mercy, so that in me as the foremost, Jesus Christ might demonstrate His perfect patience as an example for those who would believe in Him for eternal life.*
> (1 Tim 1:12-16)

I am so grateful for the jealous fury with which He took me on, because on the other side of my bitterness has been a redemption I couldn't have imagined. After the writing of this chapter, God has continued to guide me into more repentance, forgiveness, and healing. Sometimes, He chooses to free us from our sins, wounds, and bondage in a moment, with very little participation on our part. But more often than not, He chooses to walk the road with us instead. He performs miracles either way, but I think I prefer the longer road, at least in this case, because it has afforded me more opportunities to hear His heart on the matter.

Part of my process was facilitated by a healthy church body to which we have been tethered for many years now. It is a healing church where it's okay to be messy, where problems are not swept under the rug, where intimate community is encouraged, and where grace abounds. As Larry Crabb describes in his book *Shattered Dreams*, *"Church is too often a place of pretense and therefore a place without hope. When brokenness is disdained, where the real story is never told, the power of God is not felt. Where brokenness is invited and received with grace, the gospel comes alive with hope."* [9]

Within a church culture that welcomes the power of the Gospel, my experience and expectations of the Church have profoundly changed. Men and women with rich, well-nourished spiritual lives have loved and warmly accepted me, despite my unpredictable sensitivities. In observing their meek deference to others and selfless sacrifices, I have been tremendously humbled and tenderly disarmed. I'm indebted to them for their faithful love, and ever so grateful to my precious Redeemer who loved me enough to oppose my bitter rebellion. Now, I find it to be enormously ironic that I spent decades running from the Church and railing against it because, within it, I have found everyone and everything I love the most.

Questions for Reflection

1. *Janalee says she prayed for the gift of repentance (2 Tim. 2:25). Why is repentance a gift?*

2. *What does it mean that offenses are hidden within our perceptions? Is this true?*

3. *What was underneath Janalee's judgments of the Church? Have you ever had to readjust your expectations as part of the forgiveness process?*

4. *Why is it important to understand that God works through the Church, but the Church is not God?*

5. *What was Janalee's "false cross"? Can you relate to this struggle?*

6. *Do you agree that forgiveness is not only a command but also a gift? Why?*

Chapter 7

Chasing Fantasies

A Wing and a Prayer

Our first daughter was full of imagination and wonderment. She had not one, but two make-believe friends. She spoke with a British accent for years after watching Mary Martin's version of *Peter Pan*. Her mind was so full of blissful ambitions, fanciful creatures, and innocent daydreams that she danced, sang, and narrated her way through each day. It was delightfully exhausting.

One of my favorite memories of her childhood occurred during our bedtime prayers. We knelt on the floor beside her bed and folded our hands, and she followed suit by bowing her head. She waited as patiently as she could while we spoke our blessings. And then it was her turn. She sat up, cleared her throat, tightly clenched her hands together, and said, *"Lord, please give me the wisdom, and the power, and the pixie dust I need to fly!"* Far too enchanted to burst her bubble of Pixie Hollow naïveté, we chuckled adoringly, said goodnight, and submitted her sweet little prayer to Reader's Digest.

It's only human to dream. We all long to transcend the daily grind of this life. A little whimsy here and there captures our imaginations and ignites a flame of desire that the here-and-now-world tends to snuff out. It gives us a chance to soar above our circumstances, to see our world as we would like it to be, and to see ourselves the way we'd like to be. Whether we are indulging in Pinterest, bingeing on Netflix, or playing the lottery, we all appreciate a fantasy or two.

Our pretty fantasies can become more than delicious little treats in our rice-cake reality. According to the dictionary, a fantasy is *"an imagined or conjured up sequence fulfilling a psychological need"*[1]. Interesting. There's nothing wrong with a little bliss, but when we move from appreciation to *need* or attachment, when our hunger for completeness or satisfaction becomes tied to anything in this world, we have ventured into dangerous territory. As Christians, we know better than

146

to place our deep soul needs in the hands of anything on this earthen ball of clay. We know this because our experience tells us that such foolishness leads to disappointment, and because Scripture tells us it's idolatry. *"You shall have no other gods before me"* (Ex. 20:3). Nevertheless, it happens, doesn't it? Even though it's a sin, even though it never ends well, it's our wayward way. We all succumb to a little pain-numbing idolatry.

A friend of mine calls it the "If…Then World." It's thinking that *if* a particular thing happened, *then* we would be happy, fulfilled, secure, or significant. We frame it in numerous ways, but the common denominator is that we set our desires upon a particular thing with the expectation that it will satisfy us. For many of us, these little fantasies began in childhood, often in response to pain or an unmet need. In this way, unresolved brokenness often leads to such "if…then" thinking. And, whether we know it or not, whether it is logical and true or not, we carry those longings and silly expectations into adulthood.

My parents didn't endorse the make-believe, so I never dressed up for Halloween, never put cookies out for Santa, and never collected spare change for my lost teeth. But that didn't stop me from dreaming. Blame it on Disney, I imagined that marriage could bestow upon me the identity, worth, and security I craved. I believed that *If* I got married *Then* I would be safe, loved, and appreciated. *Then* I wouldn't feel lonely, wouldn't feel like a failure, wouldn't be rejected or abandoned. Long before I even met my husband, I wrote his job description in response to my heart's cry for God, my unresolved pain, and my unmet needs. Therefore, marriage was an idol, my "if…then" fantasy world, I hoped would eliminate my emotional turmoil and cure my soul sickness.

If you had asked me what my expectations of marriage or a husband were, I probably would have given you a few Bible verses. And I'd have done so sincerely, because I was unaware of my brokenness and equally unaware of my unrealistic expectations. I knew better than to think that my husband could make me happy. My head knew to anticipate frustrations. My head knew I would marry an imperfect person. But my soul had wounds that demanded attention. So I entered into marriage with unfinished business, and tried to enforce the unrealistic and unfair expectations I had unwittingly established. Even though I was not consciously aware of it, I counted on my husband to fulfill my fantasies. And unbeknownst to me, I married someone who did the exact same thing. My young husband had an "if…then" fantasy world with my name on it. We were broken in different ways and thus wanted different things, but we tried to use each other to get them. I think Proverbs describes it best: *"Those who work their land will have abundant food, but those who chase fantasies have no sense"* (Prov. 12:11 NLT). According to the Bible, we had no sense. And sadly, those with no sense must learn things the hard way.

Romancing the Stone

It couldn't have been more predictable. David Smith was the first person I met on campus. He walked into the cafeteria wearing a Christian T-shirt, a dazed look on his face, and shorts that screamed third-world missionary. I introduced myself and found out that we were both transfer students and, sure enough, he'd just arrived from Russia where he had been serving as a missionary. Reverse culture shock was written all over him. I had an aversion to complicated men, so I made a mental note to keep my distance.

Wouldn't you know it, the next morning, we were placed in what the Bible college bubble referred to as a "family group" together. For the next two semesters, I ate, went to classes and chapel, and often socialized with David and a small group of other students. Within that delightful little arrangement, I discovered that he was a shamefully bad dresser and uncomfortably shy, but also highly intelligent, easy-going, and gentle. We became fast friends.

When summer rolled around, a few of us met up at a friend's wedding and stayed up late into the night to help with the clean-up. As we headed back to our rooms, David began to inquire about the future of our relationship. Did I agree that our paths were running parallel? Did I agree that we were a good match? A little stunned by his bold approach, I told him that we were great friends and I wanted to keep it that way. When he pushed the matter and suggested that God was putting us together, I became defensive and ended the conversation with a bristled response. *"If God is putting us together, I suggest that you ask Him to convince me of it Himself."* I drove home the next day quite irritated that he had tried to tamper with things between us and wondered if friendships with men were always so complicated.

A few weeks later, he sent me a letter confessing that our conversation had opened his eyes to a harsh reality. He'd been clinging too tightly to me. Not to worry, God had pried his fingers open, which hurt, but he had released me. I was his friend, he loved me, and he was going to hold me loosely. If I decided to leave the next year after graduation, he would help me pack and take me wherever I wanted to go. Then, he'd return to Russia.

In hindsight, I see what he was doing and consider it to be an unassuming and loyal display of affection. While acknowledging his feelings, he was also committing himself to continue our friendship. Not many men could endure being in such a vulnerable position. Very few would try. Be that as it may, his humility and courage were wasted on me. I read the letter forwards and backwards and couldn't make heads or tails of it. The more I read it, the more perplexed I became. Eventually, I took it to my dad and asked him if he could translate David's "man-speak" and tell me what to do. He read the letter and stared at me from over the top of his glasses. Handing the letter back to me, he said, *"Don't give him your heart, and don't run away. Just stay on the road and be his friend."*

Those were marching orders I understood and boundaries I knew how to abide by. Happy to push that nonsense aside, I returned to school that fall fully expecting to find everything just as it had been before, but we rarely saw each other. Because we were no longer in a family group together, he had moved off campus, and we didn't share any of the same classes, our chance meetings were few and far between. But I had my hands full with other concerns anyway. It was turning out to be a turbulent semester for me, leaving me little energy for friends. My plan was to make it through exams and sort things out after returning home for Christmas break.

Unfortunately, plans change. Home didn't provide me the reprieve I had hoped for. As you may remember, I'd no sooner put down my bags than my mom announced that she was leaving. Try as I may to repair the situation and save my family, I failed. I finally gave up and sulked back to school with my tail between my legs.

The campus was still deserted when I returned, which gave me some much-appreciated space. But I quickly realized that I couldn't go through my family crisis alone and so I called upon the safest person I knew. We sat across from each other in the empty cafeteria while I told him the whole miserable story. He listened quietly until I was done, then asked what he could do. Knowing he was leading a Bible study at his church, I asked if I could join him. It was presumptuous of me, but I didn't have a church home and knew I needed one. He obliged and I was soon surrounded by older couples and grandparents who gave me a small slice of familial comfort at a time when I felt orphaned.

The Lady Doth Protest Too Much

In short order, a small conspiracy began. David would sign up for nursery duty and my name would show up on the list next to his. He would agree to babysit for one of the families in the church and they'd ask me to tag along and "help". Little old ladies would saddle up beside me after the service and ask if I'd noticed how handsome David was that day. It was all ridiculously cute, and I appreciated the respect and admiration he engendered, but we weren't a couple and I said as much whenever given the opportunity.

The absurdity of it was that I did love David and felt quite drawn to him. I genuinely liked him, enjoyed his company, and trusted him, but I wasn't *in love* with him. He was nothing like men I'd dated in the past and he didn't fit the profile of someone I imagined I would marry. Aside from that, my life had just turned upside down and I didn't know who I was, what I believed, or what I wanted to do with my life. In all honesty, I wasn't a good bet. Every one of my romantic relationships had been a train wreck, and my parents' marriage went belly-up after 29 years! Simply put, I wasn't marriage material.

With all that said, you can imagine my resistance when the notion first came to me that I should tell David that I loved him. Without hesitation, I dismissed the idea, but the discussion wasn't over. As preposterous as the idea was, I couldn't shake it. In fact, I felt a growing sense of pressure and urgency in the matter, which made me wonder if it was God's nudging. Of course, that didn't improve my readiness to comply in the slightest. On the contrary, it unnerved me. Why would God ask me to make myself more vulnerable than I already felt? Why would He set me up for failure and disappointment?

Feeling rather perturbed, I told my mentor about it, assuming she would agree with me that it was bad timing and a bad match. Instead, she suggested that I write down a list of things I would need God to do before I would be willing to act upon this intrusive impression. That seemed sound, so I laid out my fleece. It didn't take me long to compose a very impressive, bulletproof list. At least I thought it was bulletproof.

Within a few days, I was turned down for the internship I wanted, I was offered a free place to live the summer after graduation, and an old boyfriend called to apologize for the way he had treated me. Closure was a blissful relief and I realized that I wanted to cross items off my list. Regardless of the outcome, it was good for my soul. So, I wrote a few letters of apology myself and closed out some old accounts. Then, two different men invited me into a romantic relationship, one was new and the other was asking for a second chance. Without an apology I said *"no"*, and I did so with unusual confidence. Beside the fact that they were ill-timed offers, if I wouldn't pursue the man that I liked and trusted, I certainly wouldn't consider men of lesser distinction.

After a few short weeks, every item on my list had been completed. Feeling an odd combination of smug satisfaction and pleasant relief, I decided to write another one. I recited my new items to my mentor as we sat across from each other in the cafeteria. She looked at me with a sideways glance. *"You know, this isn't fair. You need to either love him back or let him go."*

That didn't sit well. If *fair* was an actual thing, I had a few things to say about my life thus far, and I was too busy trying to sort it all out to worry about a man. Unyielding, I left our meeting insisting that he was just as content as I was with a friendship.

Although I wouldn't have admitted it at the time, her words resonated with me. It was becoming more and more apparent that things were not as simple as they seemed to be, and certainly not as simple as I wanted them to be. God was answering David's prayers and changing my heart. Something was shifting and I was losing sleep trying to figure out how to control it, but before I could solve that riddle, things came to a head.

Several sleepy days later, David and I were driving home from his Bible study together, happily singing along with the music on the radio, when he reached for my hand. I'm a little embarrassed to report that I didn't pull my hand away from the man I was adamantly *not* in love with. I re-framed it instantly, telling myself that we were simply good friends who happened to hold hands. And that was all perfectly fine and good until we arrived at the parking lot of my dorm and he did something I couldn't re-frame quite so easily. He stopped the car, turned to me, and said, *"I love you."* There it was again as clear as day. No, *"you're my friend"* or *"I'll help you pack"*. Just raw and simple, *"I love you"*. My jaw dropped to the floor, immediately followed by my stomach. I picked up both, reached for my door handle, mumbled a weak, *"Thank you,"* and ushered myself out.

My mentor was right. I had a decision to make. David deserved to know if I had any real intentions. I needed to either give him the green light or send him on his way so he could find someone else. I couldn't bear the thought of losing him. He had become a fixture in my heart and my life. But, was that enough reason to throw caution to the wind and use words like *love*? Could I open the door to a romantic relationship when my soul was in chaos? Could I move forward not knowing if I was, or ever would be, in love with him? Most importantly, was I willing to risk ending up like my parents?

Like Jacob, I wrestled with God all night, begging for answers and bargaining for guarantees. He did not oblige. By the time the birds started their morning songs, I was thoroughly spent and had received neither. I should have expected as much. In my heart, I knew it had indeed been God's nudging to begin with. He had continued to impress this upon me and had graciously resolved my list of many objections. Despite my fears, that should have been enough. But I suppose nothing would have been enough at that point in my life. It really wasn't God's will I was wrestling with, but my own. Continuing with an insistence upon clarity, proof, and explanations was more like defiance than discretion, so I sat myself down, quieted my mind, and surrendered. With hands open to the sky and heart bent toward His, I made a promise. Yes, I would tell my dear friend that I loved him, and I would even marry him if that's what became of it, but for my sanity and future resolve, I needed to hear it plainly. *God, is this really your will for me? Do you want this man for me?* He broke through the silence with these words: *"This is your choice. You can refuse and I will provide another, but he is My best for you."*

The next day after class, I asked David if we could go for a walk. Without a word, we trudged through the woods, slugging through wet grass, pushing aside cobwebs and low-lying branches, until we came to a small clearing. I stopped and turned to face him. Bracing myself for impact, I expressed my heart as honestly as I could. *"I love you, and that terrifies me."* He laughed, hugged me sweetly, and said he hoped I felt the same peace he did. I'm not sure that I recognized it as such, but by the time I returned to my room, the ache in my stomach was gone and I slept like a baby.

That weekend, we drove to the mountains and walked down a muddy trail that led to the basin of a waterfall. He leaped from rock to rock, singing and laughing, then pulled out a sparkling ring and asked if I would be his wife and love him forever.

Questions for Reflection

1.   What is the "if…then world"?

2.   Can you see any areas of your life where you've fallen into this form of idolatry?

3.   Have you ever wrestled with God over an important decision? When you look back on it now, can you see Him leading you?

4.   What are/were your expectations of marriage?

5.   If you are married, how have your expectations been disappointed? How have you resolved this?

The Prophecy

Clearly, not marriage material, yet there I was in a wedding dress, with a ring on my finger. There were no butterflies, no worries about things going the way we'd planned. The pomp and circumstance were completely lost on me. Much to the chagrin of my friends and family, I couldn't care less about the decorations, the cake, or the traditions. All romantic notions of the perfect wedding were thrown out the window when my parents announced their impending divorce. Despite my emotional dissonance, I had acted on faith that David was God's best for me, and I planned to receive him as a gift. We walked down the aisle and recited our vows, he washed my feet, and we stood together to worship as husband and wife.

When we entered the reception hall, we were swept into the fervor of pictures, happy tears, and well-wishes. It was surreal and glorious, just as it should be. Rather than music and dancing, we opened the floor for a series of speeches, testimonies, and other such words of wisdom from friends and family. My father was one of the first to share, but I don't remember what he said. What I do remember is that, when he was done speaking, he came up beside me and ushered me to a quiet corner. He got out his pointer finger and told me to remember what he had to say:

> *Jana, God hand-picked this man for you. You two are like lions: strong, independent leaders. You will need to learn how to lean into each other's strengths rather than devour each other. And it's going to be up to you to break the legacy of chains we've passed down to you.*

Not exactly a blessing, and pretty tough advice to take from my dad considering the state of his marriage and the accusations leveled against him. I dismissed him before he was done talking, giving him a dutiful, *"Thank you, Dad,"* and returned to the festivities.

Admittedly, I appreciated my dad's endorsement of our marriage and his encouragement to be good partners. I also appreciated the humility it took for him to acknowledge his less-than-stellar legacy, but I simply didn't see that it had any bearing on my future. I believed that my salvation, not to mention my resolve, would be enough to protect me, from my own sin and dysfunction as well as from the sin and dysfunction of my family. Indeed, our salvation offers us far more than we may realize, but we must actualize what has been offered. Denial and self-righteousness don't bring us the life we want. Unfortunately, I didn't know that yet.

Essentially, I tried to escape my brokenness as well as the brokenness handed down to me from my family by marrying a man who would grant me my dream. It's irrational, but I equated God's stamp of approval upon our marriage with His endorsement of my expectations. Compounding the problem, David did the same thing. Together, name-it-and-claim-it style, we declared that we would achieve the dream in Jesus' name. In this way and many more, we set our marriage up for failure. Terribly wounded and madly idealistic, we said, "*I do*", then ran off to our honeymoon and almost immediately declared war on each other. We now fondly refer to the first 10 years of our marriage as "combat training." If God had not intervened when He did, we would have devoured each other for sure.

The Fantasy Hit the Fan

Before our first anniversary, the fantasy hit the fan and we were in counseling. Immediately and miserably, we failed to fulfill the unspoken demands we had of each other. My husband wanted to be involved in full-time ministry, and I wanted to hide in a corner. He was ready to go out and build something, while I was deconstructing everything I had once adhered to. Through a series of sharp and bewildering blows, he threatened my dreams of security and I threatened his dreams of significance. Injured and indignant, we held onto our fantasies and blamed each other for being selfish and unfair. Facing such blatant refusal to accommodate each other, we put up walls of rejection and judgment. Without warning, simple conversations erupted into full-blown arguments and we were both shocked and offended. It never occurred to either of us that we needed to reconsider our expectations of each other or of our marriage. Needless to say, marriage counseling wasn't helpful. We wanted out of the pain we were in, but we weren't willing to do the hard work of healing.

After a few years of this foolishness, we gave up on senseless arguments and tried to get the lives we wanted independently of each other. Although it was never discussed and probably not intentionally contrived, we began living separate lives. Since I had killed his dreams of full-time ministry either here or abroad, my husband set his sights on climbing the corporate ladder. He was offered a great opportunity by a business owner in our church. The man and his wife were close friends of ours. They had hosted the small group Bible study my husband had led while we were in college and, because neither of our parents weren't able to help, they organized our wedding. Nearing the age of retirement, the husband wanted to bring in an apprentice who would eventually buy him out, and David was only too happy to jump on board. He poured himself into the business, learned all he could, and loved every minute of it. The sting of losing his dream of missions was ever present, but he was hot on the trail of another.

Meanwhile, I had come to the sad conclusion that there was no help for my troubled heart and marriage. Whether it was God, the church, a counselor, or our circle of friends, it was painfully apparent that they couldn't or wouldn't step into the confusion. I was alone and had to find a way to manage life with my own resources. Heavy laden and grief-stricken, I jumped into the deep end of the self-sufficient life and focused my attention on building the perfect family – "perfect" being defined as the family I thought I once had and subsequently lost. Much like my mother had done, I began managing our time, energy, and money according to that script. We began a family, we made friends, and we served in local ministries. It worked like a charm. Outside of intermittent eruptions, we fought less, laughed more, and convinced ourselves that we had a good partnership and a purposeful life. To a stranger, we might have looked like we were doing well. But that kind of facade has a shelf life.

Seven Year Itch

Seven years into our marriage, my false world began to crumble, and I came face to face with the emptiness I had created. As described in the first chapter, God met me in that inexplicable crisis and interrupted my little world with an invitation to the grace-filled life. It was a revolutionary shift in my worldview as well as my relationship with Him, and I embraced it fully.

Thank God for that, because I surely needed grace for what would happen next. What followed were four long years of hardship. Apparently, God had more to teach me than grace, and He had His sights set on more than just me and my heart. While He had begun His redeeming work in me, He had specific desires and intentions for my husband, for our marriage, for our children, and for our ministry. He had big renovations in store for us, and that kind of work usually begins with demolition.

The business my husband had joined was joyfully challenging and profitable the first few years, but then things began to change. New jobs weren't coming in and some old accounts were lost. As a result, there wasn't enough income to go around. Out of loyalty to the company, David decided to gamble and go without paychecks. Perhaps it had something to do with his Navy training. The captain always goes down with the ship, and he was on his way to becoming a captain. At any rate, the next few months were very tense. We *"held our breath"* as he called it, while he streamlined processes and secured new funding sources. Fortunately, his efforts paid off and we were reimbursed the missed paychecks. We let out a huge sigh of relief, expecting that life would return to normal. He returned to his mostly mild-mannered self and all was well – for a time. A few months later, the same troubles flared up, and again he stopped taking paychecks. He doubled his efforts to bring in new clients and scrutinized every financial decision both at work and at home. My high-performing, perfectionistic husband was determined to succeed, but God was equally determined to free him from the need for it. In other words, our troubles had only just begun.

A month or so into this second financial decline, I woke up one Saturday morning feeling quite out of sorts. A strong cup of coffee and breakfast only made matters worse. By mid-afternoon, I'd had several bouts of nausea and lost a set of keys. A good long study of my calendar and a panicked trip to the pharmacy confirmed the reason. I was pregnant.

Please understand, we loved having a baby in the house, and we planned to have another as soon as our situation settled down. It was just bad timing. David was already feeling an extreme amount of pressure to provide. So, you'll understand when I tell you that I toyed with the idea of not saying anything. I thought it should wait until things turned around again with the business. But would he fault me, doubt me, for hiding it from him? All predictions aside, I knew he needed to know the truth sooner rather than later. Besides, I wasn't stellar at keeping secrets and he would find out eventually. So, when he recommended that we go for a walk with the kids later that afternoon, I saw my opportunity.

We headed out the door with two rambunctious little girls and I couldn't help but giggle with just a hint of anticipation. I was probably worried for nothing. Who could be upset about another baby? Hoping for the best, I was just about to announce my news when he broke in with a bit of his own. *"I like our family the way it is. We have two great kids! I don't think we need any more, do you?"*

I was too stunned to speak. I caught up with the girls and hid behind their theatrical chatter until we got home. Then I busied myself with dinner and vowed to keep my mouth shut until I could come up with a solution for world hunger and unemployment. Regrettably, the dam burst shortly after everyone made it to the table. Right there, in between saying grace and passing out plates, I blurted it out. *"I have news. We're going to have another baby."* The girls excitedly asked if we were having a girl or a boy and suggested the names of their favorite cartoon characters. Our oldest asked where babies come from and Mr. Beloved got up, kissed me on the cheek, and walked out of the room.

I stared into the darkness and pondered many things that night. The prospect of bringing another child into our home was causing me to look at our family with a very different set of eyes. And it occurred to me that our finances weren't the only thing to be concerned about. It was a painful realization, but I had to admit that David and I were living separate lives. We weren't really friends anymore and rarely sought out opportunities to spend time together. Outside of our children, we shared very little. He knew next to nothing about my inner world and I knew even less about his. I guess we didn't feel safe being vulnerable with each other, truth be told. We never prayed together, confided in each other, or sought ways to bless each other. Something very vital and intimate was missing in our relationship, and I felt the void profoundly that night.

Oh, how foolish I felt. I had spent the bulk of that last year tending to the mess within my soul, and it never occurred to me that perhaps my marriage required a similar effort. But I only saw symptoms. I didn't really know what the problem was, let alone the solution. What was I to do but beg for another rescue? And so I poured my heart out to God, apologizing for yet another mess. I invited Him into it and asked if He would do for our marriage what He had been doing in my heart. Would He redeem that too? Faithful as always and so near to the broken-hearted, He came for me once again.

In my mind, I saw myself seated at a conference table with Jesus sitting directly across from me. He had a leather pouch in His hand which He held out before me. Placing it on the table with finality, He said, *"This baby is like earnest money. He's my promise that I will heal your marriage."* Without thinking, without acknowledging the first gift, I asked for another. Would He also promise to heal our finances? *"Yes, that too."*

Questions for Reflection

1. ***"Indeed, our salvation offers us far more than we may realize, but we must actualize what has been offered." What does this mean? Do you agree?***

2. ***Why do you think Janalee and her husband seemed to feel happier and get along better after they began living separate lives?***

3. ***What was the result of living like that?***

By Hook or By Crook

We fought for months over a name for our newest family member. My husband had selected a boy's name long before we married, and I had agreed to it without question. I liked the name he had chosen and thought it was endearing that he had given it so much thought as a young, single man. But for some reason, when it was confirmed that we were having a boy, I balked. My husband argued well and fiercely, as did many of our friends, but I refused to budge. In the end, he gave in and I accepted my status as a bad wife. We would name him Zachariah, the only name we could agree on.

By the time I'd reached my sixth month, nothing had improved, not in our marriage and not in our finances. Tiring of the instability in the business with no relief on the horizon, David finally concluded that he had gambled enough and needed to find another source of income. He offered to go into the office if his boss urgently needed him, but a baby was on the way and he had to provide for his family. He figured his best option would be to take advantage of the booming real estate market. He had an interest in it and had been researching the market as well as various strategies for years. With newfound zeal, he took the leap, saying, *"What's the worst thing that can happen?"*

Many weeks later, he was busy working from home when we got a phone call from his boss. He sounded frantic and asked me to send David to the office immediately. Of course, I relayed the message and off he went. When he came home about an hour later, he was visibly troubled. Evidently, his boss thought someone had stolen some important documents, and he wanted David to find them. He went to the file cabinet, immediately found them, right where they were supposed to be, and took them to his boss's office. David assured him that everything was safe and sound. But there was something about the situation that didn't sit well with him. It didn't make sense. Oddly, his boss continued to insist that someone had stolen the documents; someone had set out to harm the business. David verified that there hadn't been a break-in and that everything was just as it should be, but his boss would not be consoled or convinced. Not knowing how to interpret these things, my bewildered husband took out his office keys, handed them over to his boss, and came home.

It was maybe two weeks later that we got a knock on the door. It was a private investigator. He sat at our kitchen table and accused David of stealing those documents from the business, and he even claimed to have a video to prove it. He said he had been hired four weeks earlier by my husband's boss to install video cameras, and those cameras were rolling the day David was called in to find the "missing" documents. Of course, David explained the situation in its entirety and the investigator said he believed my husband, even admitting that he didn't have a case, but the damage had already been done. With the small amount of composure he had left, David called our local sheriff's office. They came to our home that night and we filed a report. They assured us that we had nothing to worry about. No one had submitted a video as the private investigator had indicated. No one had filed a report. And even if they had, there was nothing to fear. David went back to see if he could reason or reconcile with his boss. Twice he went, once alone and once with a friend from our church. It came to nothing and only deepened the wound. All was lost.

What does one do in the face of such a betrayal? His boss had been like a father to him – to us. David loved working for him and placed his whole heart in the hope of one day taking over that business. Years of effort and investment were lost, and an arrow had pierced his heart. It was the death of yet another dream. He poured himself into his work, desperately trying to reclaim his worth, his manhood, and his reputation.

For the next year, he worked fearlessly and feverishly to buy up and renovate houses. Launching a new business is an arduous affair in the best of situations, but when you do it as we did, in the red emotionally and financially, it's nothing shy of nerve-wracking punishment. The work was often strenuous, and the schedule was unforgiving. Time was never on our side and the learning curve was steep. It didn't take long for him to show signs of wear, but he wouldn't slow down. The more tired he was, the harder he worked. He needed help, so I tried to plan repairs and paint walls with our newest addition strapped in a front pack carrier. Then I got my realtor license to improve our profit margin. As a grand and sacrificial gesture, David's father flew down twice from Wisconsin to bring tools and offer practical help and advice, but things never seemed to get easier and we couldn't catch a break no matter what we did.

When we heard about a local investor's club, we thought it would be a good idea to rub shoulders with those who knew and understood the business better than we did. David faithfully attended and learned a great deal. One particular night, he came home and told me about a group of investors who were buying and selling beach timeshares without doing renovations and with promise of higher profit margins. Intrigued by their unique business plan, he began to investigate. In an attempt to do his due diligence, he attended several more meetings and submitted the details of their business plan to his real estate lawyer for review. Everything seemed legit, a solid and rather ingenious strategy. And it was, but that didn't much matter because the value of the properties for sale were inflated, a fact that was intentionally concealed by the investors, appraisers, and real estate agents who owned them. Unfortunately, we didn't discover that until we had already purchased two. We had been scammed. Two months later, the real estate bubble burst. All properties, especially those in high-market areas such as the beach, took a nosedive. The inconceivable "worst thing" had happened, and there was plenty of blame to go around.

Call in the Cavalry

We were in trouble and agreed that we needed help, although we weren't sure where to find it. Honestly, we didn't care how God showed up as long as He did. As it turns out, He showed up as an eccentric, soft-mannered tax attorney. Fighting back tears, we sat across from him and relayed the whole shameful story: the business, the betrayal, the scamming. Ever the optimist, David finished the story, took a deep breath, and began to detail his plan of redemption. Reviewing the numbers, he proposed that we could climb out of our money pit with a little more time and a lot more work. I silently counted the cost and hung my head in exhausted dread. Our lawyer got up from his chair and grabbed his Bible. Being a Messianic Jew with profound understanding of the Old Testament, he skillfully explained how it fundamentally influenced our laws. He argued that there is great mercy within the system for those who take risks. But David wasn't interested in mercy at the time. It was an integrity issue to him. He always said what he meant, did what he said, and paid what he owed. Not deterred in the least, our lawyer persisted. *"David, are you able to pay your sin debt?"* There was a long pause as David considered the implications. *"No, you can't. You entrusted it to Jesus. And the same is true with your financial debt. You can't pay it! You'll have to entrust it to me."* In that moment, David knew he had to give up on yet one more dream.

We were given some very unconventional advice that day, and we took it. It wasn't an immediate solution and didn't eliminate our debt, but it did give us a path to ever-so-slowly walk our way out. Regarding our immediate needs, he gave us two suggestions. First, we were to move out of our rental and into the home we had just finished renovating. Secondly, we were to get jobs that promised regular paychecks.

Moving into the house we had just fixed up wasn't a simple step in our journey. Like everything else, we had disagreed over whether or not to purchase that house; David wanted it and I didn't. There was a history of water problems that scared me. I argued that water couldn't be stopped, but David argued that he had done his homework and could mediate the issues. Even though I wasn't convinced, he knew more than I did and so he had to make the call. He bought it and worked together with his dad to renovate it and mediate the water. I must admit that I was impressed with their work. They did a lovely job, so much so that it was only on the market a few days before we had a full-price offer on the table. And this, of course, became the sticking point for David. The house was under contract and we were set to clear enough from the sale to coast for a year! He wanted it when I didn't and then after it was renovated, I wanted it and he didn't. In the end, we agreed to follow the advice of our lawyer. We got out of our contract with the buyer and happily settled into our new home, thanking God for another new start.

One week later, the day before it had been set to close, we watched helplessly as a river of flood waters surrounded our house, filling our yard, crawlspace, and garage. The good news was that this confirmed our decision to move into the house. It never would have closed. The bad news was the fact that we were stuck with a house that was flood prone. Then, my friends, "the worst thing" finally did happen.

Hell and High Water

I distinctly remember sitting together on our living room couch two days after the flood. Moving boxes were stacked in the corner, a musty smell was in the air, and the sound of a water pump hummed in the distance. We stared at the ground as we waited for the heating and air technician to give us his report, neither of us daring to say a word. Everything we touched seemed to go south; everything we wanted turned sour. And here was one more example of life gone bad, one more epic fail. Only this time, there was no one else to blame. But, of course, we did. Isolated, exhausted, up to our eyeballs in debt, and only too willing to blame each other for all of it.

I tried to muster a smile when the technician came into the room to state his findings. Trying to appear solemn, he said there was nothing he could do to salvage the system. It was completely waterlogged and had to go. I nodded in full agreement. He had just described my feelings exactly. In my estimation, our marriage was completely waterlogged and couldn't be repaired. *"The rain came down, the stream rose, and the winds blew and beat against the house, and it fell with a great crash"* (Matt. 7:26-27). We had built our house upon the sand, and it couldn't withstand the storms of life. Truthfully, we had invested far too little into our marriage to think it could endure all that we had put it through.

Not being a woman known for great timing or subtlety, I drew a line in the sand and told my bedraggled husband that I would no longer abide by our rules of engagement. I wouldn't settle for separate lives, wouldn't live in chaos anymore, and wouldn't support anymore crazy schemes. I wanted a stable lifestyle with a schedule and a routine. I wanted a true partnership where we listened to each other and made sound decisions together. I wanted him to take the matters of the heart seriously and start dealing with his baggage like I had been doing. These desires were perfectly reasonable. The problem was my posture. I was making demands, with an air of superiority and a strongly implied accusation that he was responsible for the state we were in. He didn't miss it at all. He resented the implication and refused to jump through hoops for me. I assumed his refusal was due to hardness of heart and he assumed the same of me. We were both right.

Questions for Reflection

1. *Janalee says that she and her husband built their marriage upon the sand. How is this true?*

2. *Can a marriage be salvaged if it is resting upon a poor foundation? Why or why not?*

3. *How can a marriage survive hardships such as these?*

Baby Steps

The fact that we were penniless certainly didn't help matters. Our lawyer was right. We needed jobs, but the idea was more intimidating to us than you might assume. Going back into the workforce was daunting for David, and understandably so. He was still reeling from his recent experiences. Being in business for himself felt much safer, even if it wasn't possible anymore. But, in addition to that, he didn't know what kind of job to get and he didn't have references to use. It wasn't like his former boss would put in a good word for him. And before that, he had been a chemist in the Navy and a missionary in Russia. Missionary work and going back into the military were out of the question, thanks to his wife. Not knowing where else to turn, he went to every job fair and temp agency he could find. And that's when a friend told him about an office job that sounded perfect for him. He applied immediately and got an interview. Actually, he got four interviews before they made a decision. You remember the story. They hired the guy God told them to and, sadly, it wasn't my husband. We were devastated, but God had not forgotten us.

In a move neither of us anticipated, David attended yet another job fair a few weeks later and found a government-funded program that offered various technology certifications and degrees. He received a full grant to be re-trained for an entirely different career, one that utilizes his talents and gifts better than anything he had done before. He did the training in half the time required and had a job immediately thereafter.

I was even less inclined to get a job than David. I had a nursing baby and two small girls at home, and I had never wanted to be a working mom. Even though I could see that our circumstances required it, I was resentful. But God changed all that. I woke up in the middle of the night from a dream that gave me explicit directions for what kind of job to get and how to get it. More surprisingly, it simultaneously graced me with the motivation with which to do it. I started the next day with renewed energy and did exactly what I'd been told in my dream. Six weeks later, my baby had weaned himself, my mom and step-dad offered to watch the children, and I had a job.

Not a Snowball's Chance

Despite the fact that we had a routine and paychecks for the first time in years, the next six months were the darkest of our marriage. We returned to marriage counseling, but it couldn't even keep us civil. We relentlessly raged at each other, demanding vindication and validation. This was not what we had expected, not at all what we thought marriage would be like, not at all what we thought God had in store for us. We expected to be partners and to minister together, to grow together, to have more opportunities and greater accomplishments as a couple than we had had as individuals. We were so sure that God had put us together, so confident that he would bless our marriage and protect our family, but what we got was a good beating: unresolved conflicts, untreated traumas, and broken dreams. It was an excruciating example of a bait and switch, and we both felt deceived.

There is no doubt that we were both hurting, both feeling mistreated and misunderstood, alone and worn out. But the wall of judgment, hurt, and distrust between us was too thick to navigate. I could always run to God and find a safe place, but I didn't know how to translate that into my marriage. In fact, I couldn't see evidence of God in my marriage at all. I was wondering if I had really heard from Him about marrying my husband. Maybe I had fooled myself into believing it was God's will because I wanted some security in the midst of my family turmoil? Did we ever really love each other? Living together had felt like combat training from the get-go. The weight of my disappointment seemed greater than my earlier conviction that our marriage was designed by God.

After months of what seemed like an endless nightmare, it became clear to me that David didn't care enough about me to renounce the ways we had been living and relating to one another. And it became clear to him that I blamed him for everything that had happened. At our wit's end, we threw in the towel and told our marriage counselor we wanted a separation. He readily agreed. In his words, *"Your marriage doesn't have a snowball's chance in hell."* But because of our financial complications, he asked us to consider an in-home separation first. In the meantime, he told us to stop talking to each other. Really. He didn't tell us to stop yelling, stop the sarcasm, or stop making snide comments. He told us to stop all verbal communication unless it was directly related to the children or our finances. All other topics were to be discussed via emails.

I Remembered

Abiding by our counselor's very wise advice, we did not speak to each other except to discuss matters pertaining to finances and the children. And, for a while, neither of us initiated email communication. We both rather enjoyed the silence, but eventually we found other ways to push each other's buttons. And thus, the emails began. Even though we were forced to slow down and think about what we really wanted to communicate rather than simply react, our bitter tones came through loud and clear. We were still fighting, just doing it a little slower and in a safer space. For the first time, we were each sharing our perceptions and feelings about all that had transpired over the years. I use the word "sharing" loosely. It wasn't pretty. There was nothing we didn't expose in each other, nothing we didn't drag into the light. And, as we did so, one harassing thought kept running through my mind. *Did God really tell me to marry this man?* Unbeknownst to me, my husband was pondering the same question.

It wasn't until a friend challenged me on this issue that I had any clarity at all. It was a long-term confidant, someone who knew much of our history from both our perspectives, someone whom David and I both loved and trusted. He was a uniquely gifted man who saw the best in us, and often praised and encouraged us for who we could be rather than who we were at the time. One evening at a small gathering, I rehashed with him the events of a particularly difficult week, and he did something quite out of character. He cited some of our earliest sins against one another with more than a hint of condemnation in his voice and concluded with, *"You knew better. You had no business marrying each other."* Shame slapped me in the face and it burned red. I recoiled for a moment, feeling quite betrayed by his stinging rebuke. And then something rose up in me with a force that rivaled his. *"I remember what God did, what He had to do to convince me that David was God's best choice for me. I remember what He said to me. He did put us together. That's the only thing I know about my marriage right now."*

That night as I replayed my conversation with our friend, I remembered the words my father had spoken to me on my wedding day. They had been long forgotten, but now they came back in vivid detail. *"You need to remember this, Jana. God hand-picked this man for you. You two are like lions: strong, independent leaders. You will need to learn how to lean into each other's strengths rather than devour each other. And it's going to be up to you to break the legacy of chains we've passed down to you."* I hung my head in somber acknowledgment. That's right. David was hand-picked for me. He was my gift from God, but I had failed to heed wisdom. I had failed to remember. And we had failed to value each other's strengths. Instead, we were doing our very best to devour one another. We were carrying on the chains that had been passed down to us.

I wanted things to be different between us but didn't know how to make that happen. There was no way to go back and undo the damage we had done to each other. I reasoned that it was too late. There was no sign of movement from either of us and no respite from the strife. Our in-home separation and email communications weren't helping us at all. We could always find a way to hurt each other.

The thought occurred to me that we might have the time and space to decompress and re-engage on better terms if we moved forward with a separation. Just the thought of it made the ache in my chest dissipate. Perhaps if I moved out, David would fight for me and the kids? Perhaps he would see the merit of my demands? It was only a maybe, but in the meantime, I had to put an end to the rivalry between us. I drove around our neighborhood to find houses within walking distance for the kids and made appointments to take a look at them.

God Remembered

Despite the wreckage that was my marriage and my soul at the time, I was attending a Bible study at a friend's house. It was a Beth Moore study on the tabernacle. Probably because of my hardness of heart toward David, I was struggling to personalize the lessons and hear what God had to say to me. But He knows how to get my attention. In the lesson on the altar of incense, Beth pulled out a reference from Luke chapter 1, where Zacharias the priest was serving within the temple. He was lighting the altar of incense, which represented the prayers of the saints, when an angel of the Lord appeared to him. "*Do not be afraid, Zacharias, for your petition has been heard...*" (1:13). At this point in her lesson, Beth paused and told us that the name "Zacharias" means *the Lord has remembered*.

Instantly, I was brought back to the day when I found out I was pregnant with my son Zachariah, the day that God promised to heal our marriage and our finances. It was the day He said our baby boy was His security deposit for that promise. It had been two very long years since then, and we were further away from "healed" than ever before. But I got the message loud and clear: *The Lord has remembered!*

I went home that night, drenched in awe and sorrow. God was going to heal my marriage, and I was packing my bags. I believed Him and trusted that He would make good on His promise. But Zacharias and his wife waited decades for their baby John. How long was I to hold my breath? I figured God could heal my marriage regardless of our living situation; therefore, I would continue with my plans to move out, and God could continue with His plans.

That Sunday morning, just after the clock had struck a reasonable hour, my mom called. With a careful tone, she asked me to wait. She just didn't feel right about it and asked if I would reconsider my plans to look at houses. I saw past my desire for an immediate fix long enough to recognize a quiet agreement in my spirit. In short, I cancelled the viewings. As I got the kids ready for church, I wondered why God had stepped in. It didn't look like He was going to let me escape, but He certainly wasn't doing anything to fix things either. Once again, He was asking me to breathe underwater. Trembling from fear and fatigue, I paused, closed my eyes, and laid it on the altar with just a hint of sass. *Fine. Do this Your way. Just remember that it's Your job to keep me from drowning!*

He Remembered

Valentine's Day was coming up, and I was dreading it. Despite my pleadings over the years that David buy gifts and engage in romantic gestures, he had always avoided the obligation of holidays. Our first Christmas together, he had said we wouldn't exchange gifts, but we could work in a soup kitchen together if I wanted to make it memorable. Regardless of how he intended it, I had always taken it as a personal rejection of me and a lost opportunity to celebrate life and love. Well, there would be no more of that. I didn't need him in order to have a celebration. And I didn't need a man to love me in order to enjoy Valentine's Day. We had three adorable children who appreciated special occasions. There was no reason I couldn't celebrate with them! In short order, I made plans to take them out for a nice lunch and bought them each a small gift. I let David know that he was welcome to come along if he wanted to, but it wasn't an obligation he had to endure.

You can imagine my surprise when a display of beautiful red roses showed up at my office. I checked the note and discovered they were from my husband…for Valentine's Day!! He hadn't bought me a gift in years and never one for Valentine's Day. I was so flustered that I hid them behind my desk. *Why would he do something like that? What did it mean? How was I supposed to respond?* It reminded me of the time one of my girls came in from an outdoor adventure and proudly presented me with a bowl of what she described as *"black dirt, healthy greens, and poisonous berries"*. Her little face beamed with pride and eager anticipation. But, as much as I appreciated the sweet gesture, I knew better than to take a bite.

I marched myself into the bathroom, looked in the mirror, and firmly told myself to get it together! The flowers were sweet, probably extremely expensive, and they smelled glorious, but they didn't mend anything between us! He wasn't going to get off the hook so easily. The previous 10 years had been awful, and I needed to know they wouldn't be repeated. I needed to know that he understood what I had experienced as his wife. A vase of flowers was very nice, but ultimately it was probably too little, too late.

God was reminding me that He had put us together and did promise to heal our marriage, but He hadn't yet. Perhaps David had had a change of heart and was wanting to re-engage, but I wasn't willing to make nice and return to the same old, same old. I didn't want to end up like my parents. I didn't want to sweep our pile of messes under the rug only to find myself in divorce court later. I wanted to fight for a healthy marriage and that meant working through all that had happened and finding a way to do things differently. More afraid of being a weak-willed woman than I was of being rejected, I sent David an email and laid out my case. I detailed what life had been like for me over the years, explaining how I felt alone, felt taken for granted, and felt disrespected. I told him that I resented the way he spoke to me, the way he distanced himself emotionally, and the way he minimized my opinions and concerns. I reminded him of how hard I had been working on my issues, my contributions to our problems, and I wanted to know if he was willing to do the same. Would he take a serious look at the damage that had been done between us and work to resolve it?

I have no record of his responses to me and can't remember it well enough to quote him, but it was significant. He didn't retaliate with his own offenses and frustrations. He didn't defend himself. He apologized! I distinctly remember feeling heard and validated. It wasn't that he agreed with everything I said or my recollection of what had happened, but he did communicate remorse, understanding, and a willingness to make changes. I reviewed his email with a girlfriend the next day, and tearfully announced that I thought God might indeed be doing something to save our marriage.

The girls giggled with delight as they donned their pretty dresses and got their hair swept up with bows for our special Valentine's lunch. I dressed Zachariah in a darling little toddler outfit and promised him ice cream if he stayed in his chair at the restaurant. Just before we were headed out, David appeared with a cleanly shaven face and the button-down shirt I had picked out for him two years before. He asked if he could join our celebration. A little dumbfounded, I gave him a nod. So off we went, three gleeful little children and two very nervous parents.

Lunch was filled with laughter and silly antics. The girls were charming, and Zack got his ice cream. Everyone was happy to be together, something I didn't think was possible for us anymore. What a pleasant and wonderful surprise it was. After our meal, David asked if we could go for a walk. We piled into the car and he drove us through town to an area I hadn't seen in a very long time. Slowly, we made our way through the campus of our alma mater, passing by one memory after another. He stopped the car when we came to the woods we had walked through over a decade before. It was the same place where I had risked it all and told my young friend that I loved him.

He got out, opened my door, and reached his hand out for me to take. I was hanging onto my resolve by a thread. The choice was mine, just as it had been so many years before. Would I choose to love, choose to be courageous and vulnerable, and embrace an uncertain outcome? Was this man and marriage still God's best for me? Not able to justify a refusal, I slipped my hand into his, and immediately realized how much I had missed him.

The rest of the day was spent in those woods. When we returned home that night, it was decided. If God was stepping in to heal our marriage, then we would commit to join Him in that process. I'd like to say that it was more complicated than that, but it wasn't. God reminded me that He had indeed put us together, He reminded me of His promise to heal our marriage, He resisted my plans to leave, and He softened David's heart toward me. That's what it took for me to invest myself again in my marriage.

But the process of submitting ourselves to God as He walked us through healing in our marriage was indeed complicated. Even though a commitment was there, and we had rings on our fingers, our problems weren't solved. We didn't stop fighting and we didn't jump back into an intimate relationship with each other. We kept our in-home separation boundaries for months before we trusted each other enough to live again as husband and wife. And it took at least another year after that to learn how to communicate and rebuild the foundation of our marriage and family. We had spent a decade erecting a wall between us. It might have been done out of self-protection, but neither of us felt safe in its shadow. Finally, the time had come to tear down that wall brick by brick. It was time to stop devouring one another, to learn how to lean into each other's strengths, to break the chains. It was time we gave up *"chasing fantasies"* and learned to *"work our land"* (Prov. 12:11).

Questions for Reflection

1. *"The weight of my disappointment seemed greater than my earlier conviction that our marriage was designed by God." Have you ever found yourself doubting God's direction for you when things didn't turn out the way you thought they would or should?*

2. *What was it that Janalee "remembered" after her friend chastised her for marrying David?*

3. *What was it that God "remembered"?*

4. *What did David do to change Janalee's mind about the marriage?*

Working our Land

"Those who work their land will have abundant food, but those who chase fantasies have no sense" (Prov. 12:11 NLT). The day we married, my husband and I were gifted with a piece of land called "marriage". Our little plot held great potential, but it was undeveloped and not yet prepared to yield a harvest. Sadly, we were foolish enough to expect one anyway. Even though we had invested little, we expected great rewards and chased senseless and self-serving fantasies. The result was ten long years of barren fields, hunger, and disappointment.

Fortunately, the power of the Gospel is redemption and transformation. We experienced both as we learned to work our land. Guided by His Spirit, we cleared away the debris of willful sin, we broke up the hard ground of hidden sins of the heart, we received healing from the hurts and wounds that were lodged like rocks in the ground of our souls, and we began the good work of scattering seeds of love and service to one another. In all of this, His grace overcame the law of sowing and reaping in that our mustard seed faith produced an ingathering of rewards far greater than what we had sown.

This process of reconciling and rebuilding resulted in many lessons learned. The following are some of the priceless treasures found in our field of toil.

Dual Listening

One of the greatest battles in marriage is to lay aside anger and put on compassion. Using the word "battle" is not an exaggeration, because compassion must be fought for. It runs counter to our natural tendencies. In every intimate relationship, we will find ourselves feeling threatened and/or offended at times. Hot adrenaline will rush through our veins and push us toward anger and, too often, we will succumb to it. But Scripture warns us to discipline ourselves against anger and to do what feels almost dangerous in those moments: to put on compassion. *"But everyone must be quick to hear, slow to speak, and slow to anger; for the anger of man does not achieve the righteousness of God"* (James 1:19-20).

One of the first lessons God taught me was to respond to offensive words and actions with a humble and patient spirit. Walking in gentleness instead of fear and alienation is difficult and unnatural, but it is transformational. The process can begin by inviting Jesus into our conversations. Literally, I imagined Him sitting in the seat between us, then I took my cues from Him. I had to slow down and listen. It wasn't common for me to listen before I spoke, especially when I felt attacked or criticized. And on the rare occasions that I did pause to reflect before opening my mouth, it wasn't often that I asked the Holy Spirit to guide my words. I had to learn to do both. I had to learn "dual listening", listening to my husband and listening to Jesus at the same time.[2]

It was an intimidating task to attend to my husband and seek to understand where he was coming from. I was afraid of being manipulated, afraid of becoming lost in his world, afraid of losing my own point of reference. Jesus confronted my fear and pride in this area and reminded me that His reference point was the one I needed to be loyal to, not my own. He has the corner on truth and reality, not me.

The most immediate and unexpected result of this change in my approach was that, as I slowed down, so did my husband. We became less defensive with each other and our disagreements didn't escalate as quickly or severely. Probably for the first time in our marriage, I began to ask clarifying questions. *"Can you explain what you meant when you said..."* And I discovered that my assumptions about his thoughts and motives were unfair and often inaccurate. He comes at things from an entirely different vantage point, one that I needed to become more familiar with.

Next, I needed to learn how to validate my husband's feelings and perceptions. Again, a daunting task for me. I knew that acknowledging his perceptions was not the same as agreeing with them, but it still felt very risky. I feared that concession or admittance of wrongdoing would put a dent in my armor, that it would be used against me, or that he would lose respect for me. Jesus had to address my fear and pride in this area as well. He reminded me that He never shamed me, never condemned me when I was wrong. My every confession to Him was met with grace and freedom. Therefore, even if my husband responded poorly, Jesus would still grant me grace and dignity.

As an act of faith, I began to verbalize empathy and understanding, and I began to apologize. *"I can understand why you would feel that way...Yes, of course, you would see it that way. I would too. I'm sorry I hurt you.*

I don't want to hurt you." Sometimes I said these things in response to genuine conviction, but not always. Sometimes, I was simply honoring him, even if I didn't think I was wrong, even if I felt misunderstood, and even if I didn't think it was something that should have mattered. Because I knew it was what he needed and deserved from me, because I knew Jesus would hold me together, I acted in humility, set myself aside, and offered compassion. In doing so, David felt heard and validated, and he never used it against me later. Quite the opposite: I saw less and less of his anger and more and more of his heart. He began to trust me and willingly expose the story of his soul. In all these ways, compassion interrupted the cycle of rejection that was killing trust and intimacy in our relationship. It provided us with a safe place to start over and recover what we had lost.

When Forgiveness Isn't Enough

Forgiveness is a powerful thing. It can be a healing balm that ushers freedom into our souls and mends broken relationships. But sometimes negative emotions continue to rage even after we've truly forgiven an offense. I had been forgiving my husband for years, and it wasn't giving me any relief from my feelings of anger, hurt, and resentment. Arguably, forgiveness is the key to healing, but sometimes it just isn't enough. Sometimes, it's just the first step. After forgiving my husband for the wrongs I held against him, I needed to release him from my judgments.

To judge someone is to place a descriptive and conclusive label on them with an attitude of fleshly self-righteousness. This is *not* discernment. Discernment is a gift to be employed for the benefit of others. It is a gift of grace that causes us to pray for others and, in some cases, to invite them into repentance. Judgment is about self-protection and self-promotion. It reduces another person to a specific sin or character flaw and then devalues them on that basis. There is a Judge and there will be a time of judgment, but it is not my job and now is not that time.

Our marriage was profoundly compromised by judgment. I slapped critical labels on David's forehead and made discriminating declarations against him. I felt quite justified in doing this because I had ample evidence to support my judgements. He had sin and weaknesses in his life that had hurt me. He did take some foolish risks, neglect me and the kids, and treat me with great disrespect at times. But his sin wasn't my problem. While it certainly complicated matters, my problem was my response. Out of resentment and a misguided attempt to protect myself, I judged him. In my heart, I accused him. In one way or another, I said things like, *He's selfish and doesn't care about me.* So even after he acknowledged his sin, repented for it, and made necessary changes; even after I forgave him, I still found myself expecting him to fail. In fact, I treated him as if he *was* a failure.

Whether David consciously perceived my judgments or not, they were a spiritual reality and he responded to them. Romans 14:13 says, *"Therefore let us not judge one another anymore, but rather determine this – not to put an obstacle or a stumbling block in a brother's way."* David often "stumbled" over my judgments and acted in a way that was consistent with them. Like a self-fulfilling prophecy, he was living under an unholy pressure to meet my negative expectations. It was only after I removed my judgments through repentance and renounced my agreements with the "accuser of the saints" that I was able to approach him with grace. Then, I could accept him as he is: a man who is capable of making good choices and bad choices; a man who loves me but is not Jesus. I was able to separate his genuine care for me from his sin and human weaknesses. Although he continued to hurt my feelings and disappoint my desires at times, I chose to no longer allow those failures to define him or his love for me.

Unfortunately, if we open a door for judgment and give it room to speak, it will end up turning its wrath upon us as well. Scripture says, *"For in the way you judge, you will be judged; and by your standard of measure, it will be measured to you"* (Matt. 7:2). By judging my husband, I invited judgment upon myself – and I felt the weight of it. A sense of failure was my constant companion. My thoughts and words were accusatory of both myself and my husband. The merciless finger of judgement pointed back at me. But when God graced me with the gift of repentance, it set us both free. In this way, grace covered both my husband's sin and mine.

The roll of the eyes and the firmly set jaw; the *"Here we go again... that's what you always do"* attitude; sarcasm, cynicism, mockery, belittling comments, and keeping score – all these are signs of contemptuous judgment. It is the root problem underneath all failed and failing marriages, and it is unnecessary. It is a false "soulution". It couldn't protect and defend me like Jesus can. He is a far better salve for my wounds, and He specializes in broken hearts. When I allowed Him to, He entered into those dark and secret places and brought deep healing and restoration. When I asked Him to, He answered the pressing questions that arose from those places. It was His delight and His desire. He had been waiting for an invitation all along.

Questions for Reflection

1. How can compassion interrupt a cycle of rejection?

2. Why would forgiveness not be enough?

3. What is the difference between discernment and judgement?

Happy Wife, Happy Life?

A friend of mine says that God made men like file cabinets. A man opens one file drawer at a time, thinks about one thing at a time, tackles one problem at a time, and strives for one goal at a time. A man is driven to meet the specific challenges he encounters in each drawer. And he prefers to spend his time in the drawers that are going well, because he feels validated as a man when he is successful. Generally, he thinks compartmentally and relates to others objectively. He feels good about himself when he's performing well.

On the contrary, women are more like walk-in-closets. Everything is on display at the same time. All that is beautiful and orderly shares the stage with that which is dated and two sizes too small. Since a woman doesn't compartmentalize like a man does, she doesn't look at her heels with satisfaction, because they sit next to the garden boots which remind her that there's weeding to be done. She doesn't look at her folded socks and smile with a sense of accomplishment, because her nightgowns look dingy and she wonders if it's a reflection of the spark in her marriage. This life is complicated and beset with problems; therefore, every time she looks in her closet, she will find something out of place. But because she is not inherently performance-driven in the same way a man is, she is not undone by problems. They are, in fact, an opportunity to experience what makes her happy. She welcomes others into her closet and shares her life and heart with them. Feeling connected with and important to others makes her feel validated as a woman. Generally speaking, she thinks holistically, relates empathetically, and feels good about herself when she is wanted and esteemed.

God designed these differences to serve as complementary gifts to the sexes. Unfortunately, we have a tendency to take gifts and turn them into idols. This is what happens when a man buys into the lie that it's his job to make his wife happy. If she believes the same lie, things get really hairy. You've seen it a thousand times. A man draws upon his strengths as a problem solver to come through for his wife and secure her satisfaction and his success. She feels loved and pursued, so she gives him more hoops to jump through. This little dance works temporarily. But because they have placed their sense of worth in the loving but limited hands of one another, it won't end well.

We fell into this lie from the get-go. Remember my childhood fantasy? I believed that a husband could give me identity, worth, and security. I often invited my unsuspecting husband into my closet and asked him to do what only God can do: tell me who I am, bestow value and unconditional love, and infuse me with purpose and significance. He shot aimlessly at moving targets, but always failed to give me what I needed – because God had not equipped him for that job! After a few short years, he realized that my happiness couldn't be acquired as easily as he had thought. He grew weary and, in one way or fifty, checked out and moved on to other, more rewarding pursuits. I became resentful of him, thinking he either didn't understand me or he didn't care. He felt like a failure and I felt alone.

Fortunately, failure taught us a very valuable lesson. We learned to release each other from the obligation to answer each other's souls' deepest needs. We learned to shed the habit of managing each other's thoughts, feelings, and behaviors. In other words, we learned to engage one another in a way that was honest, intimate, and empathetic, but not codependent. My husband learned that marriage wasn't about performance, but partnership. He had to get his validation from God and allow me the freedom to express a vast array of emotions without trying to fix them. I learned that he can be my friend, partner, and lover, but never my source. I had to repent for idolizing my husband and give my heart needs to God instead. By releasing my husband and clinging to Jesus, I found that He is far more available, far more relational, far more insightful, and overwhelmingly more validating than my husband is. And only then did I start to truly appreciate the gift my husband was intended to be. Only then was I able to delight in him.

Rest

It was a quiet afternoon, and I was doing household chores, mulling over a conversation we'd had the night before. It was concerning an old, unresolved issue that neither of us enjoyed rehearsing. It always made him feel defensive and it made me feel insecure and doubtful of his affections. Part of me was angry and exasperated, and part of me was grieving the fact that, despite the tremendous work we had done and progress we had made, there was still sin and pain between us. The anger won out and my thoughts turned toxic. After all that we'd been through, I was angry that we couldn't get past this issue. I wondered how he could claim to love me and yet continue to let this go unresolved.

"Stop putting his love to the test." The words were a sharp interruption. I recognized the voice, but the rebuke was not well-received. *Really? He's the victim here?* That certainly didn't feel true. I was feeling quite taken for granted, and quite helpless to stop it. *"You didn't earn his love, and you can't protect or manage his love. It's been Mine from the beginning. I will grow and purify his love for both you and Me."*

My heart softened as I remembered the story. Long before I loved him, long before I was lovely, my husband had loved me. He had always been the pursuer, always offered himself to me whether I reciprocated or not. As a young wife, I was perplexed by this. I offered him very little and caused him great pain, yet he loved me. When I would ask him what he loved about me, what I did to win his favor, he would respond flatly, *"I don't know."* He couldn't offer me one reason, and he didn't know how to make one up. It was unnerving. I didn't doubt him, but I wanted to believe that I could earn his devotion and therefore secure it somehow.

Is this not what we learn in this world? There are no guarantees in love. Everyone has a limit placed on how much they will endure, how much they are willing to give, and what they expect in return. If we want to keep their affections, we must know what they expect of us and find a way to deliver. That certainly had been my experience, but God would not allow it in our marriage.

He placed a portion of His special and enduring love for me in the young heart of my husband. And it was God who was protecting and purifying that love. When I was tempted to test it, tempted to earn it, tempted to doubt it, God reminded me that His love doesn't work like that. I can't manipulate Him that way, and He wouldn't allow me to manipulate my husband's love either. I had to simply rest and receive it.

Risky Business

Toward the end of our reconciliation journey, God took me deeper. He showed me a vow I had made as a child that was having a significant impact on my marriage. I had vowed to never need a man. In my young estimation, men could not be trusted. To trust someone is to believe the best about them, to anticipate good things from them, and that felt foolishly dangerous to me. Even though I idealized and idolized marriage, I had a bucket full of negative expectations and, in many ways, would not allow myself to be vulnerable. This self-sabotage was unintentional, but it had infiltrated my thoughts and had deep roots embedded within my soul.

I had already repented for the judgments I had made against men and against my husband, and for the idol I had made of marriage. But when God showed me the inner vow that I had made to never need a man and I repented for it; a paralyzing fear bubbled up from within my heart. Among other things was the fear of abandonment and rejection. I feared that if my husband knew how much I needed him, wanted him, and depended upon him, he would reject me. Even worse, I feared that if he knew the power he had over me because of these things, he would use it against me. He would try to break me. Then I would be alone, and it would confirm the lies of the enemy: that I didn't deserve to be loved, that I wasn't good enough, that I was weak.

Because of these unconscious fears, I had mismanaged our

relationship through manipulation and control. I alternated between weak desolation and hardened domination. In some ways, I withheld myself from David and never went beyond the boundaries of reciprocity. I forgot that he needed me to be his friend, his encourager, his lover, and his safe place just as much as I needed him to be those things for me. In other ways, I was harsh and demanding, as if he didn't want to love me, didn't care about me. I appealed to his sense of duty, not knowing that duty and obligation kill love.

When God confronted me with this sin, I repented, but that didn't heal the wound. I needed more than forgiveness and freedom. I needed healing, and that required more time and several intimate encounters with Him as He brought me back to some very painful memories. Fortunately, that's often where God's love and comfort show up in greatest measure. He is so very gentle and near to the brokenhearted. He does His best work in hidden places.

Out of that healing came a quiet trust that God is in me and has given me something of worth to offer, that I have a role to play, and that my dignity is secure in Him. Therefore, I began taking risks. I put my years of intimate knowledge of my husband to good use. I sought ways to love him with more intention, choosing to do and say things that would matter only and deeply to him. I anticipated some of his needs and met them before being asked – and I did so lavishly, so that he would know it was born of love and delight, not obligation. I also began to set my needs and desires before him *softly*, giving him the opportunity to respond with love and kindness rather than duty. It cost me a great deal of courage and vulnerability, but he often responded with quiet acknowledgment rather than resentment. Thus, a kinder culture was created in our marriage and we began to experience something that could best be described as joy.

Conclusion

It is quite difficult to dredge through the muck and mire of our marital war zone. Often as I wrote, I have walked away from my computer feeling as if I needed a shower to wash away the bitterness and toxic pride that so permeated those years. But they were also a gift. Because of His mercy, God allowed us to endure those harsh and desolate years in order that, when He redeemed us, we would never go back. We have never anguished over what we once had or who we once were. Instead, we are forever grateful that He gave us a way of escape. His path is utter sweetness to us now, because it rendered unto us a longing for Him, for freedom, and for the life of abundance which only He can provide. More than a decade after saying "*I do*", I got my friend back and so much more. I could finally say that I loved my husband in every sense of the word, saw him as a gift, and would choose him all over again. By the grace of God, what began as "combat training" was transformed into "marital bliss."

Questions for Reflection

1. *Do you agree that to trust someone is to believe the best about them and anticipate good things from them?*

2. *"We learned to shed the habit of managing each other's thoughts, feelings, and behaviors. In other words, we learned to engage one another in a way that was honest, intimate, and empathetic, but not codependent." What does this mean? How is it possible?*

3. *How was "drudging through the muck and mire of our marital war zone" a gift?*

Chapter 8

Actualizing Abundance

"A book of remembrance was written before Him for those who fear the Lord and who esteem His name." (Malachi 3:16)

Captain Confident Married Completely Complicated

The drain of work and the responsibilities of life had driven us to distraction. Spent and silly, we put everything aside for the evening to talk and sip tea. While lounging on a heap of blankets and pillows, my husband and I rehearsed the previous weeks and laughed at our mishaps. One cup and two yawns later, he took a detour. Propping himself up on his elbows, he suggested we do something special to celebrate our anniversary. With just a hint of excitement in his voice he said, *"Let's hike the Grand Canyon and sleep at the bottom!"* I laughed in disbelief. The man with a serious aversion to all forms of celebration was aware that a special occasion was coming up? It took more than a decade to convince him that Christmas did indeed merit his attention. And here he was suggesting an anniversary getaway? I was delighted by his enthusiasm and eager to encourage such romantic gestures, but guilty of one slight miscalculation – and revealed it when I said, *"I didn't know they had hotels at the bottom of the Grand Canyon!"* The look on his face changed from animated anticipation to stunned disbelief. Not sure if he had understood me, I repeated myself, which turned out to be completely unnecessary. He had heard me all right. He was getting out his phone to make sure he had proof of that moment for all time. And so, we ended our pleasant evening with a geography lesson and a good belly laugh.

Captain Confident married Completely Complicated. Go figure. My husband could live in a cardboard box and eat danger for breakfast as long as he had the freedom to roam. There's nothing he wouldn't try if given the opportunity – and he's had lots of opportunities! He has lived overseas, on a submarine, in the rural Midwest, the urban West Coast, and the heart of the Bible Belt. Regardless of his specific locale, he's never failed to find avenues for perilous exploration. He's gone swimming on the equator in Singapore, shipwreck diving in Guam, walleye fishing in Canada, yacht racing in Australia, and downhill skiing in the Tetons. And of course, he's already hiked the Grand Canyon. He went down the South Rim and back again in a day. He laughs about the fact that he didn't take enough water and had a little misunderstanding with a rattlesnake over the possession of a certain rock. There's no doubt, my man would gladly leave suburbia to spend the night with the snakes, scorpions, and coyotes. In a heartbeat, he'd grab a rock for a pillow and sleep soundly next to his wide-eyed, panic-stricken wife. Because, when it comes to taking risks, I'd prefer to stick with rearranging the furniture or trying a new hairstyle. Of course, I appreciate David's need to conquer the great unknown and, because I love him, I try to support him in his bold undertakings. Because he loves me, we have a life insurance policy with his name on it.

Perilous Predictions

In my defense, I wasn't born with a geriatric mentality on life. Believe it or not, I used to be almost adventurous and carefree. Most of us come charging out of the chute assuming the risks are manageable, and the odds are in our favor. Soon enough, we discover that life gives one heck of a bumpy ride. In my experience, life bucked me off quicker than I expected and left me too disoriented to know what I'd fallen into, too naïve to have seen it coming, and far too helpless to get myself out of harm's way. I realized all too soon that the unfair, the unjust, and the unexpected are more commonplace than the grand and the glorious. Before I knew it, I was fighting fewer battles, uttering weaker prayers, and chasing smaller dreams. The fear of loss and the sting of disappointment taught me to expect little and offer even less.

Of course, I was too preoccupied with the business of life to see this for myself. Someone else brought it to my attention. It happened one fall afternoon while I was sitting in those uncomfortable little office chairs in my doctor's examination room. I watched him carefully as he scrutinized every page of the very intrusive medical questionnaire his nurse had had me fill out. The first section was my family medical history, which would give even the most humanitarian of doctors optimism about their financial future. There aren't too many diseases, ailments, or illnesses that go unrepresented in my family tree. But the fun ended there, because what followed was my lifestyle report and that was nothing but a long list of *n/a's* and *no's*. After reviewing everything, he set the questionnaire down, collected his thoughts, and matter-of-factly concluded, *"Unless you decide to take up skydiving, you're most likely to die of a car accident. Statistically, you're too careful to die of anything else."*

Didn't see that coming. I stared at him blankly for a moment, half amused by his medical palm-reading and half annoyed by his presumption. I hadn't seen him enough times to know if his medical expertise was worth much, but I was confident his pseudo-psychic powers weren't worth a hill of beans. But if I ignored the absurdity of it, I had to admit that it was an intriguing idea. Hypothetically, if he was correct and a car accident would be my fateful demise, then I could forget about my contingency plans for snake bites, shark attacks, kidnappings, and the apocalypse. Despite my very reasonable skepticism, for just a moment, I felt the exhilaration of a fearless life. And my dear friends, a fearless life would be a game changer!

After thanking Dr. Divination for his interest in my future, I drove home wondering what kind of life I had been passing up. It was such a silly way for God to get my attention, but it had worked. As clear as day, I knew that I had been living under the disorienting haze of fear. I was stuck in the survival zone, striving only for the hope of keeping my marriage afloat, keeping my kids alive, getting through the day, and avoiding catastrophe. It was nothing but fear-based cynicism, an ugly coping mechanism erected in hopes that I would become immune to disappointment and harm. Sadly, it never worked because pain always finds a way in. Nevertheless, it sure was limiting God's grace in my life and stifling my appreciation for His goodness and glory.

Read the Fine Print

Before going any further, I'd like to pause and say that this kind of shrinking back is common to all of us. Thus, the issue of fear is given much real estate in Scripture. In the NASB, the words *fear* (313), *afraid* (164), *dread* (46), *anxious* (11), and *worry* (9) are found 543 times. They are seen so frequently in both testaments that fear could be considered a theme. Not surprisingly, the Bible is equally forthright about the brutal realities that cause us to become afraid. Sin and suffering are not downplayed at in the slightest. On the contrary, war, plagues, slavery, famine, pestilence, rape, murder, incest, injustice, and persecution of every kind are on full display. And, of course, we know that the authors of Scripture had lives besmeared with sorrows. Moses was born during a time of mass infanticide and spent the bulk of his life wandering in the wilderness. Most of the major and minor prophets were martyred. The writers of the gospels, Matthew, Mark, and Luke, all met violent ends. Paul wrote Ephesians, Philippians, Colossians, and Philemon while in chains and was later murdered by Nero. Peter was crucified upside down. John, writer of the gospel of John as well as 1, 2, and 3 John, is the only disciple thought to have died of natural causes. But his final book, Revelation, was written while in exile on the island of Patmos. Consequently, we can be certain about the fact that the Bible was written *by* those who knew distresses of every kind, and it was written *for* those who were enduring much the same. It would be fair to say that the backdrop of Scripture can best be described as turbulent. Therefore, our staggered gaze at our lot on planet Earth is certainly rooted in circumstantial reality and strongly validated by the Scriptures. Yet we are instructed to not give way to fear.

I'm not a scholar, but it looks to me as if Scripture does two things. First, it honestly and specifically confirms the cruelties of our earthly existence. Then, at the same time and often without taking a breath, it heralds the existence of a greater and grander reality, one which has already begun and will continue to play out long after this disappointing chapter is finished. Set alongside narratives of abuses, woven into prophetic warnings of persecution, and contrasting stories of the harshest of circumstances are assurances of God's sovereign presence, promises of great reward, offers of ever-present comfort and strength, and the realization of abundance. These provocative passages give us an anchor for our weary souls, challenging us to defy fatalism and grab hold of hope instead. Consider the following:

> *Blessed is the man who perseveres under trial, for once he has been approved, he will receive the crown of life, which the Lord has promised to those who love Him.* (James 1:12)

> *...according to His great mercy [He] has caused us to be born again to a living hope through the resurrection of Jesus Christ from the dead, to obtain an inheritance which is imperishable and undefiled and will not fade away, reserved in heaven for you, who*

are protected by the power of God through faith for a salvation ready to be revealed in the last time. In this you greatly rejoice, even though now for a little while, if necessary, you have been distressed by various trials, that the proof of your faith, being more precious than gold which is perishable, even though tested by fire, may be found to result in praise and glory and honor at the revelation of Jesus Christ... (1 Peter 1:3-7)

Consider it all joy, my brethren, when you encounter various trials, knowing that the testing of your faith produces endurance. (James 1:2-3)

Do not fear what you are about to suffer. Behold, the devil is about to cast some of you into prison, so that you will be tested, and you will have tribulation ten days. Be faithful until death, and I will give you the crown of life. (Rev. 2:10)

Do not deliver me over to the desire of my adversaries, for false witnesses have risen against me, and such as breathe out violence. I would have despaired unless I had believed that I would see the goodness of the Lord in the land of the living. Wait for the Lord; be strong and let your heart take courage; yes, wait for the Lord. (Ps. 27:12-14)

Even though I walk through the valley of the shadow of death, I fear no evil, for You are with me; Your rod and Your staff, they comfort me. You prepare a table before me in the presence of my enemies; You have anointed my head with oil; my cup overflows. Surely goodness and lovingkindness will follow me all the days of my life... (Ps. 23:4-6)

For just as the sufferings of Christ are ours in abundance, so also our comfort is abundant through Christ. (2 Cor. 1:5)

And everyone who has left houses or brothers or sisters or father or mother or children or farms for My name's sake, will receive many times as much, and will inherit eternal life. (Matt. 19:29)

The thief comes only to steal and kill and destroy; I came that they may have life and have it abundantly. (John 10:10)

In the world you have tribulation but take courage; I have overcome the world. (John 16:33)

According to these verses, pain and loss will leave a mark on our story, but a lifetime of the gravest of difficulties cannot eclipse the greatness of our inheritance as saints. These passages and many others tell us that the agonies of this life are temporary and feeble manifestations of a kingdom coming to ruin. They are like birth pains that will usher in God's heavenly kingdom (Matt. 24). Then, according to the prophecies, when the earth is full of the knowledge of God, the reign of evil will be overturned. Death will be swallowed up and all will be made new again. We will behold the fulfillment of God's good and glorious promises. On that day, we will enjoy a new world order, one that will be infinitely better than the first.

That, my friends, is some good news. With great longing, we join all the saints who look forward to the coming glory. But there's more to the promise than that. Scripture presents to us something both present and transcendent. The offer is not just eternal life, but also abundant life (John 10:10). King David said that he would see God's favor, not only in heaven but in this life (Ps. 27:12-14). He also declared that this favor would be consistent and lifelong (Ps. 23:4-6). Jesus declared that those who follow Him will be recompensed for their losses in this life (Matt.19:29). Paul promised comfort to those who suffer with Christ (2 Cor. 1:5). Peter said that we possess not only a future hope, but a living hope (1 Peter 1:3). If I'm reading Scripture accurately, then the immense and meaningless grief that we endure can be surpassed by the joy of our salvation, the promise of eternity, and the presence of God's kind favor *today*. Fear might be a natural response to the extreme vulnerability we feel, but there's something greater and grander for us to hang onto. And that "something greater" can be tasted right here and right now.

Questions for Reflection

1. *Can you relate with the statement, "Before I knew it, I was fighting fewer battles, uttering weaker prayers, and chasing smaller dreams"? If so, when, and why?*

2. *In what ways would you say you're "living under the disorienting haze of fear"?*

3. What would a fearless life look like for you?

4. Scripture does two things simultaneously. First, it honestly and specifically confirms the cruelties of <u>what</u>? Then, at the same time and often without taking a breath, it heralds the existence of <u>what</u>?

5. What's the difference between a future hope and a living hope?

Gut Check

Here's the rub. These verses sound awe-inspiring and victorious, but do they deliver? From my vantage point, too many of us are enduring the difficulties of this present age wanting to believe these lofty assurances in Scripture are true, but we haven't seen them pan out. So, not only are we shaking in our boots because life isn't what we thought it would be, but we fall prey to cynicism because this Christianity thing isn't what we thought it would be or what it *promised* to be.

Christ's death on the cross paid for the sins of the world and He has overcome the world, but what we experience day-in and day-out can feel more like subjection to it. The cross has changed everything, yet there is nothing new under the sun. We trust and get betrayed. We take risks and fail. We invest and get cheated. We sacrifice and get falsely accused. We become jaded, we grow weary, we lose vision, and we lose heart. We feel like it's always going to be this way, and then we begin to identify ourselves by the series of sad happenings that tie the years of our lives together. It doesn't take long before the years of unmet needs, unanswered questions, and unresolved pain cause us to forget who we are and why we're here. As John Eldredge puts it, *"After a while, the accumulation of event after event that we do not like and do not understand erodes our confidence that we are part of something grand and good and reduces us to a survivalist mind-set."*[1]

I suppose, at times, we feel like the disciples on the road to Emmaus: dejected and disillusioned because they had thought Jesus was about to do something spectacular, and instead, He gave up the kingdom, got Himself killed, and decimated their dreams. *"But we were hoping that it was He who was going to redeem Israel"* (Luke 24:21). Suddenly, their hero was lying lifeless in a tomb and their chance for a Roman upset was lost. Their confidence in the ancient prophecies was shaken and their hearts broken. God did not come through for them the way they thought He would, and as a result, they were hopeless and heartsick. Proverbs sums it up well: *"Hope deferred makes the heart sick"* (Prov. 13:12).

Bind My Heart to Yours

That downcast place is where I had found myself at the beginning of my healing journey. I was utterly consumed with fear and cynicism: fear that I didn't have what it takes to make it in this world, and cynical doubts that God cared for me and would come to my rescue. But a lot had happened in my life and heart since then! Over and over again, He had proven His tender care, His faithfulness, and His compassion for me. He had pursued me with a passionate desire for my good. And wasn't I changed because of it? More than that, weren't *we* changed? For Pete's sake, it had been seven years since David and I were brought to our lowest low, spiritually, emotionally, financially, and relationally. Seven years of humble apologies, Dave Ramsey's Financial Peace and the infamous *"gazelle intensity"*, the healing balm of church community, and a heavy dose of God's redeeming love! It had been hard work, but there was much growth and fruit.

So, why was I living as if the other shoe was about to drop? Why was I haunted by a sense of dread as if, just around the corner, was a crisis so disorienting and chaotic that I would no longer be able to hear Him, feel Him, or receive His love and guidance? Despite all that God had done for me and for us in those years, why did I think that one sudden blow would cause us to lose the ground we had gained, as if I was one step away from going back to the darkness I had come from? After all we'd been through, why did I still think I had to be hypervigilant and alert to all possible threats as if I wasn't seen, wasn't surrounded, and wasn't safe?

Refusing to relinquish one ounce of that which had already been conquered, I spent the better part of the next year trying to resolve my fears and anxious insecurities. I buckled up and got back to work, surrendering, standing on truth, and praying for freedom. Preaching purpose to myself, I focused on the life and mindset I wanted to have and refused to retreat. I read the biographies of men and women who finished well, borrowing their courage to stand firm in the face of great adversity. I read *Fearless* by Max Lucado, *Radical* by David Platt, *In a Pit with a Lion on a Snowy Day* by Mark Batterson. I went through the *Breaking Free* study by Beth Moore. I employed every tool in my toolbox to eradicate this stronghold of fear and grab onto the promise of abundance.

One of my prayers during this time was that God would remove my fear of going to the mission field and that, if it was His desire for us, He would give me a passion that matched David's. Twice we had considered it in years past, and twice we had stayed. I've told you about the first time. It was when we were first married and living in the tiny duplex apartment. Whether God had wanted us to go then or not was still a sore subject between us. David maintained that, had we gone, God would have provided the community, support, and guidance we needed. And although I regretted the way I had defiantly refused to go, I still thought we were too ill-prepared and unruly to tackle the stress of an overseas venture together. In the end, we agreed to disagree.

But there was no such disagreement about the second time. It was several years later, just before I hit my "wall of works". I sensed the divide in our marriage and suspected that my killing David's dream of missions was a contributing factor. Going overseas was my solution. I figured I could suck it up and hold my breath if it meant making up for lost opportunities and giving my husband a shot at doing what he loved. Once again, we applied to go. It was a foolhardy decision to blaze ahead of God, and I quickly found myself sleepless and spiraling. In no time at all, I was in no condition to go anywhere. We withdrew our application, and I was thrown into a season of healing, beginning with what I've described as my "First Great Awakening."

Even though God had guided and protected us despite these two mistakes – defiantly digging in my heels and then heading off in the wrong direction and for the wrong reasons – I wanted to be fully submitted to God's leading. I also wanted to honor my husband's gifts and dreams. Therefore, I persistently asked God to settle my anxieties and change my desires if overseas missions was indeed His direction for us. My prayer became the same as David Livingstone's: *"God, send me anywhere, only go with me. Lay any burden on me, only sustain me. And sever any tie in my heart except the tie that binds my heart to Yours."*[2]

Thankfully, after a year of prayer and a passionate pursuit of freedom, I worried less and began to feel much more courageous and curious about life. Oddly, I also became quite restless. I was fed up with hiding in a corner and dwelling on the past. I was ready to close out our lengthy chapter of brokenness and deep soul work, ready to move on. So, when our dear missionary friends returned from Asia with stories of the many needs and growing possibilities there, I began to wonder if God would have us join them. We had long since supported their ministry and I had worked on several writing projects for them over the years. Many times they had suggested we visit, but I had always been too afraid and knew that one or two weeks wouldn't be enough time for me to get my bearings or contribute anything worthwhile. But perhaps a 6-12-month stay would be enough to get our feet wet, expose our kids to the Gospel in a different context, and give us a chance to step outside of our box. Perhaps it would be an opportunity to see if God had something and someplace different for us?

We mulled it over for a few weeks, then decided to test the waters. For the third time in our marriage, we began exploring the possibility of going overseas. We met with the elders in our church and prepared to sell our house. David spoke to his boss about working remotely. Truth be told, I didn't know if God was calling us overseas or not, but I was willing and, dare I say, even eager to find out. Thus, we decided to take some steps in that direction and see what God would do. I was ready to face my fears, itching for a change of scenery and excited to take on a new challenge. In the strangest way possible, that's exactly what happened next.

Questions for Reflection

1. *Has God ever "failed" you in a way that left you feeling like the disciples on the road to Emmaus?*

2. *Have you ever felt disappointed as if this Christian life isn't what you thought it should or would be? Where did your expectations come from?*

3. *After so many years of God's faithfulness, what was Janalee afraid of?*

4. *What did she do to combat her fears?*

Come What May

One month later, God closed the mission's door for the third time. In October of 2015, our state came to a standstill as a historic 1,000 year flood did its worst. A stalled front offshore, combined with a low-pressure system to the west and Hurricane Joaquin to the east, led to a torrential 12-25 inches of rain across the state. We were brought to our knees. Our governor declared a state of emergency and called in the National Guard. Rivers burst their banks, washing away roads, bridges, vehicles, and homes. Hundreds of people had to be rescued from their rooftops and their vehicles. Nineteen people lost their lives.

We had decided to wait out what we assumed would be another uneventful hurricane at my mom and step-dad's house, one block away and uphill from our own. David and I were sleeping on a leaky air mattress in Mom's sewing room, dreaming of our own bed. Because of the hype, we had been glued to the Weather Channel until midnight, but the last report had predicted a measly one inch of rain, so we went to bed and made plans to return home the next day. By 5:00 a.m., that one inch of rain had turned into 15. We woke up to flashing red lights, scrambled to the nearest window, and saw a fire truck parked atop the nearest hill with a crew of firemen wading through the water to the next-door neighbor's house, which was visibly flooding and on fire. We hurried out onto the front porch as the neighbor family headed up the hill to their car. Feeling quite stunned and helpless, we offered some warm clothes and our deepest sympathies. Drenched and disheveled, one of them stopped to say, *"One inch, huh? There's nothing to be done tonight. Hope yours fares better than ours."*

Experience told us that our house was likely surrounded by the swollen river that raged in front of us and was much too deep to navigate. So we returned to our deflated mattress, sank to the floor, and stared at the ceiling. In the stillness of waiting, the presence of God was palpable. I burned the moment into my mind and rehearsed all that I had been learning about courage and trust, believing I would need it for the road ahead. David reached for my hand and whispered, *"Come what may."* It was his pet phrase, a gentle reminder that he would love me despite the circumstances, that we would travel the road together. I squeezed his hand and responded with, *"I love you too."* He soon drifted back off to sleep, but I felt too awake and alive to join him. Whether it was faith or adrenaline, I don't know, but my heart felt full and expectant. There was no doubt in my mind that we were in the midst of God's perfect will and that His handiwork was on display. Uttering staccato prayers, I silently praised Him for His mysterious grace and wondered how this very unexpected story would play out.

By mid-afternoon the next day, the waters had receded enough for us to face what had become of our house. We put on our tall rain boots and trudged from one front porch to another until we reached our own. The yard was littered with rocks, debris, and a few dead fish. Our crawl space and garage were full of water and our fence was laid low. Surprisingly, the water had not gone over our floors, but they were thick and soft, as were our walls and ceilings. Evidently, the rising water had reached our floors from underneath, and the roof had failed badly.

It didn't take long to see that the damage was far more extensive than we had first thought. Things are often worse than they appear when water is involved. Fortunately, David had started demolition right away. He donned a hazmat suit and stripped walls and ceilings, took down the damaged chimney, tarped the roof, and did his best to drain and scrub the crawl space and garage. Whatever wasn't destroyed had to be bleached and dried, which fast became an overwhelming task. A few weeks later, a local company came to our aid and set up shop. Unfortunately, it took weeks for the weather system to move out of our area, and the ground was still too saturated to absorb another rainfall. Before they had finished, a secondary flood hit and all their equipment and hard work was washed away

As soon as the roads were safe again, FEMA was first to arrive on the scene. They assessed the damage to our house and personal property and announced that they would cover whatever insurance did not, provided that we first apply for a small business loan. Not knowing the difference between FEMA and our private flood insurance company, we did as they suggested and secured a loan for $25,000, hoping we wouldn't need it. Later, we would discover that the small business loan was their means of covering damages and it would also disqualify us from most sources of charitable and government aid.

Next, the county sent out adjusters to do their own assessment. They suggested we approve a "substantially damaged" declaration since ours was a flood-prone property in a regulation floodway and thus a red dot they wanted to remove from their maps. Because the "substantially damaged" status would require us to elevate, demolish, or relocate the house, we delayed a decision in order to gather more information. We did, however, take the opportunity to see if there was anything else that could be done. If we demolished the house, could we deed the land to the county? Would they apply for a federal grant on our behalf? If we simply repaired the house, would they help us find a solution to the chronic flooding problem? Claiming lack of funds and personnel, they informed us that they would not be getting involved.

Meanwhile, our private flood insurance company and our homeowner's company sent out adjusters and promptly denied our claims. Friends recommended that we contact a public adjuster to see if a lawsuit would motivate them to take our situation seriously, but finding one was more difficult than I expected. When I finally did locate one, he lived in another state and told me it would be a lost cause. I explained the history of flooding in our neighborhood, the ongoing battle we had waged with the county over its watershed mitigation policies, and the response of our insurance companies. He sympathized but discouraged us from taking legal action. A class-action suit would be our best option, but not possible under the circumstances and too costly. We would be fighting against entities with deep pockets and nothing but time and money on their side. He wished us well and asked us to let him know how things turned out. Less than one month in, there was nothing but closed doors in front of us and a rising mountain of debt and hard labor.

Shame, Fear, and Control

And just like that, we were in crisis again, abruptly stripped of all that felt familiar and safe. It was terribly disorienting and certainly not the kind of change we had been expecting. Quite the opposite. Our hope that we could close out our extensive chapter of suffering and stupidity, that we could enjoy a fresh start, ended up producing nothing but a worse case of the "same old same old." Drawing lines of correlation between the poor decisions we had made in the past and the circumstances we were enduring at that moment, it seemed reasonable to conclude that our cup of consequences was not yet full. It appeared that our request for pardon had been denied.

Just weeks before, I had been soaring on the wings of hope that God was moving on our behalf, that He saw us in the light of His favor and therefore all would be well. Evidently, I was sorely mistaken, and the familiarity of that scenario made me sick to my stomach. It wasn't the first time I had walked into a tragic situation full of naïve optimism, only to hobble away with scars. And here I was again. Without a hint of caution, without a skeptical pause, I had dared to dream, dared to trust in His goodness, and He slammed the door, bolted it shut, and swallowed the key. The other shoe had fallen, and I felt like an idiot for not seeing it coming. In my heart, I said to myself, *This is what we deserve. Once again, I thought God had forgiven us, that He was redeeming us, but that kind of foolhardy confidence has always gotten me nowhere. There are no free passes in this life and it's never safe to let down my guard. We'll never outlive what we've done, and He'll never forget who we were.*

Our circumstances were fast becoming painful, but what I felt in that moment was the tyrannical trio of shame, fear, and control. Can you hear it? *Shame* told me that God was punishing us. *Fear* told me that it wasn't safe to trust in a good God. *Control* stepped up to the plate and told me that the solution was hypervigilant, self-sufficient cynicism. If I laid low and expected nothing, I wouldn't be so disappointed.

These three forces run through most of our sin struggles and cast a dark shadow over our innermost thoughts and feelings. They were bolted to the floor of sin nature the moment Adam and Eve fell. Their deep souls, which had once been filled with a sense of wholeness and security, were suddenly flooded with the dreadful knowledge that they had become weak, vulnerable, unclean, and unworthy. This is the message behind all shame. And then just as suddenly, fear entered the scene, the same fear that grips us all: that they would be exposed for who they had become and therefore experience the pain that was due them – rejection, condemnation, punishment, and abandonment. Thus, Adam and Eve tried to meet their own needs, protect themselves, and gain some control – as we all do. They hid themselves, first with fig leaves and then with the garden itself. *"I heard the sound of You in the garden, and I was afraid because I was naked; so I hid myself"* (Gen. 3:10). This nefarious split-second domino effect became hardwired into their souls, programmed into the spiritual DNA that is passed down through every generation. (Klystra, 354)[3]

I'm embarrassed to report how easily I embraced the false and familiar narrative myself. Too quickly, I lost sight of God's good heart toward me and hailed the oppressive cloud of hopelessness. But I didn't stay there long, because my death-like descent was interrupted by some life-giving words. We were meeting with our community group, sharing what had transpired thus far. Too tired to pretend, I confessed that I felt the flood to be a declaration, a pronouncement that we had reached the limit of what could be atoned for, that the senseless madness with which we had conducted ourselves would never be outlived, never acquitted. I suspected we would need to carry the disgrace of our sins' consequence to the grave.

At first, there were only deep sighs and sad faces. But slowly our friends ventured to ask a few cautious questions and offer gentle words of encouragement. Never one to wince or look away from such displays of defenseless exposure, our friend Tammie led the way by reading aloud this passage from Isaiah:

> *"Comfort, O comfort My people," says your God. "Speak kindly to Jerusalem; and call out to her, that her warfare has ended, that her iniquity has been removed, that she has received of the Lord's hand double for all her sins".* (Isaiah 40:1-2)

I asked her to read it again and let the words sink into my soul. I didn't understand what it all meant, but it sounded like good news and I knew it was for me. Later, I looked up the passage myself and searched for the meaning of the term *"double for all her sins."* According to Ray Stedman, it is a reference to an Eastern custom.

If a man owed a debt he could not pay, his creditor would write the amount of the debt on a paper and nail it to the front door of the man's house so that everyone passing would see that here was a man who had not paid his debts. But if someone paid the debt for him, then the creditor would double the paper over and nail it to the door as a testimony that the debt had been fully paid. This beautiful picture therefore is the announcement to Israel as a nation that in the death and resurrection of her Messiah her debt has been fully paid.[4]

Even though I deserve due penalty, the Lord of new mercies has covered my shame by paying my sin debts in full. This is what Paul declares in the book of Colossians:

And when you were dead in your transgressions and the uncircumcision of your flesh, He made you alive together with Him, having forgiven us all our transgressions, having cancelled out the certificate of debt consisting of decrees against us and which was hostile to us; and Has taken it out of the way, having nailed it to the cross. When He had disarmed the rulers and authorities, He made a public display of them, having triumphed over them through Him. (Col. 2:13-15)

God has been doing this from the beginning. He covered Adam and Eve with animal skins, He covered Israel with the Passover blood, and He covers us with the blood of Christ. Therefore, our circumstances did not change the reality of His love and acceptance. It is His desire to show us compassion and unfailing love (Micah 7:18). That reminder was enough to resuscitate my failing heart and renew my confidence that God's desire was to bless us rather than punish us.

But, were we to take this passage literally? Wouldn't it be presumptuous and all too prosperity-gospel-like? I wasn't willing to make the leap that it meant He would also cover our financial debts. Honestly, I felt that this would be too audacious and short-sighted to consider. But, whether it was literal or figurative, I knew He was going to come through. This was confirmed by the letters, emails, and texts of encouragement and hope sent to us by friends and family members.

We're praying and believing that this hard time is fertilizer for dreams God is going to give you. We know he sees you and has good plans for you. He doesn't waste hard times. He's never failed. I'm excited for you. Anticipate if you can. I'm anticipating for you. He is so good! – Kris

Jesus said, "It was neither that this man sinned nor his parents, but it was so that the works of God might be displayed in Him" (John 9:3). Be encouraged! If God is for you, who can be against you? – Wynetta

God will go before you and lead you. I have a feeling that He is going to use this to get you out of the mess. It's going to take work, but you don't shy away from hard work. Be encouraged, change is happening, and I believe it's for good. I can see it! – Jenny

"But when I am afraid, I will put my trust in you. I praise God for what He has promised. I trust in God, so why should I be afraid? What can mere man do to me?" (Psalm 56:3-4). He sees you. He loves you. He has promised to be your provider. He is for you and nothing moves His heart more than your praises during troubled times. – Sandrine

The Father is so generous with His affections. He comforts, woos, and nourishes us in countless ways, but perhaps His favorite is to employ His body of believers. Throughout the course of this little adventure, we continued to receive great and timely encouragement from Christian friends. Their words and acts of service were heartening. What I cherished most was the fact that it was the first time in my life and in our marriage that we faced a season of difficulty surrounded by a loving community. I wrote all their words and Scriptures down on index cards and stuffed them into a Ziploc bag that I kept safely in my purse. More times that I could count, I pulled those kind and gracious cards out and reminded myself that I could endure with patient confidence because I was not alone anymore!

Questions for Reflection

1. **How do you suppose Janalee so quickly went from praising God, convinced that her family was "in the midst of His perfect will" the night of the flood, to thinking that their "cup of consequences was not full yet"?**

2. *How would you interpret the statement, "We'll never outlive what we've done, and He'll never forget who we were"?*

3. *What is the "tyrannical trio" of shame, fear, and control?*

4. *What does the phrase "double for all her sins" mean?*

The Gift of Pause

We never did make it to Asia, but the time we had spent going through every closet, file cabinet, dresser, and cupboard in the house wasn't wasted. In fact, a week before the flood we had had a garage sale and cleared out over 300 unwanted items from the house. Knowing what was coming, God paved the way for us, even in these small details. So much so that when our water-logged ceilings began to fall, the asbestos report came back positive, and we became sick from the mold, it was clearly time to go, and we were able to get out of our house in one afternoon!

Some sweet friends offered us their lake home, so we settled there for a few weeks and prayed for a plan. We spent two weeks in that secluded spot where our phones didn't work, there was no internet, and it was a lengthy commute of 45 minutes to Zack's school and an hour to David's work. Consequently, we decided to minimize our trips, embrace the respite, and enjoy the view. It was a gift of pause.

One particular morning, my eyes opened a little earlier than usual and I thought I might catch a glimpse of daybreak. I positioned myself in front of the lake at the back of the house and waited. As the mist rose from the water, I drank in the peaceful silence. No one stirred, not even after the morning light broke through, so I snuck upstairs to find my Bible and journal, then returned to my perch. In that delicious solitude, Jesus sat with me and led me to two different passages.

> *In repentance and rest you shall be saved; in quietness and trust is your strength…Woe to those who go down to Egypt for help*

and rely on horses, and trust in chariots because they are many and in horsemen because they are very strong, but they do not look to the Holy One of Israel, nor seek the LORD! (Isaiah 30:15, 31:1)

Did I not say to you that if you believe, you will see the glory of God? (John 11:40)

I had only just begun the arduous task of translating insurance policies, contacting government representatives, setting up meetings with community leaders, and attending informational meetings at local libraries and community centers. It was going to be an education – one I never wanted, and one for which I felt sorely ill-equipped. I had always felt ignorantly helpless in the impenetrable world of impersonal policies and unpredictable politics. The combination of my ignorance, insecurity, and unusually strong sense of justice had created eruptions on more than one occasion. Often, I became so frustrated with all forms of government and bureaucracy that I walked out, hung up, and/or spouted off. Whenever possible, I would give those assignments to David or find someone else who would either stand with me or fight for me. I had already accepted that I wasn't going to be able to push it off on David this time. He had to focus on work because we needed his job more than ever before. Be that as it may, I sincerely doubted my ability to handle it on my own.

Wasn't this Hezekiah's downfall? Just a few chapters after this passage above, we read his cautionary tale. Shaken by Assyria's arrogant and violent threats (Isaiah 36), King Hezekiah forgot about God and tried to secure a measure of safety from the king of a larger and more powerful nation. Although the Lord had already proven Himself to be just and faithful (Isaiah 38), Hezekiah acted out of fear and promiscuously exposed the treasures of the kingdom. Rather than a favorable alliance, his disloyalty earned him the loss of everything (Isaiah 39).

In the same vein, God's soft voice to me that day was both direction and discipline. It was a warm blanket of comfort wrapped around stone-cold conviction. He was inviting me to abide in His protection and find my strength in His peace, but He was also warning me that I was not to conduct myself as I had in the past, as Hezekiah did. Even if I felt outranked, outwitted, outmaneuvered, and overpowered, I was not to create alliances, to burn bridges, or to manipulate and play on the sympathies of others. I would need to sit in the discomfort while controlling my tongue and my temper. I would need to learn to copy the delight I felt in the peaceful silence of that morning and paste it into the chaos our life was about to become.

Installments of Grace

After one or two **more** beautiful sunrises, it was time to re-engage the battle before us. There was too much work to be done to enjoy the lake, and we were too far away from everything **and everyone** to justify the commute **any longer**. Our home insurance company had just agreed to cover the damage caused by our failed roof, the asbestos abatement, and our temporary housing. Even though it wasn't ideal for our family of five, we moved into a hotel suite. Our goal was to find a rental house in our neighborhood so we could be close to all things familiar, including grandparents and Zack's school.

Fortunately, we found a house only two weeks later. We made the necessary arrangements and prepared for another transition. On moving day, the insurance company called to say that we weren't authorized to occupy the house and had to go back to the hotel or pay for the rental on our own. I flagged David down in the driveway as he was unloading the last of our boxes, and filled him in. Too tired for civility, he dropped the box he was carrying, grabbed my phone, and took our complaint up the chain. It took two days for them to confirm that our agent had indeed given us verbal authorization to make the move. Begrudgingly, they agreed to pay for us to stay in that rental house for three months. We won the battle, but the war was far from over.

Cynicism is a real temptation in these kinds of moments where God provides small and seemingly weak answers to our prayers. We were praying for an all-out rescue, a breakthrough, and what we got was temporary housing with two broken toilets, a broken oven, no heat and, as we would soon find out, a carbon monoxide problem. But to dismiss this gift, to fail to pause and praise Him, would be to deny His grace for the moment. The muddy path we walked was full of uncertainty and thank God for that! Without Him, our utter ruin would have been a foregone conclusion! We had to celebrate small blessings such as this! It was proof that He was still working, still providing, and still loving us. After all, this was the same God who provided the simple grace of manna each morning, split open the Red Sea, and swallowed up the rusty chains of slavery. If He could prove Himself faithful for these small gifts, we could trust Him to provide the big ones too. As God would have it, the grace of that house was this. It gave us just enough stability and familiarity to keep us sane, and just enough discomfort and frustration to keep us moving forward.

When It Rains, It Pours

It took several months to secure a general contractor who was willing and able to give us a quote for repairs on our home. With that in hand, we appealed the damage reports from both insurance companies. As a result, they adjusted their payouts to almost fifty percent of damages. Having some seed money, we sought the advice of our county floodplain manager as well as our flood insurance representative at our local disaster recovery center. Both encouraged us to accept the "substantially damaged" status and pursue elevation of the house, assuring us that we would qualify for a specific pool of funds we had been paying toward through our flood insurance policy. As the representative put it, these ICC funds were "guaranteed." Not yet convinced it was a safe option, we hired Lloyd, a retired engineer to help us determine if elevation was plausible and, if so, to guide us through the process. I also consulted with a specialized insurance representative to make sure we understood the process and requirements. Finally, I gathered quotes from electricians, elevation companies, HVAC companies, brick masons, and our utility company. After collecting all the information I could, we sought the counsel of our engineer as well as an elder in our church and laid out our options before them.

Much to our surprise, we decided to move forward with the elevation. It was the only way to eliminate the rapidly increasing cost of flood insurance, and the only way to qualify for federal grant money and that special pool of ICC funds. We contacted the county floodplain manager, secured a "substantially damaged" status, and put together our ICC application packet.

Within a week, the same representative I had consulted earlier notified us that we did not qualify for the ICC funds. Evidently, our flood insurance provider did not abide by the same definition of "substantially damaged" as the county did. The information we received from the county and our flood insurance representative at the disaster recovery center had been *wrong*, but government entities are not accountable to each other for such errors. Quite naturally, we regretted our decision, but there was no going back. The substantially damaged status could not be appealed. Before we could get a building permit to do any repairs, we would have to elevate, demolish, or relocate our house – and we were counting on those "guaranteed" ICC funds to do that. Since the insurance payouts covered less than half of our repair costs, there wasn't enough to fund any of those options. We had taken a risk and it didn't pay off. There was plenty of blame to go around, but unless we could find someone with the position and posture to make it right, we would be stuck with the short end of the stick.

Abandoning the house and mortgage was the most sensible option, but my step-dad's name was on the note, so he couldn't allow it. Although he offered to pay off the mortgage on our behalf, we wanted to believe God would provide a better solution. Thus, we determined to get back out there and find another way to fund the elevation. But the holidays were upon us, so it would have to wait until the new year. In the meantime, we were without a productive outlet to channel our angst. It was a pitiful sight. Much like melodramatic teenagers going through a bad breakup, we spent two weeks drowning ourselves in soft blankets, sappy Hallmark movies, and Christmas cookies.

Hitting the Pavement

Since going through the traditional channels didn't seem to be working, we widened our scope and started knocking on other doors. We contacted our congressman and requested an inquiry into the ICC funds. We also contacted our state representative and asked for an inquiry into the county's watershed policies and refusal to apply for federal grants. We attended every flood-related event offered in our community and shared our story with anyone who would listen. As a result, we did a spotlight for the evening news and an interview for a local radio station. Meanwhile, several bright and ambitious members of our community decided to speak on behalf of those who had been adversely affected by the flood, and petition county, state, and federal agencies for resources. Because of the way we had slipped through the cracks within the system, they named us the "poster children" for the

2015 flood and invited us to share our story at a meeting with local, state, and federal representatives.

Multiple contractors, charities, and non-profit agencies were circulating through the area, and we vetted as many of them as possible. One in particular, the St. Bernard Project, seemed to be both trustworthy and relevant to our needs. They enter disaster areas and secure private funding to rebuild and repair homes. It sounded perfect! We invited them to do a walk-through of our house and peppered them with questions. They offered to take our case if we qualified and they were able to find solid funding. If we would turn over all insurance funds and complete the elevation on our own, they would do the repairs. Not seeing any other possibilities, we increased our small business loan to cover the elevation and hoped St. Bernard would be able to raise enough money to pay for the repairs. It looked like a plan, albeit financially devastating. Tripling our existing debt was far from what we wanted for ourselves and our children, but homelessness was even less desirable. We would have to wait on the results of our congressional inquiry and also wait to see if St. Bernard Project could get the funding to do repairs. It wasn't what we wanted, but we were exasperated enough to call it our last resort.

<u>*Questions for Reflection*</u>

1. ***What truths did God share with Janalee during their "gift of pause"?***

2. ***Where do you run and how do you cope when you feel overwhelmed and overrun?***

3. ***What is an "installment of grace"? What installments of grace are present in your life today?***

4. ***What kind of advice would you have given to Janalee and her family during this time?***

205

Hail Mary

When Zack was in kindergarten, he fell in love with the darling little girl who lived around the corner. She was irresistible; she played in the mud, wore cowboy boots, and spoke with a sweetly southern drawl. He was completely smitten and had to do something about it, so he picked some flowers and walked over to her house. She answered the door with a red popsicle in her hand and he popped the question. *"I'm cool and you're beautiful. Will you marry me?"*

Seeing an opportunity to have a little fun, her dad stepped into the conversation and chastised Zack for not having a ring, a job, or a truck and told him to forget about marriage until he could pay to have her nails done. Looking for a quick recovery and perhaps a consolation prize, Zack said "ok" and asked if he could have a popsicle. Sadly, that was denied as well. He came home and tearfully replayed the story, ending the dramatic tale with this, *"Mom, I don't understand. Why couldn't I have a popsicle?"*

In like fashion, we were still asking why we couldn't have those ICC funds when we received phone call that added insult to injury. After another change of the guard in February, the new agent assigned to our claim announced that we were being evicted from our rental home. From her perspective, we had dragged our feet long enough. It had been over four months since the flood and repairs should have been completed. We tried to explain that we could not get a building permit to do repairs without first elevating the house, and we were waiting to hear the results of our congressional inquiry regarding the ICC funds in order to elevate. She argued that it wasn't their problem. We were out of time and had two weeks to get out. Denied and rejected.

A week later, I still hadn't started packing. We had one more week to be out, but I couldn't seem to accept it and take the appropriate steps. Staggered and stunned, I grabbed the kids and went to visit my parents. My step-dad was putting sticky notes on their furniture, marking it for storage. Waves of panic and tearful gratitude washed over me as he walked me through the house and described his plan to take on my family of five. I sat down at the kitchen table next to my mom and asked if she had seen his plan. She smiled proudly and whispered, *"He's been working on it all week."* It was a profound act of sacrificial love, unprivileged generosity through and through, yet I struggled to receive it with cheer. Rather than relief, the finality of it all settled upon me like a ton of bricks. Had we really run out of doors to knock on?

That was the wake-up call I needed. Not ready to give up yet, I suddenly found myself alert and ready for action. I went home and phoned our landlord to see if we could pay her directly and extend our stay for one more month. Having an unusually high opinion of the house, she demanded an inflated price three times the amount we were paying for the mortgage on our house across the street. Our church had collected some money, available to us for the asking, but not that much. It looked like we were going to be moving again. I sent an email to our community group, rallying volunteers to help us move out of the rental and into my parents' house. Then, I followed a hunch and did some homework.

Although I wasn't convinced that it was the right thing to do, I discovered that we could file a grievance against our insurance company through our State Department of Insurance. I figured it would be a "Hail Mary" move, but everything we had attempted thus far had been just as unlikely to work out. My only hesitation was the fact that God had warned me, "...*Woe to those who go down to Egypt for help...*". Just like with the congressional inquiries, I worried that filing a complaint would be dismissive of God as our Provider and Protector. Setting my computer aside, I submitted the situation to Him and begged for wisdom. *Lord, I promised I would trust You for this whole process. Would it be disrespectful for us to take this step? Should I let it go and wait for You?* I heard nothing and felt no sting of conviction whatsoever, so I called David and we prayed together.

As I hung up the phone, my oldest daughter stepped into the room with her hands on her hips and a determined look on her face. She'd heard enough of the day's drama to conclude that it was far time someone step in and put a stop to the madness. And she presumed that person to be me. Pulling out a reference from her childhood, she put her hand on my shoulder and said, "*Give 'em your 'last resort' mom!*" How precious! She still thought I was the most powerful woman on the planet. And for just one moment, I believed her. I donned my oversized mom cape and wrote the grievance.

Stand Down and Look Up

After hitting the 'send' button, it took me all of about five minutes to fall apart. We had endured an avalanche of terribly abrupt, unfair, and seemingly unscrupulous happenings and I was scrambling to stop the freefall of emotions, starting with panic, and ending with not-so-righteous indignation. We were paying on a home we could not legally live in, rent out, sell, repair, or abandon. And we were quite likely to be kicked out of our rental home. The public service system we were taxed to support was set up to benefit the public, but it seemed to accomplish nothing of the sort. And the insurance we were obligated to purchase, thanks to the banking industry, was just about as forthright, customer-friendly, and cost-effective as the IRS. Whether it was calloused injustice or bureaucratic incompetence, I didn't know and didn't care. I felt furiously helpless and ready to pick a fight. I had a nagging feeling that it wasn't my fight to pick, but I was determined to give it a go anyway. I didn't get very far into that fantasy before the Holy Spirit reminded me that my anger doesn't accomplish His will (James 1:20) and that vengeance belongs to Him (Rom. 12:19). My job was to stand down and defer to the Father. Slightly disappointed, I put down my sword and my imprecatory Psalm-like curses, resolving to leave it at the throne.

Sometimes I believe that it is my job to fix what has gone wrong with the world. As a result, I've been known to choose the wrong battles for the wrong reasons. This would have been one of those times for me, but God has never blessed my attempts to right wrongs and crusade causes. I'm His ambassador and He does give me battles to wage. He also gives me the weapons with which to do it, but the belt of truth, shield of faith, and Gospel of peace have very little to do with my desire to exact revenge or make this world a nicer, safer, or more comfortable place to live. In this case, I was feeling threatened and blamed the powers-that-be. Anger was the easiest, most powerful emotion I had at my disposal, but it was a false "soulution" and devoid of real power. If I continued to let it fester, it would wrap itself around my heart and squeeze the courage, conviction, and softness right out of me.

As I remembered Jesus, my heart softened again. He wasn't afraid to upset the status quo or stir up a little trouble for the sake of righteousness, but He also made it pretty clear that He wasn't going to spend His time bringing about an earthly kingdom – not yet. He came to liberate the souls of men and women like you and me. He came to usher in a spiritual kingdom that would transform the world from the inside out. This mad world of ours is careening toward a cliff, racing toward a harrowing end, taking up arms against the Way, Truth, and Life it truly needs. When Jesus considered this lost and rebellious world He created, He didn't plan His revenge. He wept. *"O Jerusalem, Jerusalem, the city that kills the prophets and stones those who are sent to it! How often would I have gathered your children together as a hen gathers her brood under her wings, and you were not willing!"* (Matt. 23:37). He scattered seeds in hot pursuit of men and women who rejected Him. He did miracles for those who walked away and never said *"thank you"*, never repented of their sins, and never entered His kingdom. He put His heart on the line, making Himself vulnerable to fickle, selfish, short-sighted people, and ultimately submitted His body unto death for billions who will not acknowledge Him until He comes in glory. And He did it all for one reason: love. So, if I want to be like Him, I have to refuse the false comfort of rigid, self-righteousness and choose to love this world the way He does.

Fortunately, He loves me too and He is compassionate and generous in meeting my needs. Housing is one of those needs, and a legitimate one. I wasn't wrong to want to secure it for my family. The problem was how I expected to get that need met. Even though He may utilize human means to accomplish His purposes, I'm not meant to become dependent upon those means. I am designed to depend upon Him. Whether I place my trust in my job, my spouse, my friends, or my government, I will eventually discover that they are limited and unpredictable resources. But God's resources are unlimited, inexhaustible, and infinite; and He does not withhold them from me, because I am His child.

This is what He says: *"...do not be anxious for your life, as to what you shall eat, or what you shall drink; nor for your body, as to what you shall put on...for your heavenly Father knows that you need all these things"* (Matt. 6:25, 32). It's embarrassingly simplistic. I learned this passage in Sunday School, but freefalls make it hard to remember. Therefore, one of the most important things we can do when life falls apart is to discipline ourselves to *remember*.

Janalee B. Smith

Enough is Enough

The night before the moving van was scheduled to arrive, the state Department of Insurance called to say that our new agent – bless her heart - hadn't properly read through her notes. They would continue to pay for our rental through the end of April, giving us another two months. A few days later, we received a greeting card from our insurance company with an enclosed $25 gift card. It was a weak apology and a temporary solution, but it did buy us some time, for which we were grateful. Nonetheless, we would be right back in the same situation soon enough. Whether the ICC funds came through or not, we were going to run out of time. Hence, finding a safe and permanent living arrangement was fast outranking the financial concerns of a flooded house.

Being on the verge of homelessness does cause one to think outside the box. We were getting ready to head out the door one morning when an idea occurred to me. *"David, what if we bought a house with my parents instead of moving into theirs? What if we found one that would work for everyone and for the long haul?"* He agreed with me that it was pretty crazy, but so was asking my parents to relocate half of their belongings in order to squeeze our family of five into their three-bedroom house. Against my better judgment, I gathered up the kids and headed over to talk with them. Hesitantly, I broached the subject with my mom first. *"Mom, instead of trying to make this one work, what if we bought another house that would accommodate everyone?"* She looked at me with slight exasperation and announced that she had been suggesting that to us for over a month. I didn't know how I missed it and I wasn't about to waste time figuring it out. I had a new direction to shoot for, so off I went!

We compared lists of what we wanted and needed in a house and from each other. After a quick round-table discussion, it was settled. We committed to live together, regardless of the outcome of our flood situation, and began the search. In less than a month, we found our new house. Mom and I stood in the kitchen and told our realtor we wanted to put in an offer. Immediately, the selling agent burst our bubble by telling us there were already two offers on the table and we could not put in an offer until my mom's house was under contract. Under contract? She hadn't even listed it yet! While that little morsel of bad news was still registering, Dave, our real estate agent and elder at our church, spoke up and saved the day. Without hesitation, he announced that he would buy my parents' house. And he did! In an act of sincere kindness and generosity, he sat at my parents' dining room table that night and wrote up the papers. Then he put in our offer on the house of our dreams. The selling agent bypassed the two previous offers and accepted ours! Just like that, we had a home. It felt exactly like Christmas morning, and we hung onto the delight as long as we could.

Eyes to See

The first week of April, we loaded up our moving vans and settled into our new home. You won't believe this, but in the middle of loading and unloading on moving day, our flood insurance company called to say that they would release the ICC funds for the elevation. It was the call we had been waiting for and, if we had received it just a few weeks prior, things would have been very different. But decisions had been made and papers had been signed. We made it through moving day. Then we conferred with our engineer and decided to proceed by using the ICC funds to elevate the house, see if St. Bernard Project had the funding to do repairs, and then sell it or rent it out. After spending a few rushed weeks settling in, we dusted off our elevation plans and got back to work.

In an unexpected turn of events, St. Bernard Project announced they would not do the repairs unless we agreed to live in the house for five years. Since we had committed to live with my parents till kingdom come, this was not an option. But before we could come up with another plan, the county adopted new flood maps – which was the final nail in the elevation coffin. Rather than being required to raise the house 1.7 feet, we would need to raise it 5.5 feet. The implications of this were huge! Our elevation plan would be out of code, requiring a multiplication of materials, work, and money. And when we gave our contractors the new specs, none of them were willing to give us an actual quote since the scope and risks of the project had increased so greatly. After doing some ballpark calculations, our best estimate was three times the original cost. To put it in perspective, the cost for the elevation and repairs amounted to double our home's market value – and we still owed money on the mortgage! Naturally, there were other concerns as well, but the long and short of it was that elevating the house was no longer a reasonable course of action, let alone our best one – and there were no other options up for discussion.

Looking at life through the lens of our circumstances can cause spiritual and emotional whiplash. What God chooses to permit and what He chooses to prevent are equally inexplicable. Indeed, His sovereignty is a mysterious thing. In the fourteenth chapter of Matthew, Jesus fed the 5,000, Peter walked on water, and John the Baptist was beheaded. The twelfth chapter of Acts is much the same. James, the brother of John, was put to death by King Herod, Peter was imprisoned and then miraculously set free, and God poured wrath upon King Herod. What was God doing?

In the same way, giving us a new home was a glorious thing. God had moved mountains and given us a beautiful new home and a new household with which to put down roots. We loved everything about it, and the transition took place seamlessly. But it was not the answer to all our problems. Even with my parents' help, we couldn't keep up a mortgage, insurance, and utilities on two houses. It just wasn't a sustainable situation. Financially, we were sicker than ever, and the prognosis was grim.

Fortunately, I knew that there was far more going on behind the scenes than what I was privy to. When I wasn't throwing temper tantrums, this fact was quite calming to me and I rather enjoyed imagining what God was doing on our behalf. And the imagining did great things for my faith.

There's a fascinating story about this in 2 Kings 6. The king of Aram was losing his assault against Israel and the prophet Elisha was to blame. In an attempt to subdue Elisha, Aram's great army of horses and chariots came at night and surrounded the city where he lodged. Elisha's poor servant awoke to see this demonstration of terror and might. *"Alas, my master! What shall we do?"* he asked (v. 15). Elisha was less than impressed. He told his servant not to fear and reassured him that the show of force he saw before them paled in comparison to the heavenly legion he could not see. *"And the LORD opened the servant's eyes and he saw; and behold, the mountain was full of horses and chariots of fire all around Elisha"* (v. 17). Sometimes, the most powerful thing we can ask for are eyes to see. Because we are not as alone as we feel, our enemy is not as powerful as he claims, and the outcome is not as ill-fated as it might look.

<u>*Questions for Reflection*</u>

1. *Do you think that requesting a congressional inquiry and filing a grievance against the insurance company was being like "those who go down to Egypt for help"? Why or why not?*

2. *"One of the most important things we can do when life falls apart is to discipline ourselves to remember." What was Janalee needing to remember?*

3. *What are some of the lessons and truths God has given to you over the course of your spiritual journey, which you need to remember?*

4. *Are you ever confused by what God chooses to permit and what He chooses to prevent?*

5. *What is implied by these statements? "Sometimes, the most powerful thing we can ask for are eyes to see. Because we are not as alone as we feel, our enemy is not as powerful as he claims, and the outcome is not as ill-fated as it might look."*

Let Down Your Nets

In the fall of 2017, our county held a community forum where they announced the receipt of a multi-million-dollar federal grant. All homeowners interested in getting a portion of that pie needed to complete an application packet. I'd like to say that we were elated, but too much time had passed and too much energy had been spent on things like false hope. Needless to say, we were confused and skeptical. Those funds had been secured early in the process, while we were being told that the county would not be getting involved with buyouts, rehabs, or mitigation. Based on the information we had been given, we didn't qualify, and based on everything we'd seen and heard thus far, it wouldn't matter if we did. Those funds were earmarked for other priorities. We went home befuddled and bothered. Was this a viable option or was it just another empty chase down a blind alley?

The next morning, I was hiding away in my closet, praying, reading, and pondering, when these verses jumped off the page: "'*Put out into the deep water and let down your nets for a catch.' Simon answered and said, 'Master, we worked hard all night and caught nothing, but I will do as You say and let down the nets*'" (Luke 5:3-5). Poor Peter was spent mentally, physically, and emotionally. On the heels of the greatest failure of his life, he grabbed his boat and headed out for a night of fishing. It was the one thing that always cleared his head and gave him a sense of success and satisfaction. But his nets were empty, just like his heart. He had just decided to give up and head back to shore when a stranger standing on the water's edge ventured to offer a piece of advice. And Peter could have responded with cynicism: "*Been there, done that.*" Instead, he responded with humility and bit into a small sliver of hope. In the same way, we were ready to give up and call it quits when Jesus asked us to try again, to not lose heart, to trust Him regardless of the outcome. He asked us to suspend our doubts, our cynicism, our negative expectations, and place our full confidence in His goodness.

Holding onto a thin thread of faith, we stepped in line and began the arduous application process but expected nothing. And that's exactly what we got – a fat lot of nothing. Night after night, we pulled up nothing but empty nets. Month after month we continued to pay the mortgage, utilities, and insurance premiums on a home that was dead to us. A year and a half went by, and we were still sitting in our proverbial boat waiting for God to either bring in a catch or release us from the hope of one.

Then, as the winter was giving way to spring and death was warming to life, the county placed a sign in our front yard. It was an announcement, a public declaration that miracles still happen and grace still abounds. We had been approved for the federal grant program, and our home was eligible to be bought out at its pre-flood market value. We limped our way to the closing table with a heavy financial burden on our backs and walked away lighter than air. The sale enabled us to pay off our mortgage and settle all our previous debts. God's promises came to fruition. We received "double" from the hand of the Lord, covering our shame, and setting us free from the chains of the past.

All buyouts were finalized with demolition and re-zoning of the land as greenspace. In preparation for this, a dumpster was placed in the driveway and yellow caution tape encircled the house. Wanting to see the process through, I prayed that God would allow me to be present when they finally knocked it down. Honestly, I wanted to set up lawn chairs and sell tickets and popcorn, but was willing to settle for a private viewing. He answered my prayer one afternoon as I was driving through the neighborhood. I parked across the street and watched as a bulldozer grabbed entire walls and pulled them apart like pieces of paper. The wall with our family verse, the murals I'd made for each of our children, my bathtub…they were all snatched up and deposited into a heap of debris next to the sizeable hole Zack had dug in our side yard one summer as he attempted to reach the "Motherland".

I sat quietly in my car until it was leveled, thinking of all the things God had done for us in that house. He had taken us to our lowest low and then raised us up again. He had healed our marriage. He had given David a new career and calling. He had given me this book to write. He had surrounded us with an intimate community. I'd like to say that I cried sentimental tears and struggled to let it all go, but I didn't. I laughed! I clapped my hands in celebration and praised the God of miracles. Once again, He had rescued me! I shook my head in awe at His fierce kindness and told myself that next time life falls apart, next time a storm hits, next time my world shatters into millions of pieces, I won't be afraid. I won't allow shame to torment me and tell me that God is punishing me. I won't be afraid of missing His will or of making a mistake. Even if He denies me a tidy outcome, I won't be afraid that He has abandoned me or left me to my own devices. Instead, I will remember that He is coming for me, and He is *here*. This earthly kingdom of temporary troubles is coming to ruin and the floor of heaven is shaking with anticipation. As His rapturous love and all-sufficient grace make their way through the cracks and fall on me, I am surrounded. I am safe.

Actualizing Abundance

In the course of this unexpected and unwelcomed adventure, I discovered that my salvation had offered me more than I realized and far more than I had actualized. Salvation is, of course, the starting point. It opens the door for a relationship. It pays for our transfer from the kingdom of darkness into the kingdom of light. It takes us who were once far off and brings us near. Because of salvation, we have become royalty and a prized possession. Our hearts of stone have been replaced by hearts of flesh. But these positional truths do not guarantee us satisfaction in Jesus and the abundant life. If we want that, we must actualize what we have inherited as saints.

This actualizing comes to us as we choose to deny the many ways in which we attempt to subdue the excruciating vulnerability we feel while living in this world. When nothing makes sense anymore, when the pressures squeeze out our very breath, when the drumbeat of uncertainty drowns out every ounce of peace – it is then that the weak, helpless, empty status of the fallen human condition comes into full view. It is then that we are overcome with fear. Homelessness, financial uncertainty, lack of routine, and lack of security produced a fury and helpless sense of vulnerability within me that demanded a response. Taking matters into my own hands seemed like the necessary and natural thing to do, but God beckoned me to deny the power of my fears and the allure of smaller "soulutions" by activating His truth and presence instead. He invited me to follow His leading by receiving His comfort and hope, abiding in His protection and strength, trusting Him to provide, praying for eyes to see, and practicing gratitude for small installments of grace. As I responded to His invitations, my heart was enlarged to behold Him more fully as He is. And the result of that was – as it always is – ever-increasing abundance. The result is a miracle I like to call breathing underwater.

Life strips us naked and we instinctively reach for fig leaves. But if we want to live as if our Savior is alive and His promises are true, we must dive deeply into our union with Christ and be clothed by Him instead (2 Cor. 5:4). This is the crucible for those of us who desire to have abundance in this "meantime" between paradise lost and paradise to come. We must allow the fullness of God to dwell within every crevice of our hearts and minds. We must mortify our attempts to cover, fill, protect, and hide ourselves.

There are no formulas, checklists, or superstitious rituals that will grant us the deep satisfaction we seek, but I would like to offer a few more guiding principles as we navigate this topic.

1. First and foremost, we must seek, desire, and pursue *God* rather than His blessings. It's not wrong to ask God for specific provisions or outcomes; Christ Himself made specific requests of the Father. But sometimes we try to extract pieces of Him from the gifts He gives, forgetting that He is the greatest gift. We get so fixated on the temporary and circumstantial that we forget: *He* is the best possible outcome. In the enjoyment of Him, we lack for nothing. He is our lifeline, our greatest need and desire, and the sum total of our heart's satisfaction. When our heads and hearts are clear from the business of scratching and clawing for an earthly kingdom, we can concur with King David, who declares: *"Whom have I in heaven but You? And besides You, I desire nothing on earth. My flesh and my heart may fail, but God is the strength of my heart and my portion forever....But as for me, the nearness of God is my good; I have made the Lord GOD my refuge, that I may tell of all Your works"* (Ps. 73:25-26, 28).

   How the enemy's deceptively pious propaganda has capitalized on our insecurities to kill our intimacy with God! Where did we get this idea that He is a silent partner in this cohabitation we call *indwelling?* Who told us that He is out of reach and hesitant to make Himself known? We didn't hear that rubbish from Jesus! His presence isn't elusive. Have we forgotten that it was for the sake of relationship that He created us? And after our sin destroyed that precious fellowship, the Father sacrificed the communion He had with His dear Son in order to get us back. There's no need to hunt down or discover the presence of God. We need only pay attention to it.

   > *A spiritual kingdom lies all about us, enclosing us, embracing us, altogether within reach of our inner selves, waiting for us to recognize it. God Himself is here waiting for our response to His presence. This eternal world will come alive to us the moment we begin to reckon upon its reality.*[5]

   In like manner, intellectualizing this sacred romance through the guise of sanctimonious ideology – or even good theology – is a hellish thing to do. The loving intimacy inherent to this divine relationship can and must be *enjoyed* and *experienced*, as all good relationships are intended to be. C.S. Lewis wrote, *"The materials for correcting our abstract conception of God cannot be supplied by Reason: she will be the first to tell you to go and try experience – 'O taste and see that the Lord is good'."*[6] Suddenly or slowly, moment by moment, experiencing Him is the only thing that can awaken, define, and transform us from the inside out.

2. We must listen to God with a posture of obedience. There does seem to be one spiritual stipulation for those of us who want to enjoy the enduring presence of God (John 15:10). If we want to dwell with Him and abide in His love, then we must actually listen to what He says and follow Him. We must discipline ourselves to provide space to hear from Him, and then respond with a heart that is surrendered to Him and do whatever He impresses upon us to do.

We will not be made whole and holy prior to our grand entrance into eternity, but we can live with a clear conscience day by day. With our affections fixed upon God, His light shines brightly into our hearts and reveals areas where we are divided. Love beckons us to repent when convicted, change course when redirected, and surrender when conflicted. When the posture of our heart is bent toward His in submitted adoration, we are filled by the fountain of His goodness. Let us drink Him in deeply in unadulterated worship, until His desires become our delight.

He shows much more of Himself to some people than to others – not because He has favorites, but because it is impossible for Him to show Himself to a man whose mind and character are in the wrong condition. Just as sunlight, though it has no favorites, cannot be reflected in a dusty mirror as clearly as in a clean one…while in other sciences the instruments you use are things external to yourself, the instrument through which you see God is your whole self. And if a man's self is not kept clean and bright, his glimpse of God will be blurred – like the Moon seen through a dirty telescope.[7]

3. My family was blessed by a fairytale ending to this particular story, but not all ends well while we are living in this meantime. For now, we will know in part, understand in part, and experience in part all that God has for us. We must patiently wait for God to fulfill His promises, and some of them will be fulfilled in paradise. Hebrews

2:8 says, *"For in subjecting all things to him, He left nothing that is not subject to him. But now we do not yet see all things subjected to him."* Not yet. We are living in the tension between the already and the not yet. On this side of the veil, the redemption story is still unfolding. God is not done telling His story, and He's not done telling ours. The day of happy endings is on the horizon, but until it arrives, we must embrace the disquieting suspense of waiting. Because God is not slow in keeping His promises and because He does all things well, we can wait with confidence. When this life has passed away, we will be able to look back upon human history, upon this earthen existence, and declare with all the saints that He has been faithful. He never fails. He leaves nothing undone, nothing unresolved, nothing unsettled. Until then, while groaning and longing, we must grab hold of His all-sufficient, ever-present grace which spans the distance between what is and what is to come.

Conclusion

It doesn't make a lot of sense that I would become sentimental over my life's darkest hours. But God has so generously poured Himself out upon me in my times of heartache, so vividly revealed Himself to me within my stormy seasons, that they have taken on an odd sort of sweetness. If you remember, the first chapter fits in my life's timeline as the entrance into a very gloomy season that lasted for four years. It was in the foothills of that mountain of travail that God first became real to me. And He continued to teach me, guide me, heal me, and comfort me as I struggled to climb my way up.

When He began to heal my marriage, it felt as if I had reached the long-awaited summit. I scurried over the last few obstacles and stood up straight to catch my breath and enjoy the view. Surrounding me was mile after mile of clear blue skies. For the longest time, I stood in stunned silence, wide-eyed and a little weak in the knees. Of course, it wasn't without small setbacks and minor mishaps, but the landscape of my life was transformed. My heart was still racing, and my ears were ringing, but the turmoil and chaos were gone.

Not wanting to let any of it go to waste, I continued to reflect upon what had transpired in those valleys below, searching for hidden nuggets of wisdom and insight – which I have documented for you. But as time passed by and the distance between the mountain top and the valleys grew, I became anxious. As I described at the beginning of this chapter, I feared that I had become so spiritually lazy and ungrateful in my effortless existence that I'd forgotten how to live in the trenches. After gaining friends, family, and a meaningful ministry, I wondered if I had forgotten how to be dependent on and desperate for Him.

Therefore, I embarked on a quest to apprehend a fearless and abundant life. By the grace of God, I landed back in the wilderness to be tempted and tried. Even though I had been there before, it never gets comfortable, predictable, or familiar. Crisis always presents us with opportunities to face our fears and fight our Goliaths. In this way, our flood experience did not disappoint. There were many disorienting challenges, but as He had done so faithfully before, God distinctly and profoundly revealed more of His heart and also mine. He used my pain and discomfort to produce wholeness out of that which was unholy. But within this particular hardship, He did something new and unexpected. As He had done many times before, He exposed and healed areas of sin and wounding within me. And once again, He confirmed His love and affections for me. But this time, He also confirmed *my* love and affection for Him!

You see, I had been anxiously attempting to safeguard my life from pain and suffering – not simply because I was afraid of being uncomfortable, but because I was afraid that the chaos and pain would create a felt distance between me and God. I knew that He would continue to be present, would continue to offer guidance and protection, but I didn't trust myself to pay attention to it, to be able to decipher it. Difficulties have a way of undressing us, and I assumed that the naked truth about me was nothing other than self-love and self-worship. I suspected that the next onslaught of bleak circumstances would render me loveless and unresponsive to Him. I no longer feared that He would abandon *me*, but that I would feel betrayed and thus abandon *Him*!

I assure you that my flesh is alive and well, capable of all manner of evil – but it is not the deepest or truest part of me. This latest tempest taught me that at the very core of my heart is a steadfast affection for my precious Savior. I caught a glimpse of it. He placed a flame within me, a fiery passion and desperate longing for Him that no amount of difficulty has been able to quench (2 Tim. 1:6). Larry Crabb describes this beautifully in his book *Shattered Dreams*.

> *What He's doing while we suffer is leading us into the depths of our being, into the center of our soul where we feel our strongest passions. It's there that we discover our desire for God. We begin to feel a desire to know Him that not only survives all our pain, but actually thrives in it until that desire becomes more intense than our desire for all the good things we still want.*[8]

This is the most joyous thing I have discovered thus far! There will be no more hedging, no more passing notes back and forth asking the status of our fickle feelings – because now I know that God and I are a thing. I'm just as crazy about Him as He is for me, and we have made it official. My friends, we're going the distance! He is my favorite, my purest pleasure, my prized possession, my Beloved! And I am His.

> *Therefore, I am now going to allure her; I will lead her into the wilderness and speak tenderly to her. There I will give her back her vineyards and make the Valley of Achor a door of hope. There she will sing as in the days of her youth, as in the day she came up out of Egypt. "In that day," declares the Lord, "you will call me 'my husband,' you will no longer call me 'my master'."* (Hosea 2:14-16 NIV)

Questions for Reflection

1. ***What does it mean when Janalee says "He is coming for me, and He is here"?***

2. ***What does it mean that salvation is the starting point? Starting point of what?***

3. ***What are three guiding principles for actualizing abundance?***

4. ***What is the difference between seeking, desiring, and pursuing God rather than His blessings? How do we know which one we are chasing after?***

5. *What is the deepest, truest desire in the heart of every believer?*

6. *What does it mean to breathe underwater?*

Notes

Chapter 1: The Third Option

1. John Eldredge, *Waking the Dead: The Secret to a Heart Fully Alive* (Nashville, TN: Nelson Books, 2016), 50.

2. Henry T. Blackaby and Richard Blackaby, *Hearing God's Voice* (Nashville, TN: B&H Books, 2002), 16.

3. As quoted in Michka Assayas, *Bono: In Conversation with Michka Assayas* (New York: Riverhead Books, 2005), 159.

4. Dr. and Mrs. Howard Taylor, *Hudson Taylor's Spiritual Secret* (Chicago: Moody Bible Institute, 2009), 163.

5. Dr. Mike Plunket, "Problems Arise." *Emotional Healing: A Twelve-Week Course*, Session 2 (New City, NY: Risen King Alliance Church, 2007).

Chapter 2: Counterfeit Grace

1. Brent Curtis and John Eldredge, *The Sacred Romance: Drawing Closer to the Heart of God* (Nashville, TN: Thomas Nelson, 2001), 27-28.

2. Dr. Mike Plunket, "Problems Arise."

3. Ray Stedman, *Body Life* (Ventura, CA: Regal Books, 1972), 11.

4. C.S. Lewis, *The Problem of Pain* (New York: Macmillan, 1962), 80.

5. Dr. Karl I. Payne, *Spiritual Warfare: Christians, Demonization, and Deliverance* (Washington, D.C.: WND Books, 2011), 45.

6. As quoted in Christopher R. Little, *Transformed from Glory to Glory: Celebrating the Legacy of J. Robertson McQuilkin* (Fort Washington, PA: CLC Publications, 2015), 1.

7. Dr. Karl I. Payne, *Spiritual Warfare*, 33.

8. John Eldredge, *Epic: The Story God is Telling and the Role That is Yours to Play* (Nashville, TN: Thomas Nelson, 2004), 62-63.

9. "Struggle." *Oxford English Dictionary, 2nd Edition* (Oxford: Oxford University Press, 2002), 830.

Chapter 3: The Great Paradox

1. John Stott, *The Cross of Christ* (Downers Grove, IL: InterVarsity Press, 2006), 303.

2. Lee Dye, "Are You Angry at God?" (ABC News, 21 Dec 2010), abcnews.go.com/Technology/ angry-god-thirds-americans-blame-god-problems-survey/story?id=12540557, 6 Jan 2011.

3. C.S. Lewis, *The Problem of Pain* (San Francisco: HarperOne, 2001), 25.

4. Elisabeth Elliott, *On Asking God Why* (Grand Rapids, MI: Revell, 1989), 138.

5. Paul Kroll, "Trials: The Trial of Job" (Grace Communion International, 1992), http://www.gci.org/%20articles/the-trial-of-job/, 21 April 2020.

6. Stasi Eldredge, *Becoming Myself Today* (Colorado Springs, CO: David C. Cook, 2013), 138.

7. Joni Eareckson Tada, *Anger: Aim It in the Right Direction* (Torrance, CA: Rose Publishing, 2012), 92.

8. Joni Earekson Tada, 14 January 2013, Westmont College, Santa Barbara, CA. Chapel Service Address.

9. John Eldredge, *Epic*, 40.

10. Anne Brontë, *The Tenant of Wildfell Hall* (London: T.C. Newby, 1848), 220.

11. Isaiah 53:2

12. Matthew 8:20

13. Matthew 4;

Hebrews 2:18,

Hebrews 4:15

14. Matt. 12:24,

13:54-58;

Mark 8:14-21;

Luke 5:17, 21

15. John 7:5,

Matthew 11:2-3

16. Matthew 26:38-46,

Luke 22:42-44

17. Luke 22:48, 61;

Mark 14:50

18. Matthew 12:14;

Mark 15:3, 10, 27;

Luke 23:2-4, 10, 13-25, 41,

19. Matthew 27:46

20. Matthew 27:40;

Luke 22:64,

Luke 23:35-36, 39

21. Hebrews 12:2,

Philippians 2:5-7,

Matthew 20:28

22. Ephesians 4:8-10,

1 Corinthians 15:26,

Revelation 1:18

Chapter 4: Divine Dissonance

1. John Eldredge, *The Journey of Desire: Searching for the Life We Only Dreamed Of* (Nashville, TN: Thomas Nelson, 2016), 144.

2. DeVerne Fromke, *Unto Full Stature* (Coverdale, IN: Sure Foundation, 1985), 34-35.

3. John Eldredge, *Waking the Dead: The Glory of a Heart Fully Alive* (Nashville, TN: Thomas Nelson, 2016), 44.

4. *"Nous." Strong's Concordance: NASB,* https://www.blueletterbible.org/lang/lexicon/lexicon.cfm?Strongs=G3563&t=NASB, 28 April 2020.

5. Bruce Lipton, Ph.D., "Epigenetics" (BruceLipton.com, 7 Feb 2012), https://www.brucelipton.com/epigenetics/ (excerpt from Leigh Fortson, *Embrace, Release, Heal: An Empowering Guide to Talking About, Thinking About, and Treating Cancer* [Boulder, CO: Sounds True, Inc., 2011]), 1 May 2020.

6. John Eldredge, *The Sacred Romance*, 49.

7. C.S. Lewis, *A Grief Observed* (New York: HarperCollins Publishers, 2001), 7.

8. Nancy Leigh DeMoss, *Lies Women Believe: And the Truth That Sets Them Free* (Chicago: Moody Publishers, 2007), 32.

9. Hannah Whitall Smith, *The Unselfishness of God* (London: J. Nisbet & Company, 1903), 14-15.

10. As quoted in Dale L. June, *Introduction to Executive Protection* (Boca Raton, FL: CRC Press, 2008), 291.

11. John Owen, *The Works of John Owen, D.D,* edited by William H. Goold (London: Johnstone & Hunter, 1851), 105.

12. Neil T. Anderson, *The Bondage Breaker* (Eugene, OR: Harvest House Publishers, 2006), 166.

13. Ibid, 69.

14. John Eldredge, *Waking the Dead*, 120.

15. "Cognitive dissonance." The Merriam-Webster Dictionary (Martinsburg, WV: Merriam-Webster, Inc., 2000), 365.

16. Frantz Fanon, *Black Skin, White Masks* (London: Penguin Books, 1967). As quoted in Jaan Islam, *Political Philosophy in the East and West: In Search of Truth* (Wilmington, DE: Vernon Press, 2018), 18.

17. C.S. Lewis, *The Problem of Pain*, 81.

18. Stasi Eldredge, *Becoming Myself: Embracing God's Dream of You*

(Colorado Springs, CO: David C. Cook, 2013), 185.

19. Simon Tugwell, O.P. *Prayer: Living with God* (Springfield, IL: Templegate Publishing, 1975). As quoted in Rueben J. Job and Norman Shawchuck, "A Guide to Prayer for Ministers and Other Servants", *The Upper Room* 1983, 161.

Chapter 5: Mirrored Realities

1. As quoted in Richard H. Bell, *Seeds of the Spirit: Wisdom of the Twentieth Century* (Louisville, KY: Westminster John Knox Press, 1995), 104.

2. John & Stasi Eldredge, *Captivating: Unveiling the Mystery of a Woman's Soul* (Nashville, TN: Thomas Nelson, 2011), 7.

3. Brené Brown, "Listening to Shame" (TED.com, March 2012), https://www.ted.com/talks/brene_brown_listening_to_sha me?language=en, 4 May 2020.

4. John Eldredge, *The Sacred Romance*, 85.

5. Robert S. McGee, *The Search for Significance: Seeing Your True Worth Through God's Eyes* (Nashville, TN: W Publishing Group, 2003), 18.

6. John Eldredge, *Waking the Dead*, 35.

7. Beth Moore, *So Long, Insecurity: You've Been a Bad Friend to Us* (Carol Stream, IL: Tyndale House Publishing, 2010), 35-36.

8. John Eldredge, *The Sacred Romance*, 89.

9. John Piper, "Thankful for the Love of God" (DesiringGod.org, 18 Nov 2001), https://www.desiringgod.org/messages/thankful-for-the-love-of-god, 7 May 2020.

10. John Eldredge, *The Sacred Romance*, 88.

Chapter 6: Pardon the Parish

1. William Carey, who is considered the Father of Modern Missions, initially set off for India to answer God's call leaving his pregnant wife and two of their sons behind.

2. John Pavlovitz, "Dear Church, Here's Why People Are Really Leaving the Church" (ChurchPlants.com, 2015), https://churchplants.com/growth/8774-dear-church-heres-why-people-are-really-leaving-you-john-pavlovitz.html, 14 May 2020.

3. C.S. Lewis, *Mere Christianity* (New York: HarperCollins, 2001), 115.

4. Chester and Betsy Klystra, *Biblical Healing and Deliverance: A Guide to Experiencing Freedom from Sins of the Past, Destructive Beliefs, Emotional and Spiritual Pain, Curses and Oppression* (Bloomington, MN: Chosen Books, 2014), 33.

5. C.S. Lewis, *The Weight of Glory* (New York: HarperCollins, 2001), 178.

6. C.S. Lewis, *The World's Last Night and Other Essays* (Boston, MA: Harvest Books, 2002), 8-9.

7. Edward M. Smith, *Healing Life's Deepest Hurts: Let the Light of Christ Dispel the Darkness in Your Soul* (Ventura, CA: Regal Books, 2002), 123.

8. John & Stasi Eldredge, *Captivating: Unveiling the Mystery of a Woman's Soul*, 101.

9. Larry Crabb, *Shattered Dreams: God's Unexpected Path to Joy* (New York: WaterBrook Press, 2016), 63.

Chapter 7: Chasing Fantasies

1. "Fantasy." Dictionary.com, https://www.dictionary.com/browse/fantasy?s=t, 19 May 2020.

2. Chester and Betsy Klystra, *RTF Issue-Focused Ministry: Minister's Guide.* (Hendersonville, NC: Restoring the Foundations Publications, 1999-2017), 3.

Chapter 8: Actualizing Abundance

1. John Eldredge, *Waking the Dead*, 9.

2. As quoted in Alvin L. Reid, *Introduction to Evangelism* (Nashville,

TN: Broadman & Holman, 1998), 103.

3. Chester and Betsy Klystra, *Restoring the Foundations* (Hendersonville, NC: Restoring the Foundations Publications, 2014), 353-357.

4. Excerpted with permission from "True Comfort", © 2014 by Ray Stedman Ministries. All rights reserved. Visit RayStedman.org for the complete library of Ray Stedman material. Please direct any questions to webmaster@RayStedman.org.

5. A.W. Tozer, *Renewed Day by Day* (Chicago: Moody Publishers, 2011), 23.

6. As quoted in Patricia S. Klein, *A Year With C.S. Lewis* (San Francisco: HarperCollins, 2003), 6.

7. C.S. Lewis, *Mere Christianity*, 164.

8. Larry Crabb, *Shattered Dreams: God's Unexpected Path to Joy* (Colorado Springs, CO: WaterBrook Press, 2016), 4.

About the Author

Janalee is a sentimental people person with an intense hunger to learn and love deeply. She's been married to David, her favorite person, best friend, and soul mate since 1998, but says their first ten years were more like combat training than marital bliss. It was through a long season in the wilderness that God gifted them with profound personal transformation and the miraculous restoration of their marriage. The grace that was shown to them has grown into a passion to teach, encourage, and walk alongside others who are weary and wounded in the body of Christ. They reside in the Carolinas with their teenagers, furry friends, and her parents.

www.ingramcontent.com/pod-product-compliance
Lightning Source LLC
Chambersburg PA
CBHW061511120726
48001CB00004B/1295

9 798705 753215